The Romanov Cache

Dimitri Gat

www.lulu.com

The Romanov Cache can be obtained in .PDF file format or as a trade paperback at **http://www.lulu.com/dimitrigat.**

All the action, characters, and plot devices are original works of the author's imagination. Connections with actual historical events are intentional and as accurate as research and care can make them.

First edition
ISBN 978-1-84728-055-8
Copyright© 2006 Dimitri Gat

www.lulu.com

Other books by Dimitri Gat

Fiction

Child's Cry, 1995
Programmed for Peril (Writing as C. K. Cambray), 1993
Conditioned to Death (Writing as C. K. Cambray), 1992
Personal (Writing as C. K. Cambray), 1990
Where Is Crystal Martin? (Writing as C. K. Cambray), 1988
Nevsky's Demon, 1983
Nevsky's Return, 1982
The Shepherd is My Lord, 1971

Non-fiction

*Some Are Called Clowns: A Season with the Last of the Great
Barnstorming Baseball Teams* (with Bill Heward), 1974

10/28/06

For Vince

Whose comments about
internet print-on-demand
possibilities put me back in
harness where I belong. You
asked for more "wolf of the
steppes" but will have to settle
for a wolfhound. All best to
you

Dimitri Gat

In memory of my father, Vsevolod Dimitrievich

"Russia cannot exist without a czar."—*Grand Duke Alexander Mikhailovich, in an unsent letter to Czar Nicholas II*

"In Russia everything is secret, so nothing is secret."—*Russian proverb*

"We must put an end once and for all to the Papish-Quaker babble about the sanctity of human life."—*Trotsky*

"So it always has been, and so it always will be."—*A. A. Makharov, Minister of the Interior, April 1912*

THE ROMANOV CACHE

OLGA NIKOLAYEVNA

1

Pittsburgh, Pennsylvania—June 1998

Yuri Nevsky surveyed the post-poker rubble. Ashtrays were heaped. Dirty glasses crouched in sunken cutouts around the octagonal table. Ashes dusted the felt. The air inside 138 Morlande's spacious living room was an environmental nightmare. It smelled worse tonight because he had lost a couple hundred bucks. Even though it was 4:30 AM he started to clean up. He didn't want to have to face the job after too little of the uneasy sleep that always followed ten hours of concentration. He brushed the felt, cleaned off the table, and folded its legs.

He heard footsteps on the creaky wooden front porch. Someone knocked on the aluminum storm door. A player had forgotten something. He crossed the smaller of the two living rooms and stepped into the entrance hall. He flipped on the porch light and heaved the heavy front door open, expecting a familiar face.

A young Russian Orthodox priest stood under the dim porch light. By the curb at the foot of the long sloping lawn waited a taxi.

The priest was short and broad chested, his beard wide. He spoke Russian. "You are Yuri Vladimirovich Nevsky?"

Nevsky said he was, cranking up the language he knew well, but used seldom.

"I am Father Alexei. I have come from Russia to speak to you about some important matters."

Nevsky invited him in and closed the door. "Matters like what?" he asked.

"The guilt of an ailing priest whom I have brought to Pittsburgh."

Nevsky smiled. "In America we don't generally visit one another at this hour. Custom of the country."

Father Alexei smiled back. He well understood. "This isn't a time for mannerly delays, Yuri Vladimirovich. The priest I mentioned survives yet, but who can say for how much longer?"

"What priest?"

"That one who played a part in your father's murder."

Nevsky froze. After forty-six years *this?* Tonight? His father had gone to Portugal in 1952 to do some translating for his employer, U.S. Steel. He had disappeared. Efforts were made. They proved meager and fruitless. He was declared dead after the statutory period. His wife, overwhelmed with grief, moved all his possessions out of the house to their Murrysville property and turned her energies to raising young Yuri.

Father Alexei gave Nevsky a letter from a Bishop Paulos. Typed on a Moscow diocese letterhead, it identified the priest as the bishop's personal emissary. It urged Nevsky to listen "with an open heart" to what he was told and to "consider the anguish of one of God's servants."

Nevsky led the priest into the larger living room and waved him toward a soft chair. He was still stunned by the news, even though over the years he had of course come to accept the likely possibility of his father being dead. Now... "Let's hear what you have to say," he said.

Father Alexei explained that the ailing priest, Father Ruslan, had pleaded with Bishop Paulos to help him seek the Nevsky family's forgiveness. So far as the Church had been able to discover he, Yuri Nevsky, was the family's only surviving descendant. He was the one person who could put the priest's soul to rest.

Nevsky cut him short. "Why did he kill my father?"

"A terrible error! Your father, Vladimir Sergeyevich, was part of an expedition to a remote area of the Kirgiz Steppe—"

"*What?*"

"Only after the attack on the expedition did the guerrillas discover that your father was there with the M.G.B., soon to be the K.G.B. You cannot imagine Father Ruslan's horror. Because it was *he* who had engineered the attack. To have killed a Nevsky!"

Nevsky frowned. This was getting deep and coming fast. "A priest commanding guerrillas? And why does he still ·care about killing an American citizen nearly half a century ago?"

"He had a *great* attachment to your family. Yours was an old aristocratic one, you must know, that prospered for centuries." The priest hurried on. "Whatever the reason for his torment, he fled his ecclesiastical responsibilities, became a religious hermit, and bore his guilt like a massive weight. And bears it still!"

Nevsky rose and found his glass. It still held some stale beer. He sipped it and made a face. "Why was my father with the M.G.B. and in Central Asia?"

"I don't know."

"Why did a priest lead an attack on government men?"

"I was told he was protecting Church property from the hands of the state."

Nevsky had spent ten years on the edge, and sometimes slightly inside, private detective work. He knew people. He often knew when they lied. He didn't think this young man was lying—even though what he said didn't make much sense. "So this Father Ruslan is languishing near death, waiting for me to forgive him?" He shrugged. "OK, I forgive him. I forgive him! Go tell him. Or use the phone if you want." He waved at a portable phone sharing a small table with the padded box of poker chips.

Father Alexei at once looked ill at ease. "The bishop gave me particular instructions about how your forgiveness was to be expressed."

Nevsky's eyes narrowed. "Meaning...?"

"The failing one wants you in his presence, wants to hear the good news from your own lips."

Thoughts of his father, long dormant, bubbled up in Nevsky's memory. He remembered him crouched over his old Vari-Typer doing his technical translations, always wearing a tie and jacket to dinner, eating raw bacon on thick slices of black bread, puzzling the tyke Yuri by telling him to remember "that water seeks its own level..." Nevsky muttered, "He killed my father..."

"And regrets it with all his heart," the priest said.

"You brought him to Pittsburgh all the way from Russia?"

"All expenses were arranged," Father Alexei said.

Nevsky frowned. "I understand the Russian Church doesn't have rubles to spare. At least not the wheelbarrow full you'd need for plane fares to make sure an obscure priest dies happy." He drained the stale beer. "If you don't mind me saying, all this doesn't ring quite right. Now that I really think about it, I'm not sure I want to forgive this Father Ruslan."

The priest's anxiety rose. "You aren't willing to go to his bedside?"

Nevsky's eyes met the other's in a shrewd, hard glance. "I won't even consider it...unless you tell me the rest."

Father Alexei was now an honest man on the spot. Color rose above the generous shrub of beard. "I *beg* you to accompany me, Yuri Vladimirovich. A few hours of your time and you'll be back here in your bed."

"I'm not sure I want to go with you."

"If you could see him..." Father Alexei shook his head. "It was my intention to bring him to you. But he had another seizure. Now, who knows how long he'll live?" He raised his eyes to Nevsky's face. "You *must* go to him."

"Putting aside the forgiveness issue for a moment, something else is bothering me about all this," Nevsky said.

The priest heaved a heavy breath. "What?"

"I don't think you're telling me everything you know."

"I assure you..."

Nevsky shook his head. "Tell me *everything.*"

The priest's color deepened further. "I wasn't told much more..."

"Aha!" Nevsky grinned. "Father, I want to know all you do. I don't think your evasion and my forgiveness mix well, do you?"

Father Alexei asked to use the bathroom. When he returned, he had made his decision. He sat down and met Nevsky's eyes. "The little more that I know is that Father Ruslan won't discuss certain Church business with the bishop unless his mind is freed of his anguish."

Nevsky growled suspiciously, "That's it? That's all? 'Certain Church business?'"

"Yes."

"What Church business?"

The priest flashed an embarrassed smile. "I swear that was all that I was told. I'm afraid I know nothing more exciting."

"Then I don't think I'll go with you."

Father Alexei rose from his chair and sat on a low table. From there he could stare directly into the American's face. His eyes were a penetrating dark brown, almost black. They met Nevsky's gaze and didn't blink. "Does a Russian care nothing for a dying priest's soul?" he asked.

Soul! Or in Russian, *dusha. Dusha* was big stuff in Russia. Well, they were in America. Nevsky made a vague gesture of denial. This kind of talk didn't apply to him.

"Then what of your own soul, Yuri Vladimirovich?"

"My soul is fine." The moment he spoke he regretted it. How stupid that sounded! Few souls were fine. In fact, his wasn't that healthy at all. If soul meant wealth of spirit, he was hurting. Who wasn't? *Dusha, dusha...*

The priest's chuckle was hearty, rumbling even. He saw through Nevsky like a man before a swinging bead curtain. Not hard for him to tell the American's life hadn't been a stroll down Easy Street. Take a look at those lines that fifty-odd years had worked into his face. Don't miss the deep parentheses bracketing the mouth, the hairline receded all the way to the back of his head.

How quickly could the priest read his face? Could he see the divorce? Could he see three children scattered, estranged? How about a dozen careers that never flew because of his personality, his inability to suffer fools, the perverse tendency to lead when he had never been hired to do that?

Then there were the six years with widow Charity Day in this big house. The two of them had been in the information specialist—read private snooper—business. They were called a romance waiting to happen. Well, the waiting was long over. Ten years ago Charity married a rich man and moved away. Who could blame her? After that he had a bad run of luck that left him in late middle age still living in this old, airy ark. Information work? He hadn't been too active lately. He had enough money put away to ease through until... Well, he wasn't sure until what or when. Not for the rest of his days, that was certain.

If Father Alexei was clever enough, he could draw the obvious conclusion from the ample evidence.

Nevsky's life had disappointed him greatly.

The priest spoke carefully, sensing he could well lose the American. "I feel...you need a change, Yuri Vladimirovich—one that turns you toward the country where your family's blood once ran. Come meet Father Ruslan. He needs your forgiveness. Come for the humblest reason: to do good works—as our Savior urged us to act!"

Nevsky shaped his mouth to say no. But he didn't. In fact he knew his life needed...something. He didn't know what. He dreaded living it out as he was, like an old bachelor rattling around in seventeen rooms. He was better than that. A lot better. Prove it! he thought.

He said to the priest, "I need some time to think it over."

Father Alexei frowned. "Father Ruslan may well be dying. How much time can I give you?" He hesitated. "Later today I must have your answer. I'll come back some time in the afternoon. If your answer is yes, I'll take you to the holy man."

The priest rose. He understood matters had swung his way, even if he wasn't sure precisely why. He didn't use his small victory to goad Nevsky. He embraced him and went out through the rattling aluminum screen door into the early dawn.

Nevsky watched the cab pull away down the hill. For a moment he felt guilt at having turned the priest away, even if it proved to be for just a few hours. Then he quickly buried that thought. The ailing Father Ruslan had played a part in his father's murder.

What kind of fool would rush to forgive him?

2

Nevsky slept four hours and awoke dry-mouthed and nervous. He had dreamed of Russia, which hadn't happened in memory. His brain delivered wild surreal careenings—nightmares, really, worse ones than those serving as that country's history. What could he expect after a priest had told him his father had been murdered and inquired about the condition of his soul?

Very likely on tap for future nights were dreams of his father, the man moving again after so many years close to the center of his attention. Murdered! How? *A terrible error?*

He was eye-to-eye with a nearly fresh garlic bagel and a cup of French roast when the porch creaked. He heard the click as someone tried the dead door buzzer. Cup in hand he opened the door to face a couple. He was squat, bald, and bullet-headed. His Slavic eyes looked over cheekbones as thick and jutting as Himalayan outcroppings. His arms were only slightly thinner than Nevsky's legs. She was a pert brunette with a narrow waist that gave way to womanly swellings north and south. Her short-sleeved blouse and light print jumper weren't American. She carried a worn leather briefcase.

Well, well, things *were* starting to happen to Yuri V. Nevsky, weren't they? "What is this? Russian Week in Pittsburgh?" he asked.

They stared for a moment, uncomprehending. Wrong language. The woman held out her hand. "I am Lyudmila Mogadam," she said in Russian. Nevsky was surprised by the strength in her slender fingers. "This is Shmelev."

Shmelev had obsidian eyes set in a penetrating glower. The shape of his face and body and bristly graying hair gave him the look of a wild boar.

Once inside, the two lit cigarettes with the economical motions of confirmed addicts. Nevsky guessed post-Soviet Russia, though called new and improved, didn't have a surgeon general. Before he could ask them what was on their minds Shmelev was moving purposefully through the first floor's rooms, not skipping the kitchen and half-bath. He returned as stony-faced as ever. Nevsky realized he was Lyudmila's bodyguard in addition to whatever other roles he played. "Who did you think might be here?" he asked.

"One never knows." Shmelev spoke with a voice like a stone rasped against a cheese grater.

Lyudmila eyed Nevsky through a swirl of smoke. He put her age short of thirty-five. Under heavy brown brows her gray eyes were shrewd. He guessed her to be no fool. Her gaze measured him inside and out, up and down. She wanted to know what kind of man he was. Nevsky smiled inwardly. A complicated one, he could tell her.

She was loaded with lots to say. Her eyes shined with the brilliance of belief and commitment. Nevsky didn't have to wonder long about the source of her zeal. She couldn't wait to tell him about a man named only "Korchevko" whom she thought was destined to lead Russia with wisdom and compassion. He would raise the country to heights worthy of its promise. Presently he was living in a Spartan cell in St. John's Monastery near St. Petersburg.

"What's he doing there?" Nevsky asked.

"He seeks to center himself with God and Mother Russia," she said without a trace of sarcasm.

Shmelev said, "Korchevko is an extraordinary man touched by God. He rises far above the mob. Above even the best of us. His personality and will are stronger than *this!*" He made a fist thick as a chunk of rock. "God has marked him above all the opportunists, false patriots, and schemers who seek to lead our floundering country—such as the diminishing incumbent, Yeltsin!"

The two explained that the members of their organization, the Force for Leadership, were devoting their lives to seeing that Korchevko rose to the Russian presidency. Broad efforts were underway on all political and populist fronts to make this happen.

Last week Lyudmila and Shmelev had made one of their regular visits to their leader. As usual they conducted lengthy business and he led them in prayer. Also as usual they left the monastery with many orders to follow.

Lyudmila had been pacing aimlessly about the living room and smoking. Now she turned to study Nevsky's reaction to her coming words. "The most important matter discussed was your grandfather's diary. Your grandfather *was* Sergei Nevsky, the czarist called 'The Cunning,' was he not?"

Nevsky shrugged. "Well, he was Sergei Nevsky, all right. But I don't know much about him. 'The Cunning?' You sound like experts on the man." He frowned. "What do you care now about his diary written—when—before 1920?"

Shmelev scowled at him and then Lyudmila. "He dissembles, Lyudya."

"Watch yourself!" Nevsky said. "When I say I hardly know anything about the man, never mind his diary, I'm telling you the truth. If you came 7,000 miles to call me a liar, you wasted a lot of time and money."

"The diary records his activities in service to the czar." Lyudmila looked expectantly at him, as though she had just delivered an obvious cue.

"What services?" Nevsky said.

"Surely you know!"

Why the emotion in her voice? Nevsky wondered. "Sorry, I don't."

Shmelev began an abusive outburst. Lyudmila cut him short. To Nevsky she said, "We ask you to be frank with us about your grandfather's service to the Romanovs."

"Look, friends, I *am* being frank. I don't know what you're talking about!"

Lyudmila drew Shmelev into the next room. They lit more cigarettes. The air was taking on that poker night scent again. Their conversation came to him in mumbles, Shmelev's tone annoyed, hers pacifying.

The two returned. Shmelev opened Lyudmila's briefcase. He removed a photograph and a stack of photocopy sheets. He gave them to Nevsky. "Look. Read. Improve your memory," he said.

Nevsky didn't like Shmelev's tone. He didn't like Shmelev. "Maybe I have something better to do right now," he said.

"I think you will find the diary very interesting and informative." Lyudmila smiled.

Nevsky studied the color photograph. It showed that the original, a leather-bound volume, had been well preserved, likely in a cool dry place.

Nevsky riffled the photocopy sheets. The diary had been opened onto the copier's glass plate and copied two pages across. There were maybe a hundred hand-written pages to be read. "I need some coffee to get through this," he said.

"Shmelev would like some vodka with his," Lyudmila said.

"Here we usually take cream and sugar," Nevsky laughed. "But, hey, the guy is a Russian." He got the bottle. That Shmelev was heavy-handed didn't mean Nevsky couldn't be a good host.

With his favorite Superman mug filled with French roast he sat down with the diary. He looked across the kitchen table at the Russians. "Where's the original?"

They exchanged guarded glances. Before either could speak Nevsky said, "Stole this, made a copy, did you?"

Shmelev bristled. "I bought it! It suddenly appeared on the market. The original had been hidden for seventy years."

"Who'd you buy the copy from?" Nevsky looked at Lyudmila.

"That needn't concern you." Her strong face was set. He wouldn't find out right then. First Father Alexei. Now these two. He sensed much Russian intrigue over—what? Too soon to know.

The diary should make an interesting read.

It did!

His grandfather Sergei Nevsky, a wealthy landowner, began to keep the diary in 1908, the year he joined the monarchist group, the Sons of Continuity. Growing unrest and increasing political instability in the Motherland had convinced the Sons that Nicholas II might for a time have to exile himself and his family. The group planned to fly the entire family to Sweden in small airplanes piloted by French mercenaries. Sergei was asked to organize financial "resources" to support the czar in exile. The Sons of Continuity's thinking proved too fuzzy for him. He drastically revised their proposed plan. His improvised one involved setting up an agency within the government bureaucracy to aid him. The diary was deliberately ambiguous in describing precisely how he went about it—the first among the many other deliberate ambiguities to follow.

When the Sons of Continuity showed signs of dangerous incompetence, Sergei chose to carry out his responsibilities in complete secrecy. The diary was chiefly a record of his travels between 1909 and 1916. And travel he did, under a variety of aliases. The diary revealed that he had found his way to more than 150 of the world's major cities over the seven-year period. In each he made purchases. What he bought wasn't described. Nevsky was vexed to read such phrases as "...Buenos Aires, bought well from a half-dozen reliable merchants," and "...Chicago, steered to a tradesman of admirable discretion, bought extensively..." Also somehow involved in Sergey's plan was a transshipper somewhere in Switzerland to whom he sent his purchases. From Switzerland they were forwarded. Where? The diary didn't say.

Also in Switzerland he visited a design firm with some plans for a number of devices which its engineers improved. The devices were manufactured, but not assembled. Their parts were shipped "to the requested destination."

In early 1916 he paid one visit to a Countess Natalia S. living in a château well south of Paris. She was a friend of his youth, seemingly a very good one. His motive for making the journey was connected with his monarchist project. Her agenda was emotional: to revive their love, though both had married others. The visit was a taxing one for the couple. It was unclear whether or not Sergei accomplished what he set out to do which, annoyingly, was not described.

Later in 1916 Vladimir noted two vacation trips, one to "the desert region," another to "the south." Accompanying him was some personal freight transported under canvas.

The diary's final portion was less vague and more sorrowful. The Sons of Continuity's conspiracy was uncovered just as Nicholas II's government began to collapse in the late summer of 1917. Sergei gave his son Vladimir, Nevsky's father, and his daughter Anya "certain instructions." Each also received a Bible printed to his order. He sent Anya to Ukraine and Vladimir to America. Regional soviets made their presence felt. Great Meadow, the land and property accumulated by the Nevsky family over 400 years, was taken over by "the people." Sergey's wife Izabel was executed against a garden wall by a ragtag firing squad. Only by luck did Sergei escape to Paris. He lived there modestly in the guise of a German journalist.

In the summer of 1922 he learned that Cyril Vladimirovich, oldest son of the senior surviving branch of the Romanov family, intended to set up a government in exile. Sergei made arrangements to meet Cyril in Brittany where he could "at long last remove the massive responsibility that I have borne alone for so many years."

The last diary entry, June 21, was a curious one, Nevsky thought. "Countess S. contacted me. I must go there first!"

Nevsky put down the sheets. Now *there* were a few things to think about. What in the world could anyone make of all that?

He looked at his visitors. Their gazes were riveted expectantly on his face. The gray brilliance of commitment in Lyudmila's eyes had intensified. When Nevsky said nothing, Shmelev prompted, "The diary must have brought to mind all that your father Vladimir Sergeyevich shared with you."

Nevsky rose and shook his head. "He never said much about Imperial Russia. Losing everything to the Bolsheviks as a young man and running for his life wasn't a pleasant experience."

"The diary *must* fill in the blanks in what he shared with you, *swore* you to keep secret..." Lyudmila's voice rose. "Matters having to do with what the Romanovs hid away?"

"I told you. He didn't say much about old Russia. And nothing at all about any Romanov possessions. If they exist, I don't think he knew anything about them."

Nevsky couldn't mistake the disappointment on his visitors' faces. "This...cannot be," Shmelev growled. He moved closer, his shoulders hunching threateningly. "You have been reached by the others searching for the czar's treasure!"

Others? So that was it, Nevsky thought. All this was about a hunt for old treasure. Very likely Father Ruslan's visit to America was also connected to it, though Nevsky was certain Father Alexei had been kept in the dark. He drained his mug. "Sorry to disappoint you, friends. I'm sure you went to some trouble to find me—"

"Much investigation had to take place before we reached your door," Shmelev growled.

"All for nothing then."

The couple traded glances. That was all the warning Nevsky needed. When Shmelev came in hard and fast, he was ready with his assortment of bottom-of-the-deck defensive moves. He sidestepped the oncoming Russian, grabbed his ear and gave it a savage jerk. Shmelev howled and turned back into a heel of the hand driven into his nose. Something crunched inside and the fight went out of him in a gush of blood and tears. Palms pressed to his ruined face, he staggered and cursed.

Nevsky was about to throw them out. Lyudmila began to cry. He had read her as one tough lady. That she was moved to weep meant her most important hopes were being crushed. Like most men, Nevsky couldn't bear a woman's tears.

He went to the fridge and got some ice. He wrapped it in a towel and gave it to her. "Nurse him. He'll live." He added, "Even if he had the chance to give me the old K.G.B.-type interrogation, you wouldn't have found out anything more. Some people still tell the truth most of the time." He nodded toward the kitchen. "I'll make some lunch. We'll talk."

While slicing Muenster and salami, out of the living-alone habit he turned on the TV news-at-noon. The talking head had an ugly surprise for him. A dead Russian Orthodox priest had been fished out of the Allegheny River near Oakmont—not all that far from Nevsky's borough. He had been dead only a few hours. Marks and mutilation told a tale of torture. No ID. The description was close to that he would have written for Father Alexei.

Nevsky put down his knife and leaned on the kitchen counter. A shudder ran through him, nearly rattling his teeth.

"How is your soul, Yuri Vladimirovich?" he imagined a certain bearded wraith whispering. *How is your soul—now?*

A good priest had been tortured and murdered. Somewhere in Pittsburgh another was very ill, possibly dying. He awaited Nevsky's forgiveness for murdering his father. Now flip denial of what abruptly *did* seem his responsibility failed to come so easily. Father Alexei's words, *Come for the humblest reason: to do good works*, carried the weight of a moral authority that Nevsky hadn't felt since his days of innocence.

He saw he had an additional responsibility—find out who had killed the priest, and why. And see that justice, rough or otherwise, was done.

What am I thinking? he asked himself. He would have to be the world's worst ex-detective not to gather that Father Alexei's murder was connected to what the visiting couple called the czarist treasure. That meant that the "others" Shmelev had feared were also in the hunt. To seek justice Nevsky would have to tussle with treasure hunters. His instincts told him that would be risky business indeed.

Still, I should do something, he thought. *Do good works...* He groaned to have such simplistic thoughts at his age. Bad luck followed those who set out on missions. They took too much energy, enthusiasm, and persistence. They often started out as right, but turned out wrong. Their routes twisted and doubled back. Good tore off its mask and stood as evil. An ocean of complexity, cross-purposes, opposition, and physical danger diluted a single drop of reasonable commitment. He was too wise to set out on a dangerous mission aimed at mere wealth.

Unless it might also be a mission of personal salvation.

He revived himself and set to finishing the sandwiches and brewing tea. As he worked he recalled events of more than fifteen years ago when he had pursued missing Nicholas Markov across Pittsburgh's Russian Slope. In that search he had found not only Nicholas, but also himself. He had learned that the ties of blood and nationality were not so easily severed, either by the scythe of time, mere physical distance, or even generations passing.

Since then, though, he had lost that track leading into himself. After Nicholas, for a while his life had angled up. Then, down... To where he languished now. His visits to Russian Slope were infrequent. His time spent among the many recent émigrés was meager, no matter the fresh convulsions that shook their oft-shaken native land.

He needed to restore his perspective. More: he needed to test himself in ways that had real meaning. Did that include taking on those whose greed and savagery had already been revealed, even if their identities hadn't?

Was he up to so much? To his surprise he thought about...

His grandfather, Sergei Nevsky.

To whom he had given not five minute's attention totaled over his entire lifetime. It seemed he had gone on a mission—one for the czar. See how well he had carried it off! More than seventy years had passed and people were still looking in vain for whatever he had hidden. So, missions could be accomplished. What had Lyudmila said they had called Sergei? "The Cunning!"

Nevsky carried some of the same genes. He hadn't survived as a detective by lacking cunning. Just how much was in him he didn't know. Maybe to find that out he needed to work in a whole different arena.

A tempting idea presented itself: conclude what his grandfather had begun. Cross the bridge that led from the era of doomed waltzing aristocrats to the edges of the new millennium—and from his indifferent middle age to a later one of inner tranquility born in self-satisfaction.

Then there was the matter of 138 Morlande needing a new roof. What good was slate? Fifty or sixty years and one had to put new ones up there. And the whole ark needed painting. Handling those problems would take some scratch.

Dollars? He grinned. Maybe...a few rubles would shake loose somewhere.

"Lunch is served," he bellowed.

Shmelev's nose, when he lowered the ice pack, looked like a ripening mango. There was grudging respect in his still watering obsidian eyes. "I'm sorry, Yuri Vladimirovich," he growled. "It was hellish hard to find you. The journey here was long and tiring—"

Nevsky offered his hand. He always operated on the theory that one should have as few enemies as possible.

Over the meal his two visitors further described their leader Korchevko. He was a pious man guided by a calling to lead Russia, not for his gain but for that of its people. Though God-fearing, he was most practical. He had worked hard to create a place for himself as the only uncompromising critic of current leadership. He wasn't content with safe carping from the sidelines. He dared to be a visionary. Through his books, articles, and media appearances he communicated his principles. He spoke of linking the best qualities of the Russians, generosity, strength, and spirituality, with government. He firmly anchored these concepts to the political and economic realities of the post-Soviet era. Over time political support had coalesced and grown. He was poised to take over the main arena.

"What's holding him back?" Nevsky asked.

"Money," Lyudmila said. "Even he requires it to further expand his views and support a nationwide political organization."

"That's why you're looking for the treasure."

She pursed her lips. "Korchevko is skeptical about its existence. He was willing to take only two preliminary steps and see what developed. If they prove fruitless, he'll consider the horde a chimera. The first was to talk to you."

Nevsky couldn't help but laugh out loud. "Well, so much for *that* lead."

His visitors weren't amused. "The second step was to locate kin of the 'Countess S.' mentioned in the diary," Lyudmila said grimly. "If possible."

"An even more difficult task than finding you." Shmelev's rattling voice buzzed with his nose blocked by swelling. "Luckily Korchevko has friends in the French government. They are earnestly searching."

Lyudmila insisted on cleaning away the lunch's remains. Cigarettes and matches came out.

"Let us have the bottle." Shmelev lowered the ice pack and smiled painfully. His first show of humor. "My nose has need." He winked at Nevsky. "There is still one matter remaining before us. Korchevko armed us for every eventuality. We told you he is no fool." He poured three fingers of Stoli. "He told us what to do in the event you were not able to help us as we hoped."

Nevsky stared blankly. "What's that?"

"You are the grandson of the cunning one, are you not? Korchevko felt you would be a fine ally, not just in the search for the cache, but afterward as well. He invites you to join his political organization in a role of your choosing."

Nevsky hesitated, for the moment speechless.

Shmelev turned toward his companion. "Lyudya, two more glasses, if you please."

Nevsky understood Shmelev had every intention of the three of them emptying the nearly full bottle. "I'll have one drink with you, but that's it for right now," he said.

Shmelev's craggy brow erupted into a frown. "Do you not know our proverb? 'If you want to know a man, get drunk with him.'"

"Another time. Right now I have some important business to take care of."

Lyudmila pressed her palm to Nevsky's shoulder. Invitation shaped her face, its degree and direction left to his interpretation. "Will you join Korchevko and us?"

Nevsky took a little walk around the kitchen. "I'm not ready to decide that now. And if I do decide to help you, how will you reward me?"

Lyudmila's eyes narrowed shrewdly. "I don't think you're a man to be moved by money. We can offer you only...a chance to do good works."

Good works! Again! Nevsky thought, *Watch out!*

3

No sooner had Nevsky's visitors closed their rented car doors than he was on the phone. He called Russian Slope's Mr. Information, the ballet teacher Ivan "Volodya" Tschersky. He owned and operated the Petrograd School of Ballet Arts. "Volodya, this is Yuri Nevsky. How go pliés in these days of gangsta rap?"

"*Real* art survives. Trash comes and goes. When did you last see a break dancer?" Tschersky's heavily accented English rolled down the line like big stones in a drainpipe. "We haven't seen you here since Gorbachev ruled."

"You'll see me today, if you have the time..."

Driving to Russian Slope on a balmy morning in early June, Nevsky was reminded that greater Pittsburgh had done well the last dozen years. Bustle and construction were everywhere. The convulsions of the departure of heavy manufacturing—the sprawling steel and rolling mills clustered along the rivers, the slag heaps—were by now long departed. Those sooty days survived only as themes for new malls, in the papers of historians, and featured in the anecdotes of the retired nursing beers in gloomy Rankin gin mills. The new generation had forged ahead into light industry, medicine, and health care. The air was clean. Prices were low. Housing was affordable. Pittsburgh: once voted America's number one city in overall quality of life. There were worse places to live.

He drove fast in his battered Rabbit diesel. He sensed haste was needed if he were going to succeed in his errand of mercy— the first of the "good works" with which he seemed to have charged himself.

Tschersky, now in his seventies, was standing on his accustomed perch above a studio where a dozen leggy girls and two boys stretched and bent at the barre. He hadn't changed over the years. He still wore a turtleneck and gold-rimmed glasses below the gleaming sheen of his baldhead. Seeing Nevsky, he grinned until his gold-capped incisors gleamed. His handshake was as crushing as ever. When Nevsky told him he was in a bit of a hurry, they were in his office in less than a minute, the door closed behind them.

The photos of ballet greats still lined the walls. Missing, however, was the length of barre identified as having been removed from the original Petrograd Ballet Corps Studio in 1918. Nevsky asked Tschersky where it was.

"I have returned it! The Studio in Petrograd re-opened." His lined face lit up like fireworks on Bastille Day. "I attended the ceremony! Can you imagine I lived to stand inside the building for the first time? Its roof leaked. I could do nothing less than make a generous donation..." He damped his delight. "Yuri Vladimirovich, how can I help you? And what is your hurry?"

"My hurry is that I want to stay ahead of ugly things starting to happen." He gave the ballet master a laundered outline of Father Alexei's visit and his fate. Tschersky's face fell. Father Alexei spoke no English, Nevsky explained. He likely had sought Russian speakers with whom to leave his charge. So Nevsky had a feeling the surviving priest who awaited his forgiveness might well be on the Slope. "I'd be most grateful, Volodya, if you could do your magic and help me find him."

The ballet master rushed to the telephone. To do what Nevsky wanted required just three calls and the younger man's promise to return when he wasn't so rushed. Volodya sent Nevsky on his way to—he should have guessed—the rectory of St. Basil's Russian Orthodox Church that crowned the Slope. The frame building's four gilded onion domes gleamed in the early summer sun. Those domes... Nevsky remembered his mother said they represented holy flames: the Spirit of God, souls reaching toward their Maker, faith, and salvation. His mother... And now his father! Virtually forgotten for so long, he had stepped back into the middle of Nevsky's life. Here his son was, pressing forward in search of links to the past, hoping that finding them would validate his threadbare present.

A young priest answered the rectory doorbell. He had a thin beard and slightly protruding brown eyes. "I am Father Teodor, assistant to Father Mikhail."

Nevsky heard shouting upstairs. When he introduced himself, Father Teodor's young face wreathed with relief. "Well, this *is* a timely visit."

"It is?"

"I assume you've spoken with Father Alexei."

Nevsky nodded. Father Teodor hadn't heard the bad news.

"Father Ruslan's done little but ask for you. He has a visitor whom he's treating most rudely. He's been asked polite questions which he answers with unpleasantness."

The priest led Nevsky up a wide staircase. A voice cracking with age and agitation broke a short silence, speaking Russian.

"...does not matter to me that you're a friend of the Church! That you say you saw to the cost of our travel—"

"Don't excite yourself, Holy Father," replied a rolling mellow voice. "Your health is precarious. Excitement is—"

Nevsky was invited by Father Teodor to enter before him. He saw on the bed an emaciated man whose white beard and hair swept like a blizzard around his aged face. From the drumhead of taunt skin stretched over fleshless facial bone stared incredible green eyes. Some of their disturbing gleam arose from illness. The greater part came from obsessive guilt linked to great piety. The eyes moved and found Nevsky's face—and widened further. Father Ruslan's stick hand rose to bless himself. "Vladimir Sergeyevich Nevsky!" he shouted, his voice cracking.

"No, father. I'm his son. I am *Yuri* Nevsky." The words caught in his throat. What kind of holy soul was this?

The other man moved forward and lightly restrained Father Ruslan. He had a thick head of curly hair and luminous blue eyes. He wore a curly beard and an expensive business suit. His hands were long and smooth.

Father Ruslan sat up despite the restraining hand. His strength was the manic one of those teetering close to death. A bony finger pointed at Nevsky. "Come closer!" Nevsky advanced. "Yes. Yes!" the holy man cried. His cold fingers tweaked Nevsky's cheek, brow, and chin, as though to uncover disguises. He threw himself back on the bed, turned his face upward, eyes closed, and extended his arms horizontally. "I thank the most Almighty God! *I thank the most Almighty God!* He has granted my wish made *every* day for more than forty years!"

He sat up slowly and shook off the hand of the well-dressed man. He wore a loose shift. Sliding off the bed exposed his feet. They carried the heaviest calluses and scars. He had gone barefoot in the wilderness! He sank slowly to aged knees. He tried to walk on them across the floor to Nevsky's shoes, muttering, "Your forgiveness, Yuri Vladimirovich. Your forgiveness as the last of the Family Nevsky!"

Nevsky's eyes filled with tears. He hurried to the old man and pulled him up. "I'll forgive you. I know what you did—"

"No! *You must hear it all!*" Father Ruslan was racked with coughing. He staggered. Nevsky held him. The body under his hands was as light as a sack of sticks. He carried the holy man back to the bed. Father Teodor met him there, attentive with a light blanket and pillows. The old man's face had gone ashen.

His eyes closed. Two hot red spots marked his cheeks. He wouldn't die this moment, Nevsky thought. But how much longer would he live?

The coughing fit passed. The holy one breathed deeply, gathering his strength.

Nevsky turned to the well-dressed man. "You know my name. What's yours? And where do you fit into all this?"

The luminous blue eyes twinkled from a thicket of hair and beard. "I am Timofy Teodorovich Grushkin," he said. "I am a Moscow politician with an interest in the Church. I paid for the two priests to fly here. I took the same flight. Father Alexei—surely you have met him—knew of my generosity. Possibly he mentioned it to you." He nodded at the motionless priest. "I came to speak to him because I'm afraid something's gone wrong. After talking to you, Father Alexei was to meet me early this morning. Your being here means you two did talk."

Nevsky nodded. He volunteered no information about the priest's ugly death or about having found his way here by himself.

"When I received no message from Father Alexei, I grew anxious," Grushkin said. "I came here for information."

"We know nothing," Father Teodor volunteered. "We promised Father Alexei to care for the holy one here until you came back with him. We assumed it would only be a matter of a few hours."

Nevsky swallowed. If he had returned with Father Alexei last night instead of taking time out to sniff his damned melancholy *dusha,* the man might still be alive. One decision made. One decision wrong!

"Shortly after we arrived Father Ruslan took a turn for the worst." Grushkin frowned. "I knew vaguely that there was some important Church-related information locked away in his head. I was afraid that he might die and what he knew would be lost to the pious for eternity. Over the last hour I tried to persuade him to tell me what he knew. As you no doubt heard, I was unsuccessful. He will unburden himself only to you, Yuri Vladimirovich."

Father Teodor left the room and returned with wine in a tumbler. He raised the ill priest's head and wet his lips. He drank in feeble swallows. The grape did its magic. The magnificent eyes opened, their brilliance intensified. They found Nevsky. "Vladimir Sergeyevich..." he murmured.

No one corrected him. Let him confess to his victim in delusion, Nevsky thought.

Father Teodor explained that his regular duties for today had so far remained undone. He excused himself. Nevsky and Grushkin drew up chairs and leaned forward.

Father Ruslan began to speak.

He chose not to begin with his life's great misdeed. Instead he talked about the resulting crushing guilt. It transformed his life. Up to then he had lived the simple life of a priest ministering to the very few believers in small scattered villages on the edge of the Kirgiz Steppe in south central Russia. Subsequently he became a driven man seeking only to purify his soul. He traveled to the far north, spending much time beyond the Arctic Circle. There over years he met God. In his infrequent dealings with men they came to think of him as a holy man. Healings and supposed resurrections were credited to him. Some sought in vain to make him their *starets*, or spiritual counselor. All hung on his meager words like shipwreck survivors to a lifeboat. So the years given to him passed.

"But God, whom I love with all my heart, did not relieve me of my guilt, no matter the length and substance of my prayers," the holy man whispered. "He told me that only by confession to one in whose veins ran the blood of my victim could I be set free from my torment. And this wasn't possible. Time, upheavals, and the Great Patriotic War had scattered the Nevskys far beyond my hobbled reach.

"Several weeks ago, while wandering the taiga in the far north, I grew ill and found my way to a small nameless village. Fever seized me and for days I lay close to death. In that time a man from the village traveled far to reach a radio. Word of my illness reached the Church."

As a result he received a visitor from a thousand miles away, Bishop Paulos traveling in disguise as a simple priest. Even in his fever Father Ruslan knew here came his only chance. Possibly it could be arranged for him to make his confession, be forgiven, and then die in peace.

He guessed what the prelate wanted to know. Since the death in 1944 of Father Ruslan's father, himself a priest called Father Konstantine, there had circulated through the Church rumors of hidden czarist wealth. He knew no details. He guessed that what had happened on the Kirgiz Steppe forty-five years ago was connected with that horde. So he played his only card: he would tell what he knew only to a member of the

Nevsky family. In that way also he would be given a chance to beg for forgiveness. And the relative of the man he helped murder, if God willed it, might somehow be made a rich man. He proposed his bargain to the bishop. "And thus I came to this bed and this moment," the holy man breathed.

Nevsky drew a deep breath. "Tell me how my father died."

The halo of white hair around the holy man's withered face shifted and shined as he leaned from his pillow. He resumed his story. After Father Ruslan's ordination in 1935 Konstantine, no matter the weakness of the Church and the rule of the commissars, arranged for his son's assignment to the steppe communities. This was a cunning design because there were few Christians there. This largely freed him from great responsibilities, allowing him to remain constantly vigilant in regards to a certain small shallow canyon. In strictest confidence Konstantine charged his son with a vague but important responsibility. Added to this charge were instructions involving possible eventualities...

Nearly seventeen years passed without event. During this time he married. His wife bore him a son. Then came the summer of 1952. Early on a morning in July one of the local lads was taking his turn at lookout, as had dozens like him stretching back over the years. He saw movement on the grasslands! He ran to report three cars and a heavy flatbed truck had appeared in the far distance. They were headed in the general direction of the canyon. The difficult terrain would make their ultimate arrival a lengthy business.

Following long-established procedures reinforced by earnest drills, six men joined Father Ruslan on a vantage point inside the canyon. All were Muslim or shamanist Red Army veterans who had seen heavy action in defense of Leningrad. One peered through battered field glasses at the approaching vehicles. "Not the military, Holy Father. Worse. I remember their kind from the war. Internal security. 'Cheka,'" he said, using the old name of Lenin's now transmogrified secret police.

The priest reviewed in memory his father's instructions. The approaching agents were not among those to be favored. His men looked toward him for instructions. "Stay hidden among rocks on both sides of the canyon," he said. "Ready yourselves."

With familiar ease they hefted their weapons and adjusted their belts of ammunition and hand grenades. One asked, "Why have they come here?"

"I swear I don't know," the priest said. "We will find out. Be ready!" He kept one man with him and pressed his shoulder. "If this one opens fire, so shall you all. By then you'll know you're aiming at enemies of God and Mother Russia."

The vehicles stopped beyond the canyon. Men got out and used gleaming navigational instruments. When they finished, one pointed ahead at the canyon.

On they came.

There was a rough track leading around a tumble of rock nearly blocking the canyon entrance. The eight-wheeled truck lurched over the massive rocks, angling onto four wheels for a moment and nearly tumbling. At the canyon bottom the navigational instruments were used again. The group's leader, who wore a gray homburg despite the heat, waved ahead toward a level sandy patch free of rock.

The cars emptied. Ten men with shovels roamed over the patch and began to dig random holes. Homburg returned to the first car where he sat beside another man, possibly his superior.

The digging continued for three hours. In time men were up to their waists in the holes, then shoulder deep. One cried out.

A chill scampered like an icy spider up Father Ruslan's spine.

The others rushed to the shouter. His hole was widened, deepened. Dirt flew as though from the work of a pack of dogs. The cries of excited shovelers echoed in the canyon. Homburg walked to the edge of the hole and looked down. Only their leader remained quietly in the lead car.

There was a distant consultation, its words lost to Father Ruslan. Shovels trimmed the hole into a square. They resumed work, but only along one edge. The priest was puzzled. In time he understood.

They were fashioning a ramp.

Up it they would drag whatever they had found.

Two more hours of hard labor were required before the object edged out of the earth.

It was a gleaming metallic cube.

Its sides were higher than a man. Each bore the stenciled red Romanov double eagle and black lettering: *Olga Nikolayevna*. She was Czar Nicholas II's eldest daughter, the first of the four grand duchesses. When the cube finally stood completely free on the sand, the M.G.B. men cheered.

Their jubilation proved somewhat premature. Father Ruslan did not have the field glasses, so could only gather that the cube was tightly sealed. The tools needed to open it were lacking.

Three of the men with shovels began a clumsy attack on the shining surface.

After another hour they were able to twist back an edge of metal. Within the cube lay some kind of lattice structure. There were additional cheers as Homburg stepped forward and peered into the shadowy interior. Through the hole he thrust a hand, groped about, withdrew it.

Holding nothing.

He spun and snatched a shovel from the nearest man. He jammed it into the latticework and heaved viciously. Metal creaked, bent. The shovel handle snapped. What remained in his grip he threw into the sand. Whirling back to the opening, he levered out the shovel blade. He was now able to thrust in his head and one hand. Again he groped, now with increasing wildness.

He spun free of the cube. "It's empty, comrades! *Empty!*" he shouted. He flung his arms about wildly. "Enemies of the state have beaten us to the czar's wealth!"

Father Ruslan drew a heavy breath. He knew as well as he did his own name that this site had never been disturbed. Surprise had followed surprise. Even so, his father's instructions whose vagueness had evaporated this day under the summer sun still remained to be followed. The next moments would determine the fate of these M.G.B. men.

Homburg shouted. "Load the cube onto the truck. We will take it back with us. It will be examined for clues and analyzed."

And so they must die.

Father Ruslan blessed himself. Sometimes doing the work of God and Mother Russia tested His servants. He touched the ex-soldier's shoulder. "Shoot the man in the hat," he whispered.

It was all over in twenty seconds.

The priest's men crept warily from among the rocks. Coups de grace were administered.

Grenade shrapnel had riddled the lead car. A flat-faced ex-sergeant threw open the passenger door. Father Ruslan was summoned. He found the vehicle's dead occupant was handcuffed to the steering column. His body showed signs of extensive torture.

Uneasiness over the death of the seeming innocent stirred the priest. In the back seat he found a briefcase. In it were papers relating to the odyssey that had brought the M.G.B. men to their death.

It began with a directive from Stalin himself. The persistent rumors of the czar's un-recovered wealth goaded that paranoid into believing his beloved Revolution was not yet fully complete. The treasure *must* be found, or many more would be guests in his gulags. So the search began. Among the papers the priest found one, then another—then more!—bearing a certain family name.

One that chilled him, no matter that the sun remained a hot disk in the low western sky.

The name was Nevsky.

It was the Family Nevsky that his father Konstantine had served! He had lived at Great Meadow where he saw to the spiritual needs of aristocrat and peasant alike. He and the landowner Sergei Nevsky might as well have been brothers!

More papers revealed a worldwide hunt for family survivors. Sergei Nevsky, it was clear, was dead. His daughter Anya had been traced to Ukraine, but the chaos of the Great Patriotic War had left no further record of her. His son Vladimir had immigrated to the American city, Pittsburgh. The M.G.B. found him and contemplated kidnapping, but this crime at least was delayed at higher levels. He was watched continually. When business took him to Portugal, the lucky M.G.B. dared pounce. They whisked their captive to Russia and tortured him until he told them what they wished.

At this Nevsky was baffled. His father *was not involved!* His grandfather was surely too clever to weigh down his son's future with the heavy anchor of the czar's double eagle. Yet he must have told him...something. Nevsky was too shaken with re-living his father's horrid end in torture and shrapnel to sift his memories for what little that decent man had heard before forever departing from his own father.

With a steadily sinking heart Father Ruslan had the handcuffed corpse searched. Its pockets carried no papers. But Homburg's inside coat pocket bulged with them. Among them was a foreign passport. One of the priest's men recognized the seal of the United States. Another knew the Roman alphabet. He squinted at the document, at the photo, then at the corpse. He nodded: paper and man matched. He ran his finger along the line of type that was the man's name. Slowly he read, "Vladimir...Sergeyevich...Nevsky."

The priest howled and threw himself on the ground. He tore at his hair and robes. For long moments he was indeed mad. What he had done undermined *everything* that his father had promised. One day, he had told him, a Nevsky or someone sent by a Nevsky might come here. One road from the czar's days to Russia's present would forever lead through the Nevsky family.

In the thrall of arrogance and error Father Ruslan had ordered a Nevsky's death!

The M.G.B. corpses were carried away, destined for deep, invisible graves. The body of Vladimir Nevsky was prepared for travel. The useful automobiles would be repaired, disguised, and put to domestic use.

His father had left him with a final major task.

"Return whatever might be found to Great Meadow."

With the aid of Homburg's papers, the truck, and the nerve of loyal believers the covered cube and Vladimir's body found their way in secret across thousands of miles. Their destination: what was now the Red Banner Collective Farm east of St. Petersburg. There pious men with long memories and no love of the regime met and embraced a recently arrived young man. He directed Vladimir's burial in the former family cemetery. After long consultations with the oldest of the trusted men who had known Father Konstantine, he hid the cube somewhere on the sprawling acreage. When that old man died, he would be sole master of all Great Meadow's secrets.

He, Gregory, son of Father Ruslan.

All that done, Father Ruslan cast off his worldly garments and donned the rough rags of repentance.

The ailing priest lay back on the bed, his strength spent. Only his eyes kept their luminous vigor. He beckoned to Nevsky. The American came forward and bent over him. "Am I truly forgiven, Vladimir Sergeyevich?" the old man asked.

Nevsky's eyes burned. He swallowed tears. He felt he spoke for his father whom the old priest now imagined he was, as well as for himself. "Forgiven...with all my heart, holy one!"

Stick fingers pressed Nevsky's hand. The old man's flesh was so cold! His thin lips moved within the silvery shower of beard. "Behold the kindness of God!"

He fell asleep.

Outside in the shadow of the church Nevsky shared with Grushkin the news of Father Alexei's ugly death. The Russian's mouth fell open. He blessed himself. "How horrible! The lad had *dusha naraspashku,* an open heart."

Nevsky nodded. "I had two visitors after he left. They represented a man named Korchevko. Maybe they're mixed up in his death."

Grushkin touched his shoulder. "Yuri Vladimirovich, we must talk."

Nevsky shook his head. "Not now." He was too shaken by the priest's tale and the ugly circumstances of his father's death. He had no desire to share any of his morbid speculations.

"Tomorrow then."

"We'll meet here on the Slope." Nevsky named the place. Surprising himself, he went on. "Be careful. People who murder priests will murder friends of priests, too."

4

Moscow

Boris Petrovich Detrovna slipped into his armored limousine's back seat. The driver closed the door behind him and Gennady Efimovich Rishnikov, the man called the Attorney. Detrovna was in a rage. Repeatedly he had tried to make the herd of political sheep *move.* Repeatedly they had quailed at swift seizure of the presidency from the comic Yeltsin—the bold action from which would eventually emerge a significant leader of Russia.

He, Detrovna, would be a major contender. Should he achieve the presidency...many would tremble.

Oh, the hack politicians were a glib, dancing bunch, secretaries-of-this, prime ministers-of-that, directors-of-screw-all! They spouted reasons for caution like the Ob River spewed its waters into the Arctic Ocean.

They feared damage to the economy. The *economy!* What was the Russian economy but a hybrid hulk cobbled together not by plan but circumstance? Take five parts ingrown Communism, mix with three of novice capitalism and seven of opportunism exercised in the outright theft of state property. Dust heavily with foreign brigandage masked with pretty names like "venture industries" and "resources development"—and behold the tottering monster!

They feared instability, though civil wars raged, Russia's borders were violated at will, and relentless inflation impoverished the population. *Instability!* When orders, no matter where they originated, were obeyed only when convenient and few feared either government or God. Add to this his country's age-old traditions of sloth, corruption, drunkenness, and incompetence and one understood why no nation now trembled at the footstep of the Russian bear.

In fact Detrovna knew the only thing his political associates *really* feared.

It was the power of the military.

Only when General Gaichev—never mind what bureaucrat in theory commanded him—agreed to back the civil coup to topple weakened Yeltsin would they dare to act.

Detrovna's colleagues within the Duma and beyond thought Gaichev, a long-standing patriot, aloof from the pettiness of politics. The only public statements he made were in praise of the Motherland couched in phrases so vague that no one could disagree—or imagine what was truly on his mind.

Detrovna knew.

It was rubles.

A great many rubles. Only after torturous arrangements had one of the politician's emissaries come to sit down over vodka with the general's aide-de-camp. Over a two-day drinking bout the flunky let it be known—in the guise of a joke, of course— just how much money the general expected for his support and his armies.

An amount out of the question.

Detrovna growled to his driver to speed up—damn the traffic that had come to clog Moscow streets! Yet one more affliction spawned by that long-gone impossible curiosity, perestroika.

The Attorney tried to draw Detrovna into conversation without success, so dark was his mood.

It wasn't improved when they emerged from his private elevator into the living quarters atop his five-story building in the Patryarshi Ponds area. He, the Attorney, and the two trailing bodyguards all wrinkled their noses.

The stink belonged to failed plumbing. Detrovna growled in frustration. The entire suite of nine rooms with its three baths had been completely remodeled by Swedes and Finns. Their labors at least could be relied upon. Foreign work teams had also re-plumbed and rewired the entire building—not to mention Detrovna's dozen lucrative apartment houses. All had been refaced and re-roofed as well.

Nonetheless, stink!

He knew it wasn't the building's perfect plumbing that had failed. The corruption was beyond his property lines in the city's crumbling ancient piping. Behold the reality of the "new" Russia! He slammed his briefcase down on an antique marble table. No matter how he built, remodeled, and hoped, in the end his feet sank into...crap. Not just the crap in jammed pipes, but that of bankrupt municipalities and the necessity of bribery to accomplish anything. Add the crap of delays and of the impossibility of getting major sewers—or anything else— promptly and properly repaired. Transform the pipe problem into any industrial, social, economic, or scientific challenge. Send it in any direction! The result was the same. Across the face of Russian life ultimately there was no escape from *crap*. There were not enough Finns, Swedes, or the accursed Germans on earth to do Russia's work for her. To free her from crap.

Russians must do it.

Led to do it. By someone who didn't fear to make the people tremble. How else could matters be managed? When else had matters *been* managed in this timeless, vexing land except at too few periods in which feared leaders took power and used it? Peter, Catherine, Stalin. History had shown there was no other way to lash Russia to greatness. Yeltsin was no such man.

Call him a president, a czar. Call him a salamander! Names didn't matter. The point was a *true* leader was needed.

He could be that leader. To be sure there were many problems to be overcome. It was a long leap from respected member of the Duma to the head of the nation. Nonetheless, much might be dared—save for the stumbling block of General Gaichev.

His communication pad buzzed. His secretary reported that Mr. Ivanov was on the line. "Ivanov" was Daniel Tserborov, a man never seen with Detrovna. A Moscow-wide private telephone system installed by Americans for an extortionary fee assured confidentiality and reliability. Daniel Isadorovich was brief, as usual. Some operatives under his control were failing to turn over their full share of receipts. They were "skimming."

"You're certain?" Detrovna asked.

"Reliable sources, Boris Petrovich. I sense Vseva Sesnikov is at the heart of it. The other three likely nodded their assent. Our men-at-work under them know nothing."

"Your suggestion?" Detrovna asked.

"Seva should be punished. The others will get the message."

Detrovna cursed. "You're getting to be an old woman, Daniel Isadorovich! Here is what you will do—and the lesson will not be lost on men-at-work in other districts. You will liquidate all four. Hear me clearly. *All four.*"

Tserborov did not hesitate. "As you like, Boris Petrovich."

"No one steals from me. I have done too much and gone too far to even dream of permitting it. Understand!"

The Attorney, looking on, allowed himself a thin smile. As Detrovna's confidant and advisor, he had always advocated a strong hand in dealing with the brigades of hoodlums under his master's control.

Boris Petrovich needed little convincing.

Moments later the secretary buzzed again. A visitor, one Josef Harsky, wanted to see Detrovna. No appointment.

Detrovna ordered him away. The secretary reported that he refused to leave. He said he had come for both Detrovna's gain and his own, but refused to amplify. Detrovna was about to order him thrown into the street, then thought better of it. He had learned to his great benefit that one never knew from which direction opportunity came to knock. He nodded to the Attorney. "See what he wants, Gennady Efimovich. I'm not to be troubled unless it's to my advantage."

After five minutes the Attorney returned. "He's being frisked now, Boris Petrovich. You should talk to him."

Detrovna frowned. "Why?"

The Attorney, who was privy to his master's recent frustrations, smiled as broadly as his narrow face and thin lips permitted. "He says he wants to make you 'far richer than you are.'"

Josef Harsky was a short, slight man past fifty. His carefully kept beard was graying. He wore rimless glasses. Behind them his eyes were anxious but determined. He was well aware of Detrovna's rank in government and business. Possibly he had heard the rumors of the man's third empire—organized crime. Whatever the case, he drew himself up and advanced through the lavish suite.

"Speak fast, Harsky," Detrovna growled.

Harsky's face was expressionless. "As you wish." He explained he was a government accountant. Like so many of the multitudes formerly employed by the great, inefficient state, he once had much "work" time to use as he pleased. He chose to learn to find his way through the vast domain of ledgers and balance sheets belonging to earlier regimes. He amused himself by sifting through historical financial archives from the days of Lenin—and before. Yes, even those belonging to the governments of the czars. While countless documents had been destroyed in the heyday of the infant Revolution, many still remained, shunted off to moldering storage or turning to confetti in inadequate libraries.

"I'm a man quickly bored, Harsky. Come to the point," Detrovna said. "How am I to be made rich by rotting hundred-year-old ledgers?"

The little man whitened. Nonetheless, whatever determination had carried him to this point didn't fail him. "Some small patience, Mr. Detrovna—"

"And why did you come to *me?*"

"You'll understand quite soon."

Detrovna made an impatient gesture. "What did you find for me?"

"I found...the financial records of a government ministry that utterly failed to perform its function."

Detrovna and the Attorney burst into laughter. "This is the *only* kind of ministries our country has!" Detrovna howled. "Those that steal and fail!" To himself he added: *this too will change!*

Harsky did not smile. He began his story.

The Ministry of External Survey and Evaluation had been set up in 1909 by unclear authority. Money was transferred to it from Czar Nicholas II's personal accounts and siphoned from scores of other bureaus. This was managed in ways that only careful internal audit and review could expose. Audits were seldom done—then or now. The ministry's staff was small. Its expenses were chiefly financial wires sent to a few men who traveled to most of the world's major cities. Much smaller amounts were sent to two Zurich companies to pay for services. One was a precision engineering firm, the other a transporter.

"All financial entries for the wires were for 'survey and evaluation services,'" Harsky said.

"What of it?" Detrovna's characteristic impatience bubbled. "It was a survey and evaluation ministry!"

"The amounts transferred were too large merely to pay for surveys," Harsky said.

"How large?"

"Generally between two hundred and three hundred thousand rubles."

"Altogether?"

"Each time!" Harsky made no effort to hide his excitement. "They kept careful accounts. The ministry began operations in January 1909. It was dissolved in September 1916. An average of 50 wires were sent each year, say just fewer than 450 over that period. The average disbursement was, as I said, around 275,000 rubles. Simple multiplication gives us a total something over 123 million rubles."

Detrovna frowned. "If the money wasn't sent for services, what was it sent for?"

"We must step back a bit to answer that question," the accountant said. "A curious fact about the ministry—its head was a man with no known political ties and no credentials as a bureaucrat. He was a landowner, a member of an old aristocratic family. Very possibly he was a monarchist." Harsky paused and cleared his throat. "One who had a great interest in the welfare of the Romanovs."

The Attorney pointed to a chair. "Sit down," he said.

Harsky smothered his small smile of satisfaction and sat quickly. He continued. "I suggest he was on a seven-year assignment for the czar—either personally or as an impresario. The ministry was created for his use."

"To do what?" Detrovna was mystified. In what way would all this turn his way?

"To make purchases for the czar," Harsky said.

Detrovna laughed loudly for the second time. "To *buy* for the Romanovs? Whose exploitation of the people and decadence made them owners of a quarter of Russia? They ate off *gold*, you idiot, and danced minuets while peasants starved! What could this man buy that the Romanovs didn't already have?"

"I don't know. All I know is the cost."

"You pose a puzzle with no solution," Detrovna said.

"Nonetheless...nonetheless..." Harsky pondered how best to continue. "The same thoughts came to me. Yet heavy use was made of the Swiss transporter, shipper, what-have-you. Transporters transport *something.*"

"*What?*" Detrovna barked.

"As I said, I don't know." Harsky hurried on before Detrovna could bark again. "A more rewarding question might be...whence? Where were the purchases sent? I have an idea about this. If I'm right, then I'll soon have some hard evidence to show you." The little man swallowed. "If you agree to my bargain."

"What 'bargain?'" Detrovna was at once on guard. He had not become what he was by being swindled.

"Let's talk financial appreciation before any negotiations," the accountant said. "Suppose the 123 million rubles were used to buy something of hard value—art, precious metals, jewelry, any fine work. Imagine how much the purchases have increased in value in more than eighty years! Ten times? Twenty? Fifty? Possibly even times hundreds. We speak then about a massive fortune."

"Possibly so," the Attorney said. "But who can say what happened to whatever was bought and shipped. The winds of the Revolution blew everywhere."

"I believe the aristocrat gathered everything in a single safe place. I also believe it never reached the czar's hands. Nor those of the Revolution." The little accountant stood up. "I've talked enough. Hear what I'll give you as my part of the bargain." He paused.

The Attorney nodded for him to continue.

"Mr. Detrovna will get all the financial records and other documents from the Ministry for Survey and Evaluation and the name of the aristocrat," Harsky said. "If he agrees to my terms, later I'll bring him some hard evidence of the vicinity of the valuables. I don't offer any guarantees. Work will have to be done to find what, over my years of digging and dreaming, I've come to call the 'Romanov Cache.'"

Detrovna rose scowling. He was no stranger to setting the stage for making a favorable bargain. "Such will-o'-the-wisps aren't worth much to me." He made a dismissing gesture with his right hand. "What do you want in exchange? And don't ask for much. Because you offer little."

The little man's eyes burned behind his rimless glasses. "What I want I don't believe will greatly inconvenience you. I don't want my daughter Alessya to be your mistress any longer."

5

Boris Detrovna would have liked to have put Josef Harsky and his will-o'-the wisp czarist fantasy out of mind. But he couldn't do it.

Because he needed wealth.

More so than ever. The reason: he had made a decision. He wished to divest the darker portion of his enterprises. It was time to say goodbye to the highjackers, protection peddlers, rent gougers, extortionists, thieves, whores and panderers, arms sellers, smugglers, and hired killers who, whether they knew it or not, owed him allegiance and paid handsome tribute. If he were to have a chance of seizing the ultimate prize—total leadership of the country—these activities had to be put behind him in favor of additional legitimate businesses.

To the expense of so doing add that needed to overcome the *crap*. To put right jobs done wrong. To pay far more for reliable imported equipment than for its shoddy local equivalents. To compensate reliable middle managers, effective technocrats, and shrewd market analysts. To employ *anyone* who knew how to do good work day in and day out and make profit. Spending money this way was no luxury. It was a necessity. Because the crap was everywhere. And would be—until he led Russia to wiser ways.

He had just finished an arduous session with his two financial men. Their figures told him that it would take years, even in an expanding economy, for him to make his present profit honestly. To be honest meant obeying the laws, particularly those of the whimsical tax agencies.

To be honest had one thing in common with dealing with the crap. It too was expensive!

Add to this shortfall the amount needed to bribe General Gaichev at the right moment. Look also at the expenses required to expand his political constituency. Substantial "investments" had to be made in certain powerful Federation Council members to guarantee their future support. He had to pay his street workers to do the spadework that delivered votes. Votes not just for him, but also for those he had chosen for office and public responsibility who would expand his power base and act on his behalf at the right time. Oh, it *could* be done. This was a volatile era in the history of the Motherland; everything could be bought.

Even an empire.

If one had the rubles.

He had been hard-nosed with Harsky. He had told him he wouldn't even consider his proposed bargain until he provided the promised "hard evidence" of the cache's approximate location. Off he had gone to gather it. Several weeks passed without word from the man. Detrovna was surprised at the level of his own disappointment. Then a few hours ago Harsky's call had come. He had "some things" to show him. Detrovna quickly summoned him. Possibly too quickly. Greed had seized his lips and spoken for him.

Harsky was preceded by one of Detrovna's larger men carrying two wooden boxes of different sizes. At the little man's order he placed them on the carpet in front of the gleaming desk. They carried a familiar odor that Detrovna couldn't immediately place. Not until Harsky greeted him and loosened the box lids did he recognize it.

Dampness.

Harsky began an exposition on the boxes' contents. Detrovna cut him short with a wave of his hand. "Let's *see* what you've brought me. Talk as you go." From the corner of his eye he saw the Attorney lean forward for a better view. Gennady Efimovich well knew the vaulting state of his master's ambitions and also was having trouble reigning in his expectations.

Harsky took the lid from the smaller of the two boxes. From it he pulled a shapely waist-high vase, its colors faded from immersion. "Everything in both boxes was under water," he said. "To retrieve the objects I had only the help of a single amateur diver. It doesn't look it, but gathering what little I have here required much work—"

"Don't try to impress me to strike a better bargain, Josef Yurievitch," Detrovna growled. "What else do you have there?" He passed the vase to the Attorney for examination.

Harsky's white hands withdrew three identical ceramic elephants larger than fine melons. They were empty planters. Detrovna examined them as well, his frown growing. For the moment he held his tongue.

Next out were ten life-sized doll heads, a few flecks of paint still dotting their clay. The fabric bodies meant to dangle below evidently had dissolved in watery rot. Harsky's nervous glance found Detrovna's face. Seeing the growing glower sped him to open the larger box. He beckoned Detrovna forward. "Look!"

Detrovna saw what seemed at first to be a crusted jumble of rust. After a moment he recognized the object. It was a badly oxidized suit of armor. "You see?" the accountant said excitedly.

"I do *not* see a treasure," Detrovna said.

"You can't deny these were once valuable items," the accountant insisted. "I believe they were part of the cache. If you'll remember, I didn't promise to deliver the riches. I'm offering *you* the chance to find them. Frankly, if my suspicions are correct, uncovering the full cache is beyond my means."

"Why so?"

"Much labor, much danger." Harsky smiled cryptically. "Certain...logistical problems." He removed a photograph from his pocket and gave it to Detrovna. It had been taken with a cheap underwater camera. It showed a submerged slope angling down. Its silty surface was littered with indistinct objects. All were covered to some degree with sediment. Detrovna had to assume that many hundreds, possibly many thousands, of items lay down there, survivors of eighty years of incessant corruption by water. Who could guess their initial number—or their value?

He understood that what Harsky had brought him was salvaged from this site.

"Where did you find these?" Detrovna waved the photo at the objects.

Harsky smiled. After several moments he said, "I believe there is only one reason for them to be where they are. As I said, they are part of the Romanov Cache." He replaced the lids on the boxes and faced Detrovna. "You now know as much as I do—except the location of this body of water and the name of the long dead aristocrat behind the effort. If we're able to complete our bargain, I'll give you that information and his map. I'll also turn over to you the financial records of the Ministry of External Survey and Evaluation." Harsky drew a deep breath and stepped closer to Detrovna. "And that of course brings us to my daughter, Alessya."

Alessya. Alessya, *indeed!*

Women had mirrored his life, Detrovna thought. When he had been a young member of the Kremlin nomenklatura, far from sucking on the tit of power, Lydia had been his lover. Nervous Lydia smoked incessantly and dreamed of riches—she with never two kopeks to rub together. They were matched in only one way: their purposelessness.

Detrovna awoke one morning with a clear idea of where in truth he was going—nowhere. He went to his supervisor, a minor minister afflicted with the un-Russian disease of gout, and asked to be transferred to a post in Afghanistan. *Yes*, and he knew it was 1983 and that a war raged there.

Detrovna was made a political officer in a ministry nominally in charge of supervising military materiel distribution. Over the next eighteen months, through both energy and opportunism, he rose in the ranks of the Kabul bureaucratic cadre. He took an Uzbek typist as a mistress. Taka was far more self-possessed and prettier than poor Lydia. She was an improvement, like his new post. She was fond of driving over the country's ugly terrain to watch fire fights in progress. She squirmed at the detonation of mortar shells and grenades. With tongue tip thrust between broad teeth, at each *crummp!* and *kruussh!* she hissed like an adder.

Physical and psychological casualties thinned Detrovna's cadre ranks, even as frustrations, desertions, and too many exported zinc coffins demoralized the army. Before long he was second in charge. He was ordered to make a tour of posts and supply areas. Amid some torturous foothills outside Herat in the western hills he arrived as scheduled at a reserve post and small arms depot—and found only two frightened soldiers on duty. Ten men had deserted yesterday and their commanding officer had disappeared.

Detrovna started for the communications bunker to report what he had found. Halfway across the dusty compound he stopped. No! He had a better idea.

Now he understood why he had come to this evil country.

He used his political position to requisition five trucks and drivers from a previously visited depot. When the convoy arrived, he ordered the men to load up with cases of small arms and ammunition. With the help of the soldiers they finished plundering the post's magazine as dusk fell. With a map and compass he climbed up beside the driver of the lead truck.

"Where are we going, commissar?" the driver asked.

"Iran."

The dangerous two-day trip avoiding main roads took them through narrow passes and along scarcely marked tracks. That time seemed weeks, thanks to having to avoid bands of increasingly well-armed *dukhi*, mines, and landslides. In the end luck favored Detrovna's daring. A few kilometers across the unguarded Iranian border he found those he sought—rebel tribesmen, enemies of the militant Islamic regime. Time and tea drinking brought him eventually to the rebel leader, curving knife and AK-47 clips stuck behind his belt.

Detrovna read his mind: kill the Russians and take what they had. He was ready. Pay for these weapons, he said, and there would be more—many more. The leader boasted about his access to hard currency. In the end a deal was struck.

Detrovna was paid in C.I.A. dollars.

Now he could bribe his drivers and the military men most useful to him. He repeated his little Iranian roundtrip more than a dozen times. In the final stages he no longer rode the trucks. He stayed in Kabul, struggling with licit responsibilities as the military situation continued to deteriorate. The greater the confusion, the easier went theft and smuggling. His superior's Moscow friends summoned him home for an offer of reassignment and a medal as "an honored hero in the international struggle."

Detrovna chose to stay on a while for two reasons: further swelling his West German bank account—and Fatima. A Russian-speaking Afghani educated at Cambridge, she had been the mistress of an English diplomat. Detrovna met her at an embassy function. After Sir Reynolds departed for safer climes, Detrovna reassigned Taka to a distant city and made a social call on the lustrous-haired Fatima.

Unlike Lydia and Taka, Fatima had expectations, and so instructed Detrovna in the matter of keeping a woman of quality. She expected to live where the shells were least likely to fall. She expected to be well fed, though good food was often in short supply. She was fond of music and expected him to provide first-rate sound equipment and recordings. She did not expect to be paid, only to be cared for. Above all, she expected to be treated as his equal.

In his inexperience and anxiousness to please he made mistakes which she corrected with tact. In the bedroom he blundered as well, but she provided a first rate primer in carnal matters from which he learned much. He was still young enough to wish to improve himself.

And so he did.

Gorbachev came to power. And in time orders arrived to depart. The exodus clogged the airports and the road to Termez on the Soviet side of the border. Detrovna arranged a private flight to take Fatima and him back to Moscow. The day before departure a car bomb exploded on a side street off the Maivande, the main market area, where she was shopping for a gift for him. Her leg was blown off. She bled to death under the hot sun.

Once back in Russia a sobered and now well-heeled Detrovna began to move in wealthy circles. It was in them that he learned the true condition of the Russian state. Despite the lessons Afghanistan had taught him about his country's lethal inefficiencies, news of its present political fragility came as a shock. By the time the word perestroika was publicly uttered he was poised to enter business—imported cigarettes would be his first capitalist venture. A wealthy friend suggested he prepare to join in a banking venture. Banking! *In Russia!* Such times were these! Then came 1992 and a Motherland in turmoil.

Not all apparatchiks and political hacks could make the jump from the ironbound sinking ship of the Party to the pirate vessel of political and economic free-for-all. With some of his hard currency very favorably exchanged for rubles on the black market he bought these desperate men's dachas for pittances and held them. He knew a new class of rich would arise. To them he would sell at a princely profit. Of course he would demand hard currency.

At the same time his rougher Afghanistan lessons had not been forgotten. Theft and audacity were keys to quick wealth. He set up squads to loot emptied government buildings and idle state-operated factories as soon as official eyes looked elsewhere, sometimes for a price. In other cases quick deals and ready cash made him the owner of profitable enterprises so recently run by the state. New businesses, particularly Western ones, quickly learned to pay Detrovna protection from his hastily assembled cadre of thugs and bone breakers. While rubles poured into his coffers, he much preferred hard currency. So much so that lives were sometimes ended to get it. He never forgot the power of those C.I.A. dollars.

Like dachas and imported automobiles, fine women too could no longer be afforded by the dispossessed nomenklatura. His growing wealth allowed him his pick of these pearls. He came to command a parade of increasingly desirable women, discarding them one after the other as the next seemingly superior creature entered his sphere. They marched by with the months: Olga, Taisiya, Galina...

Then a few months ago he met the finest of all—Alessya.

She had been no one's mistress. She was an actress in a Moscow improvisational comedy group. She stood out on the dingy stage. Tall, graceful even when contorted to provoke mirth, she was magnificently proportioned. Her dark almond eyes spoke of blood from Sarmarkand or Turkestan. She was under thirty. After seeing her perform he sent for her. She had no idea who he was. They stared at one another. A current passed between them. Her fierce eyes burned. She didn't lack audacity.

Those first few weeks were heaven! He played the ardent lover, she the somewhat mystified but appreciative beneficiary of his energies and attention. Her appetite for physical love was voracious. Before it his excursions with her predecessors faded in memory like dying echoes. He called himself a lucky fool.

Shortly however he found her physical appetites were matched by hunger for his attention and time. He entered her apartment, which he had provided and furnished, to find his expensive gifts in their unopened packages. "I missed you, Boritchka," she said with a *moue*. "No one to play 'turtles' with." His words about the demands of his business and political affairs fell on her shapely, deaf ears.

He boldly introduced her to his social world where, in clothing worth ten laborers' yearly wages, she turned men's heads and evoked envious women's whispers. Those who spoke with her found a brain within her well-formed skull. On her own she made friends, not all of them well known to him. These gatherings were among her happiest moments because she was with him—a situation, she made clear, that was far too rare for her satisfaction.

In coming days he entered what he had dreamed would be their love nest to find her reading books and listening to music rather than preparing for his arrival. He had provided champagne, caviar, wine, and meat. Even fresh vegetables! All sat untouched in the new West German refrigerator, though his lover was a skillful cook.

He recalled dear dead Fatima's lessons: this one, too, wanted to be an equal.

Considering his life, it was not possible. That life could not be changed for her. The stakes of the game in which he played were too high.

He couldn't blame her for her anger. Like her passion it burned hot and honest. His age—for he was in his middle fifties—intruded itself onto the bed, ugly as an ape. Once the initial excitement of his new conquest had spent itself, his sexual energies returned to the normal state for one his age. Oh, he was still a runner, but the days of the marathon were far behind him. He began to feel himself less of a man.

Alessya was too kind-hearted to even mention this. Possibly it didn't concern her. What she could not overlook was his failure to provide sufficient emotional intimacy.

To be sure he should rid himself of her. Yet it wasn't easy for a greedy man to toss away a woman of beauty and—yes, character, though he had largely forgotten what that was. He had also forgotten how difficult it was to deal with such principled people. Increasingly he understood he could not have her on his terms.

But he could not afford hers.

Then, enter the father! Insightful Detrovna had read his eyes. Harsky had not talked to his daughter. He thought Detrovna an evil monster who would bring to her only tragedy. Not *quite* right. Mistakenly, then, Harsky had come to the rescue bearing a chance of riches.

Not a bad trade for a relationship that had *no* chance.

Harsky had promised Detrovna the only kind of push away from Alessya that could be effective—a golden one.

As the little accountant stood before him, shifting foot to foot in his anxiety, Detrovna made a great show of deliberation, though he had already decided. After suitable delay he agreed to the man's terms. He would end his relationship with Alessya at once, and say nothing about his reasons.

Harsky departed. Shortly he returned at the wheel of a truck loaded with file boxes. The crumbling records of the ancient ministry now belonged to Detrovna, as did a map bearing careful markings, the name of a defunct old family, the vase, the ceramic planters, ten doll heads, and a rusty suit of armor. Harsky bid a hasty farewell and departed.

Detrovna turned to the Attorney and bellowed with laughter. "Does this all not have the look of a confidence game, with me the pigeon, Gennady Efimovich?"

"No games could be played by a man with such earnest eyes, such concern for his beloved..." The Attorney paused, gauging his superior's frame of mind. "Arrogant bitch!" he finished.

Detrovna laughed still louder and nodded. He pointed at the doorway through which the relieved Harsky had so recently departed. "We don't need him to go elsewhere with like merchandise and create rivals for us. See that he has a fatal accident," he ordered.

6

Pittsburgh, Pennsylvania

From the moment Nevsky said goodbye to Grushkin his mind churned like a rocky stream in flood. There was so much to sort out! He tried to slide apart from his emotions—sorrow for his gentle father's horrid death and compassion for the man who ordered it. Instinct told him violence ran like a red vein through the Romanov treasure. So it was: twelve men dead in a sandy canyon forty-six years ago and another in the Allegheny earlier today.

He sensed there would be more, in the past and in the present.

Then there was the shiny cube! *Olga Nikolayevna.* What was that about? Evidently it was the "personal freight" that his grandfather's diary said he took to the desert region. So that document tallied with Father Ruslan's anguished personal history. Whether or not the cube was a cunning Sergey's red herring or a part of the puzzle he couldn't guess. Either way, however, it was real. That meant his grandfather had in fact carried something else to "the south," possibly the real cache. Where had that been stashed? Who could know? And what was in it? Gold? Art work? Anybody's guess.

Back at 138 he found an answering machine message from Lyudmila. He wasn't ready for her and her Force for Leadership. He opened a bottle of Sam Thompson Pennsylvania Rye Whiskey and went up to bed. Before Charity Day had departed ten years ago he would have gone into the kitchen and made coffee. They would have talked everything up and down. He would sit at the table jotting in his Harvard Coop notebook. She would perch on the Lamont Library circulation desk chair that long ago had followed him home from Cambridge, Massachusetts.

White-blonde and pale, the pre-Nevsky Charity had been the well married mother of three. An ugly auto accident blasted her into an orbit of childless, grieving widowhood. She found work as a junior partner in a downtown law firm and cheap lodging with him. She was a cool detail-oriented WASP, a good balance for Nevsky's emotional freewheeling. Together they handled some vexing problems of missing persons and money.

Communing with his rye, Nevsky tried to play both his part and Charity's. He could hear her say, "It needs to be lined up and reasoned out..." Hmmm. He dug the old Harvard Coop notebook and Bic pen out of the bottom bureau drawer. Let's see if he could be precise and brief about where he was in the confusion that sprawled across half the world and the century. He wrote:

I don't really care about possessing the treasure.

I want to find Father Alexei's killer.

All I know about the treasure came from others. I bring nothing to that feast.

But the Church, Shmelev, Lyudmila, and probably every other treasure hunter thought he held key information. That was his lever. With it he would pry out the killer. No mistake it would be hairy business. Just the same, he knew how to play it.

He had learned that over years at the poker table. Sometimes the lesson needed relearning, most recently at the Caesar's Palace Casino in Las Vegas. He was playing twenty-forty hold 'em. His stacks of chips were suffering serious erosion. He woke up when he was twenty-two hundred down. And knew what was wrong.

He was playing it too safe.

He was making it too easy for the table to read him.

The time had come to play a little crazy. Forget what cards he held! Bet huge, shove in those chips, and keep them off balance.

He did, hit some hands, and walked away a winner.

Treasure hunters, meet the *crazy* Nevsky, the sandbagger and bluffer—the guy who plays the men and women and not the cards. That was the way to go with this greedy lot, all of whom he guessed he hadn't yet met. Yes, he had found the right groove, and would stay in it. So much for his mind set.

He put down the notebook. He sipped rye and adjusted his pillow. Memories of practical Charity persisted. She would slide her bare, shapely feet over the library chair's curving foot rest and say, "What are the facts, Yuri? The actual *facts?*"

The facts? He wasn't in an empirical frame of mind. Blame the rye and his essential personality. What had clung most from the last two days was that his present, this day of hard computer drives, cell phones, and 500 TV cable channels, was chained to a past of Imperial winter balls and horse-drawn troikas. The chain's links were hammered from the permanence of blood and culture. He sensed coming events would be marked by changes looping so swiftly and repeatedly between past and present that time disappeared.

Maybe he *was* his grandfather.

Magic promised to fill a full future...

The phone woke him shortly after eight the next morning. Lyudmila. Was he going to join the Force for Leadership? Partly because of his suspicions that she and Shmelev might have been involved with Father Alexei's murder he put her off. She didn't like it. If he had hoped she and Shmelev would leave Pittsburgh, he was disappointed. Korchevko's French connections were still hard at work trying to track down Countess S. Only if they turned up descendents anywhere in the world would the couple be dispatched to find them. He cut Lyudmila a bit short and later felt sorry for it. He had already disappointed her by not having the information she wanted and roughing up her sidekick. Brought her to tears, he had. Nevsky, always a killer with the ladies.

He went to the ATM and withdrew a thousand dollars that he really couldn't spare. He took it to Father Teodor. "I imagine Father Alexei's remains will end up on your doorstep," he said to the priest. "Put some of this toward his funeral. Use the rest to cut the expenses of taking care of the holy one." Nevsky motioned upstairs where he understood the wild old priest still lived. "Sorry it can't be more. At least not right now."

He interrupted the young priest's thanks. He explained he was meeting Grushkin at the Garden Ring bakery-café and running late.

He needn't have hurried. Ten o'clock came and went. So did ten-thirty. An ominous tickle began to work on his belly— and it wasn't just his third glass of strong Russia tea with lemon on an empty stomach.

Grushkin had been anxious to talk to him. Now he hadn't made it. Maybe he had been unlucky in the same way as Father Alexei. Maybe his body was racing barges on the Monongahela.

Nikolai Mogarian, owner and master baker, came out to shake Nevsky's hand and chat. Happily he reported that Russian Slope had received a healthy infusion of émigrés. From Ukraine, Armenia, and Odessa they came, businessmen, artists, musicians, and skilled craftsmen. After years of erosion the Slope was growing. He beamed under the handlebar sweep of his glorious moustache. "Business has never been so good!"

"Keep making those rye loaves big as throw pillows and you won't have to worry," Nevsky said.

He went out with one of those loaves under his arm. Mogarian didn't share recipes, but people said chocolate was in there.

Thing was, Nevsky wasn't hungry. He was worried about Grushkin.

He climbed into his Rabbit and turned down the Slope. Stopped at a red light, he turned his head to check out recent changes in the neighborhood. His eyes found a tall figure standing alone across the street. He froze.

The man wore the uniform of Czar Nicholas II's Imperial Guard!

He beckoned to Nevsky.

The driver of the car behind laid on the horn, distracting him. When again moving, he looked back.

The uniformed man was gone!

Who in the world was *that?* Was he seeing things? His hands trembled on the wheel and slimed with nervous sweat. He shook his head and drew a deep breath. What was going on?

Back at 138 he made phone calls to Slope hotels and motels. No Timofy Grushkin had registered. He called Mr. Information. Volodya had not heard of the man. He would make some calls and get back to Nevsky if he learned anything. Otherwise....

In late afternoon Lyudmila arrived with a grocery bag. In it were two bottles of vodka and herring filets. She also had been clothes shopping. She wore a knitted peach top and linen slacks. No mistake, she had a figure. The light of determination in her eyes had cooled. She said she had come because she was tired of Shmelev and wanted to be social.

Before sociability Nevsky had a few questions about the murder of Father Alexei that he put to her.

She turned an angry glance at him. "And at about what time did this murder occur?"

He told her and she snorted with derision. "Our flight didn't get in until an hour before we arrived here. We had no time for murdering—or anything else except renting a car. Would you like to see our airline tickets?" She turned toward her purse.

"Forget it," Nevsky said. "I'm angry, grabbing at straws."

"Understandable," Lyudmila said. "You see the danger, the need for you to join us quickly in action."

Back on stride she sliced the herring and heavy rye bread thin. Nevsky watched her dexterous, short-fingered hands work on the cutting board set into the sink counter. He studied the curve of her neck and its fine dark hair. His gaze moved down her back to the flare of hips below the white cord belt.

It was nice to have some feminine companionship.

She talked about life in Russia in the last few years of confusion and uncertainty, the wildly successful few, the miserable many.

"What were you doing, Lyudya, before you joined Korchevko's people?"

She laughed deep in her chest and looked away. "I was neither a candle for God nor a stick for the Devil," she said.

That meant useless—or worse. She flicked her fingers to chase away that subject. She poured the vodka and offered the first toast. He was obliged to offer a second. The vodka flowed, as Nevsky supposed she had intended. Were they then becoming drunk together in the time-honored getting-to-know-you custom of that mad country he had never seen?

They talked. His eyes moved across her face with its angled Slavic planes and promising lips. He found himself thinking of women from his past. It had been a while since he had shared his bed. The vodka stirred up embers—earlobes he had tongued, flat bellies with perfect navels into which he eased a curious fingertip, fanned hair spread like a sheaf of black grain on a paisley pillow...

Lyudmila shook her head. "This affair of your grandfather's, this czar's treasure. We had much hoped you would tell us—something."

"I told you the truth. I don't know anything."

She rose and put her palms on the table and leaned forward. "Tell *me* if you don't trust Shmelev."

"I thought this wasn't a business meeting," Nevsky said.

"It wasn't intended to be," she said. "It's that I can't believe there isn't *something* you can tell us."

Nevsky had had enough of this niggling after clues he didn't have. "Lyudmila, do you want to know what my father brought from Russia? It was a family joke! People would say, 'What did you bring from Russia, Vladimir Sergeyevich?' And he would say: 'What my father gave me. Forty-seven, fifty-two, sixteen, sixty-two, eleven, thirty-three. Six numbers that mean nothing. And the word of God.'"

Lyudmila started, "What—?"

"What does that mean, you want to know? How do I know? The last part is likely about religious faith."

"Why did he come to live here in Pittsburgh?"

"His father told him to. 'A good city in a safe country' were my grandfather's exact words."

"Your father *must* have told you more. *Known* more."

"He didn't." Nevsky poured more vodka. "Let's both have one more on that."

In time Lyudmila Mogadam was in his bed, her mouth tasting of straight vodka, herring, and cigarettes. Ah, the Russians make love! And love, or at least lust, did seem to be on the agenda. The biological conditions were correct: firmness and soft wetness. Inhibitions had fled in alcoholic flood. So all that remained was to...

She turned her shadowed face up to him. With a hand behind his neck she pulled him closer. Her bright gray eyes were hooded. She grimaced in pleasure. Her white teeth gleamed. Her eyes closed. She ordered, "Do anything you want with me!"

Those words clanged, even in Nevsky's drunken mind, like a rejected slug dropping out of a vending machine. Lyudmila Mogadam was nothing if not strong-willed. Not a woman to just roll over, in public or in bed. Was she acting? Go ahead, you idiot! he told himself. Yet it wasn't so easy now for him. Somebody said the brain was the chief sex organ. His *Love Boat* had taken a torpedo hit. He wondered if he was going to be able to keep that abruptly fragile craft afloat. Lyudmila's eyes opened. She had said it was his move, but he hadn't acted. She tapped his teeth speculatively with a short-nailed index finger.

The phone rang.

"Let it—" Lyudmila began as Nevsky sprawled toward the bedside instrument. He picked it up. "Hello," he said, his voice crusty with lust.

"At it again, Yuri?" asked the woman's voice

Nevsky drew it a sharp breath. It was Charity Day! She was crying. "Oh, my God!" he said.

"Yuri, Yuri, I want to come home—I mean back. *I want to come back!*"

"What's wrong with Texas?" he said.

"Too much chicken fried steak. That's what it is." Charity paused for a moment, sniffling loudly. "That woman you're in bed with. She's not your *wife*, is she?"

"No, and she doesn't live here either."

"Shame on you then! Don't you know the kind of things going around these days?" Her breath caught. She was battling weeping. Nevsky could scarcely imagine *her* in tears. She had always been so cool and composed over all the years she'd lived with him. Having had such bad luck with her family had toughened her. Well, nothing like ten years of what now seemed to have been a bad marriage to bring on the bawling. "When are you coming?" he asked.

"I don't know. Maybe soon. I better hang up before I really get silly." Pause, deep heaving breaths down the line. "Yuri, *thank you.*" She hung up before he could reply.

No fool and evidently knowing some English, Lyudmila said, "So you have a lover then?"

The sound of Russian again in his ear now sounded strange. "No. Haven't seen her for ten years. Never slept with her."

She chuckled.

He persisted in his denials.

"Don't you know our proverb?" she asked. "'Look for real love in the heart, not among the sheets.'" She began to grope for her clothes.

Nevsky began, "She really isn't my lover. Your don't have to—"

She held up her hand. "We will have another time, no?"

He wondered. About that and about why she had come. Motivated by loneliness or design? Looking for love or information?

He couldn't guess.

He got no help from her. She said she'd be back with Shmelev sometime soon. By then she expected his decision: join the Force for Leadership or not.

That night he stayed awake deliberately, taking the time to ponder the puzzling plenty that had fallen on him over the last two days. Overarching it all was the delightful news: Charity Day would be part of his life again! At four in the morning he dug out the letter written by Bishop Paulos. Eight hours difference to St. Petersburg. He phoned. Four tries needed to get through. When he mentioned his name and that of Father Alexei, he was put through at once.

The bishop's voice on the hissy connection was brittle with age. Nevsky told him about Father Alexei's torture and death, and Father Ruslan's confession. The bishop fell silent for a handful of heartbeats. To Nevsky's surprise he said nothing about the young priest's death. Instead: "*You* heard Father Ruslan's story?"

"All of it. And very interesting it was. Afterward I forgave him. He was very grateful. He's living temporarily in a rectory here. You'll have to do something to—"

"Of course. Of course." The bishop rushed ahead. "What exactly did he tell you?"

Nevsky realized that only he and Grushkin, if he were still alive, knew tormented Father Ruslan's story. The ancient priest had dealt him another high card to pair with that of everyone's belief that he already held a piece of the puzzle. He knew what had happened on the Kirgiz Steppe and the fate of the strange cube marked *Olga Nikolayevna*. "I'm going to keep that to myself for a while."

"Do you dare interfere with Church affairs, Yuri Vladimirovich?" The bishop's tone was threatening.

"I already know too much for you to try such tactics, Excellency," he said coolly. "The 'affairs' have more to do with Caesar than Christ. We both know it's about treasure. One that likely will belong to those who find it first, whether they wear robes or rags."

The bishop quickly changed his tack. No mistake, he was a smooth, polished tactician. "Someone else representing me will come and negotiate with you."

"If you like," Nevsky said, his tone neutral. He went on. "I'm afraid I have some additional bad news, Excellency. Your layman representative, a man named Grushkin, is missing. He might well be dead, too."

"Grushkin?"

"Timofy Grushkin. The man who paid the two priests' fares for the good of God, and came with them."

"I don't understand," the bishop said.

"The three of them flew here together."

"Yuri Vladimirovich, the Church paid all transportation costs. I don't know anyone named Timofy Grushkin."

TATIANA NIKOLAYEVNA

7

A private meeting hall on the Levasnovsky Prospekt, St Petersburg

More than a dozen times the two hundred rose to their feet shouting approval of General Sviatoslav Slavkovich Ostrovsky's words. The Raptor was telling them *his* truth. And they heard it!

Why not? He stood before them a uniformed, be-medaled hero of the fading Afghanistan fiasco. He had salvaged from that war the nickname "Young General Victory." He had brought not just that home from the horror. He returned, as few had, with pride and honor because he had resigned his post in outrage over the state's incompetence. Now that state was gone. He emerged from the following years of confusion as a hero and patriot. He stood by this image—aloof from politics.

But he was not aloof from grand, daring planning. All his efforts over the last ten years aimed in a single direction: to one day seize power and use it.

Ostrovsky had recently heard the latest news from Moscow. Once again he had spat contemptuously. The "latest" news was all too much like all that of the last ten years—yet another crisis in authority. Russia still thrashed like a Siberian fairy tale's mythical beast. The bullfrogs creeping forth from the pond of candidates were of the weakest breeds: Gorbachev, Yeltsin...

Such idiots could never deal with the problems of a staggering economy, a laughable ruble, Western exploitation, crime and wide-ranging corruption—to say nothing of the many civil wars. In some, brave Russian soldiers fought against troops. In others they faced unseen guerillas upon inhospitable terrain. Increasing numbers of fanatics and terrorists played grisly cards from decks fashioned from religious lunacy. Elsewhere counter-ambitions festered quiescent between inevitable outbursts of violence directed at Russian citizens. Some restive republics attempted different kinds of civil war through political bargaining and waving their asses at the West in commercial or militarily strategic enticements. Whatever their stripe, all the rebels were cut from the same cloth: to hell with Russia! We wish to stand alone.

Humiliation for the Motherland!

It would not be thus much longer!

As he formed familiar phrases for the appreciative audience, his attention drifted over the last years. In that time he had brought the Sons of Continuity back to life, like the firebird, from eighty-year-old ashes.

When the Sons of Continuity's 1917 plot failed to whisk Czar Nicholas II and his family to safety, some of its members were lucky enough to scatter beyond Russia's borders. Not his grandfather, though. Though head of one of Imperial Russia's greatest families, he had been prepared with a new, modest identity established beyond the Urals. It was he who had guarded the torch of belief in autocracy, passed it to Ostrovsky's father who in turn had bestowed it upon his son with the words, "The day *will* come..."

And in 1989 real hope began.

By 1992 the day had indeed come!

Secret records had been maintained over the decades. Keeping them current had been dangerous work. The pervasiveness of the commissars, though unimaginative, called for the most stealthy and indirect communication. The task had been managed well enough that a useful list existed. On it the deceased were so marked, their sons and daughters noted, and their eventual deaths, too. Grandchildren were born, even some great-grandchildren in whose veins still flowed the best blood.

To Ostrovsky fell the task of transmitting the long-awaited command: *loyal children of loyal parents come home!*

Circumspect methods of making contact were found, so that little was risked. Over months these men and women came to Russia from across the world. Not all of course. In the descendents of only twenty of the original fifty-two Sons of Continuity had the seeds of political faith sprouted and flourished. When they first gathered, they made an inevitable decision. The Romanov line of succession was to be abandoned as utterly bankrupt and long inconsequential. Ostrovsky's fine bloodlines, iron will, and charisma easily made him the Sons' choice as their autocrat. More possessed zeal and commitment than he had the right to anticipate. He was not an emotional man, but his heart warmed as he worked with them. They, too, had special ways. In a few years they had gathered under his umbrella countless thousands of supporters. Many of these were already taking active roles contributing to his certain ascension.

Much more still would be done with them under his bold leadership.

. Not just Sons' descendants had come home to Russia over the last six years, but some objects that linked the painful past with the promising present. Chief among them was the diary of

Sergei Ivanovich Nevsky. It had returned in the hands of Sasha, Alexander Petrovich, great-grandson of one of the original Sons. Several months ago he had brought it to Ostrovsky's modest home.

Ostrovsky recalled the first time he had held the precious volume. Its eighty-year-old leather binding gleamed. He riffled the pages. The paper was still white and creamy, the precise handwriting clearly legible. "Excellent condition!" he marveled.

"My family knows how to keep a treasure," Sasha said. "Initially storage in a cool cellar, later climate control."

"Well done." Ostrovsky hefted the volume. His excitement refused to quiet. He swallowed and looked at the other. "You've...read it?"

"Many times, Raptor. *Many* times. Its fascination lies in what it *fails* to say. Don't think it's the complete key to what we seek. If it was..." He turned a frank glance to the general. "I might have succumbed to selfish temptation."

"As I gathered..." Ostrovsky put the diary down on the table, but felt it drawn back to his hand. He resisted the urge to pick it up. Instead he laid his palm on the gleaming leather. He said, "We understand that by itself it's not enough. But without it..." He shrugged before the impossibility. "But we have it! So we've good reason to go forward energetically."

Then treachery had struck!

Ostrovsky raised his voice and hands. As on cue, his audience stood. He summed up, sounding the themes increasingly identified with him personally: end the civil wars speedily, discipline the profiteers, focus on fashioning a new Russia based in part upon old values, establish "an aristocracy of talent," work toward an independent Motherland. To hell with the West! Use the firmest measures against the criminal element. Reorganize and re-equip the armed forces. Forge them into smaller, more potent entities. Maintain a nuclear capability.

Yes, first put Russia's house in order, then look to the lands at her borders. Which would retain historical ties, which would be partners, which would choose collaboration, which independence? With Russia powerful again, leaders in Ukraine, Azerbaijan, Turkestan, Armenia and the nook-and-cranny republics, like Nagorno-Karabakh and Chechnya-Ingushetia, would not be so quick to jump to their nationalist agendas. It *could* be done if true leaders came forth.

He closed this speech as he had all in recent months with the words: "Who will lead us to greatness in the coming new millennium?"

Without the prompting of judiciously distributed Sons the chant went up. It was soft at first, but built and grew upon itself. Ostrovsky saw fists and right arms raised to the horizontal. The voices fairly *booomed!* Os-trov-sky! Os-trov-sky! *Os-trov-sky!*

He applauded during the long minutes it took for them to quiet. He left the lectern and eased into the crowd of admirers. Among them moved his bodyguards carrying concealed weapons. Media people were present. See their cameras and tape recorders! Ostrovsky had studied the West. These pushy men and women were fools and tools of the clever. They were like whores begging to be used, asking for it. He always found time for them.

Tonight their questions were the same. As were his answers. No, he was not interested in public office. He was a proud former soldier anxious about the fate of the Motherland. His plea must be boring them by now: *Russia needed leadership.* Where were those who would guide her out of the resistant rubble of Marxist-Leninist bankruptcy?

He personally thanked the women in the audience for attending. While he had little personal use for them, he knew no movement could succeed without their support. He was not a man to underestimate them. They brought gentleness and empathy to his burgeoning base of support. Bless them!

As the crowd thinned, two mustached young men moved closer. The bodyguards slid between them and Ostrovsky. In the lads' clear eyes the general saw the passion of commitment to the path he blazed. He signaled his men to allow the duo closer. He drank in their youthful zeal like an elixir. These were the kinds of soldiers he needed! "Sviatoslav Slavkovich, what must we do until you consent to lead us?" the taller one asked.

Ostrovsky didn't bother with his customary self-effacing denials. He leaned forward and whispered. "Have patience, be energetic! Spread word of hope. Gather support for our ideas—"

He might have gone on, but for a touch at his elbow. It came from Sasha the Swiss who had just arrived. He whispered, "We have finished with him, Raptor."

Ostrovsky nodded. In minutes they were in the big Lada wheeling through the late spring night out of the city toward the countryside. Behind the glass partition Sasha spoke tersely as always. "He isn't affiliated. It was his own, bad idea."

"You're sure?"

"We broke him, Raptor. Take my word for it. He has no secrets—or crap—left in him."

"You're certain he didn't sell our identity, our purpose, too?"

"I am."

Ostrovsky had come to trust the Swiss. He was a reliable man given to understatement. For these reasons he had made him his chief lieutenant. "Then we'll survive his treachery," he said.

The car nosed off the main road and slowed by an isolated low building made of roughly shaped timbers. Evening was falling. Shadows from the woods touched the man in a business suit who stood guard by the door. At Ostrovsky's approach he said, "Mother Russia will be great again!" His arm shot out like a piston.

"If her Sons dare make her so!" Ostrovsky replied, returning the salute.

Sasha led Ostrovsky inside. Four men and two women were gathered around a seated figure. Rope held the young man to his chair. Even though in the prime of life, around twenty-five, he wasn't pretty to see. Ostrovsky's people had worked on his teeth, fingers, and nails. His head sagged and his breathing was heavy. The room stank of loosened bowels.

"So here I find the fool," Ostrovsky muttered.

Though dazed, the young man raised his puffy head at the sound of Ostrovsky's voice. "You..." he breathed.

Ostrovsky stared down at him with burning eyes. See the traitor! "If you didn't find the Sons of Continuity to your liking, you would have done better to quit our cause," he said, "rather than trying to reap a shabby profit at great personal risk."

"You're...idiots living in the past." The young man winced at the pain from split lips. "Worshipping an old dream of the bankrupt nobility. Thinking there's a vast treasure somewhere. Madmen!"

Ostrovsky seized the man's ear lobe and twisted it. The ruined head rolled on its neck. "And what're *you*, pig?" he asked. "Scum without ideals or traditions, without concern for our country. A 'modern' man, are you? Quick to make a selfish profit. Quick to be a 'capitalist.' When you came to us from the West, you should have left Western ways behind you. They've cost you your life."

The young man's swollen eyelids twitched. *"My life..."*

"We are in a war for the leadership of Russia. Your act was treasonous. The penalty for treason in wartime is well known."

The young man howled. His eyes shut tight with despair. He heaved weakly against the rope. Ostrovsky realized his inquisitors had broken one of the man's legs. The traitor composed himself. He drew a deep breath and raised his chin. Ostrovsky saw he had good blood in him. How sad it had been polluted! He didn't relish losing one of his twenty Sons.

The young man twitched his fingers. "Come closer. I have a question." There was no danger. Ostrovsky moved his head toward the ruined lips. Beyond them lay the debris of crumbled teeth. "Tell me: how could you *possibly* have found out I sold a copy of Nevsky's diary?" the young man whispered. "I didn't leave any clues, any traces whatever."

Ostrovsky grinned thinly. "Would you be happier knowing how before you die?"

The young man nodded.

Ostrovsky shrugged. "How? The simplest way: you underestimated the cause you betrayed! The diary was watched around the clock."

The young man grimaced at his stupidity.

"You were followed to the copy shop and then to your rendezvous. Your transaction revealed the identity of a rival group. We allowed the purchase; the diary by itself is not the key."

"Why do you bother?" the young man asked. "The diary's nothing but a strange antique. It has no practical value. I felt like a confidence man selling that copy. In fact, you're *all*...antiques!" he cried. "Looking back to times, ways proven impotent."

Ostrovsky curbed his swell of rage. "You who know so much! You aren't a student of history, are you? You listen to the 'commentators' instead of thinking for yourself. What is history, fool, but a wheel that turns around and around, but delivers nothing ever truly new or different—"

"You're the fools!—"

"You don't see that the time has come again for a czar— called by whatever name you choose."

"A czar!" The doomed man laughed harshly. "The last one died in 1918—"

"Correction! I believe Comrade Stalin died in 1953."

Ostrovsky had ordered high-powered rifles for the

execution. He owed the betrayer a swift death. The young man was dragged out and tied to a thick oak. Six of Ostrovsky's soldiers made up the firing squad, two of them women.

Light had fled. A third woman held a hand lantern. She centered the beam on the young man's chest. Ostrovsky stood at the end of the line of six. He raised his fist. The doomed one didn't cry out. He had refused a blindfold and now his eyes stayed open. Yes, good blood. A pity...

He dropped his arm. The rifles of his disciplined corps crashed. Pieces of skull and chest flew off into the darkness. Such a waste! Ostrovsky thought. Nonetheless, traitorous acts must have the severest consequences. Cruel, but how else had men ever ascended to power anywhere but by climbing a ladder of corpses?

Study history.

Sasha gave orders for the disposal of the body. Then he and Ostrovsky met alone in a corner of the building. The Swiss asked if others having a copy of the diary had damaged their cause.

"I know what group has it," Ostrovsky said. We now know we have a rival where before we searched alone. Even so..." He shook his head. "Much must be done before anyone can claim whatever Sergei Nevsky gathered." He smiled and touched his lieutenant firmly on the shoulder. "We have some valuable information our rival doesn't have."

The Swiss's eyebrows rose. "What?"

"An unsent letter of great interest written by a peasant working at the orders of his master, Sergei Nevsky."

"And?" the Swiss asked.

"Translations. To be finished within a few days."

"Translations from what language?" Sasha asked.

"German."

The Lada's car phone buzzed. Ostrovsky picked it up and listened in silence for a moment. Then he ordered his driver to stop. He sent Sasha into the front seat beyond the soundproof partition. The car rolled on with the Raptor listening intently. After several minutes he said, "Then how do you read this grandson of the Cunning One, this Yuri Nevsky?"

8

Ecclesiastical offices, off Prospekt Mira, Moscow

Bishop Paulos paced his carpeted office. His legs moved even more stiffly than they had some weeks ago before he had made the long trip north of the Arctic Circle, across the taiga, to meet the legendary Father Ruslan of Kirgiz. The business seemed simple then. He planned to catch a thread from the past and follow it to a lucrative present.

That thread stretched better than forty-five years.

The Church's attention first had been caught during the last hours of the life of a Father Konstantine who, before the October Revolution, had served the Nevsky family on its estate called Great Meadow. His end had come in 1945 in a bullet-pocked monastery near St. Petersburg with monks at his bedside. Fever and fits racked him in turn. His maddened mind flew willy-nilly between past and present. He babbled of a "great service" Sergei Nevsky had done for *Batiushka*—Czar Nicholas II. It wasn't clear if the aged priest was aware that the czar and his clan had perished in Ekaterinburg. He talked vaguely of Sergey's swearing him to a lifelong assignment connected "to *Batiushka* or whoever comes after him with the blessing of God."

There were more puzzling outbursts concerning Germans and "Anyitchka's" misfortune in Ukraine in 1942. He cried out that there was blood on his own hands as well. Woven throughout all his ravings were the names Olga Nikolayevna and Tatiana Nikolayevna, the czar's first and second daughters and grand duchesses. Had they been in his presence then, not dead at the hands of the Bolsheviks twenty-four years earlier? Confirmed historical facts said otherwise.

Intrigued, the confessor pressed the dying man. What had Sergei done for the czar? He leaned down to better hear Father Konstantine's whispered response. He was disappointed. The landowner hadn't told him. He knew only that Sergey's work would "allow the czar to live like a czar" wherever he was.

And of course the czar had lived well indeed.

In time Father Konstantine's tale became legendary Church gossip. Particularly when it was linked to a long-standing rumor supposing that much Romanov wealth had been unaccounted for in the wake of the dissolution and terror following the Revolution.

The bishop had first heard the tale when a novice. It found a home in his imagination. It seemed a fascinating curiosity, like an insect sealed in amber, clearly seen from all sides, but inviolate. Or so it appeared.

Then a curious thing happened on the Kirgiz Steppe.

Men had died. A priest bore the responsibility.

Father Ruslan.

The son of Father Konstantine!

The Church had heard this through rumor: a dying former soldier's partial confession to a Muslim cleric. He described something of what happened in the Kirgiz canyon—an American, excavation, ambush, and slaughter... He answered the question, "What was in the cube?" with his death rattle.

What had been recovered was certainly something valuable, the bishop reasoned. That Father Konstantine had been involved meant that the Church had been represented in this "service" done the czar. Therefore to the Church rightfully belonged a substantial part of what had resulted from the effort.

So he had journeyed to the edge of civilization only to be frustrated by Father Ruslan's guilt and need for forgiveness. Afterward he had arranged for Father Alexei to escort the ailing old man to America. He had told the young priest to arrange for Sergei Nevsky's grandson Yuri and Father Ruslan to meet. He was to remember the old priest's every word and report it back verbatim.

Yesterday Nevsky's phone call had brought news of death—and of an unknown man masquerading as a friend of the Church... Unhappily nothing that had left the ill priest's mouth had reached the bishop.

The bishop's housekeeper, a squat woman whose impressive ugliness was death to any lewd rumor, brought him his morning tea and dry roll. He sat and sipped, thinking thoughts for which God wouldn't love him.

For example, Father Alexei's torture and murder could only mean that others were most seriously in pursuit of the czar's wealth.

The old rumors, it seemed, were founded in truth.

These unknowns, whom the bishop was now thinking of as rivals, had already played the card of ruthlessness, as though to warn him to leave the quest to the soulless and hardhearted. And well he might do so except...

In the forefront of the bishop's mind stood the seventy-odd years of abuse and humiliation of Russian Orthodoxy at the hands of the Communists. Believers had been forced to endure the outlawing of religion and to suffer random martyrdom. Priests and Church officials correctly had feared for their lives. Church property was confiscated. The monster Stalin sentenced clerics to death by forced labor in bitter cold. The weakened ecclesiastical hierarchy then was forced to bear the crushing cross of the intrusive Council for Religious Affairs...

Then there was history writ small—*his* history as a religious through fifty years of state contempt and personal humiliation. To do God's work he had to weasel before Party bosses and endlessly wrestle the nomenklatura. Much begging, deal making, and accommodation had been absolutely necessary to eke out the smallest favor, the few crumbs to throw to the faithful— when their spirits cried out for whole loaves. At the darkest hour he had burst out weeping before a commissar, confessing that he could endure not one day more of Church vilification and personal humiliation. The mustached apparatchik grinned knowingly. From his hidden holster he removed a revolver, put it on the cleric's desk, and departed smirking with contempt. Paulos handled the dreadful device, but was too much the coward to use it. It went into his desk drawer, a constant reminder of his weakness.

Living such a miserable life, he had long imperiled his *dukhovnost*, the exercise of his spirit after the highest Christian model. How long could one swim in swill and still smell sweet? He wondered. When the Soviet system collapsed, he had been filled with gleeful hope that things would surely change. And so they had, with new freedoms and opportunities for the religious. Even miracles of a sort were worked: some evil caterpillars of former oppressors emerged from cocoons of guilt as spiritual butterflies championing the Church.

To him, though, all this freshness was not enough. He had expected...more. The Church was owed much for what it had endured. Cathedrals, chapels, and monasteries had been destroyed and neglected over decades. Today everywhere across Mother Russia paint and gilt peeled from ikonostases, wood rotted, and stones separated. The cost of the Herculean work of returning the Church to its proper condition had to be paid. Was it wrong to expect...reparations? But from whom? From the state, now a confusion of shifting forces and values? Or from God Himself—whose face to Bishop Paulos had become less distinct as he aged, not clearer, as his dreamily pious peers professed?

He swore to himself that if there was anything to be gained for the Church by way of Ruslan of Kirgiz, he *would* see to it!

What might be thought of as a higher voice suggested to the bishop that the Church's focus should be on the present, not the past. In Christ's spirit one had to forgive even the unconscionable savaging of the religious. Time and again one was tested in trying to follow His teaching: turn the other cheek.

The bishop broke his roll. His knuckles ached. Arthritis. He was getting old. That brought with it a certain kind of impatience. He needed to leave...something for the Church and its faithful. Christ himself had left the monument of his Church. Possibly he could leave it the far lesser one of meaningful wealth.

He would not break off his pursuit of the czar's treasure just yet, he rationalized. He would advance it, and then take measure of the situation. Too much was unknown to allow a final decision just now.

What he needed was a younger man.

A very special kind of man.

Possibly he already knew him.

For some years he had borne the burden of a "unique" priest. This man, who no one could force to wear the customary beard, had distinguished himself in service during the late days of the Soviet empire. He served as informal liaison with the organs of state security. When practical he cooperated with these agencies. At the same time he pursued the Church's interests. He knew many secrets on both sides of that quiet, determined struggle: atheism versus belief.

It was understood that he used violence and other unacceptable means on behalf of the Church, later sincerely begging forgiveness. For many months he was a man on a tightrope. On at least one occasion he had the misfortune to feel the bite of torture instruments. The effect of such agony on his character was impossible to determine. Looking back, the bishop could not imagine how anyone could have better handled such testing responsibilities.

Since the collapse, though, this priest was at loose ends. No assignment given him long held his interest. He was seen among the rabble lately washed into Russia from neighboring countries. Gossip said he drank and caroused. He barely avoided charges of dissolution. Even so, Bishop Paulos had been forced to discipline him several times for unbecoming conduct. The last occasion carried the threat of expulsion from the priesthood. The priest was ordered to bend his head to the wishes of his superiors and the spirit of his vows. There could be no doubt that good and evil raged in battle for the prize of his soul—as they did in all men.

Despite this priest's considerable service to the Church, the bishop had long been certain there was no real future for the man within holy orders. Like a tool too sharp and irregular for use, he would have to be discarded. But today the prelate smiled broadly. He spoke aloud. "*See* how God works! He has provided me with an agent to do His will."

It was this ill-formed priest who would be the bishop's representative in this affair of the czar's wealth. His first task would be to go to Nevsky, find out what he knew, and try to make him an ally of the Church. If he was unsuccessful—well, he was a resourceful soul, if nothing else. The priest would think of something.

The bishop swallowed heavily and turned to the telephone.

9

Zurich, Switzerland

Gennady Rishnikov, the man called the Attorney, had spent a week in the city's libraries and government offices, making good use of his knowledge of the German language. The location of the Romanov Cache indicated by the late Josef Harsky had presented major problems. Certitudes were needed before his master Detrovna dared proceed further. He ordered the Attorney to track down the precision engineering firm and transporter doing Sergei Nevsky's bidding eighty years ago. The diary's oblique references proved of only general use. The Attorney had to identify all such businesses active at that time, and see which survived to the present.

His efforts to find the engineering firm ran up on the reefs of business failures and consolidations. No luck.

He did better with the transporter. There were three possibilities.

He had no choice but to appear hat-in-hand at each of their offices in turn fortified by several hearty sniffs of cocaine, a carefully crafted lie on his lips. The lie accounted for Sergei Nevsky's likely use of an alias. It also rationalized analyzing the records from the years 1909 to 1916 with reference to number of shippings. It was very likely, he suggested, that the transactions arranged during those years constituted the bulk of the firm's business. He made it understood that he was prepared to pay for copies of the records and for any inconvenience.

The first two firms indeed had complete records. In some ways the Swiss were marvelous! Unhappily the pattern of accounts and copies of bills of lading were not those hinted at in the diary. With polite bows and clicking heels he was sent on his unhappy way.

At Schweizdrang GmbH, formerly Moguer Carting and Rail, a Herr Koswig, in pince-nez and silk suit, gave the Attorney cause to hope. He was ordered to return in two days. At the appointed hour he found Herr Koswig at his desk. Beside him were orderly piles of photocopied documents. The Attorney stopped himself from snatching them up to discover what form the czar's riches had taken. Cocaine helped him sit back and smile expectantly.

Herr Koswig rose and circled the desk, a heavy mahogany box in his hand. "Cigar?" he asked. "Cuban. The best." He opened the lid. The scent of prime tobacco filled the office. "May I suggest the Mouton Rothschild?"

When both had lit and puffed, Koswig was now prepared to talk business. "Making the copies was nothing more than a clerical chore. All records were in order," the Swiss said proudly. "But as we studied them, some...curiosities became obvious."

The Attorney grew inwardly vexed. Would nothing be simple with this czarist business? "Such as?" he asked.

"At the time these records were made this was of course a much smaller firm. Its head was Hans Moguer, our founder. The records show that the bulk of the transactions you describe he handled personally for..." He glanced at a sheet of notes. "Herr Ivan Ivanov." He smiled thinly to footnote the obvious alias.

"To be brief, Herr Rishnikov, Moguer kept all the records for transactions involving Ivanov. I further suspect, though I can't prove it, that he physically handled both incoming shipments and prepared the items transshipped. Financial records show that Herr Ivanov willingly paid very high rates. Rates so far above those normally charged for that era that one makes certain assumptions."

The attorney held his breath. Damn the details! His eyes turned hungrily toward the piles of photocopies.

"Some illegality, for instance," Koswig said. "Very likely somehow shipments were arranged to avoid customs duties or similar taxes, and all attention. The amount of material arriving and departing indicates a sustained, methodical operation. One that left Ivan Ivanov happy and this firm well endowed from that time forward. Our founder and his client were in some way dealing with valuable items. No mistake."

"Anything else?"

"Moguer was a man of high principles. Only a chance to grow *very* wealthy would make him compromise himself."

"How does that all effect us?" the Attorney asked. "I said I was willing to pay for copying plus any reasonable surcharge."

The Swiss studied his cigar. Its bluish smoke curled toward the gold curves of his pince-nez. He said, "The question is what is 'reasonable?' I took the issue to my partners during our regular morning meeting."

"So then...how much?"

"We decided it would not be unreasonable to expect ten thousand Swiss francs. Surely a trivial amount should your efforts be rewarded. You *are* trying to locate the shipments, aren't you?"

The exquisite cigar now tasted like smoldering dung in the Attorney's mouth. These damned Swiss! Forever driving hard bargains from positions of strength.

He asked to use the bathroom. Once there he removed the threaded pillbox from his vest pocket. In it were his golden spoon and a mound of white powder. He refreshed both nostrils. The exhilaration was instant. The very best! The drug was secured from a black American dealer with a startling white smile at the rear table in a certain Moscow coffee shop. What did Detrovna always say? "Russia is now crap! All good things come from the West." In a flash of drug-sparked insight he saw what he must do with the carte blanche his master had given him.

He must pay.

A bank check was required, of course. In Swiss francs or German marks. Not rubles. And a contract to be signed! The records were not to be recopied or distributed beyond the Baikal Resources Group, one of Detrovna's dummy corporations that the Attorney claimed to be representing. He scribbled his name. He would have signed if it were the Devil himself who offered the papers.

He arranged all and departed. On the train to the airport he pulled out the first neat folder box. His eager eyes found the bills of lading for what Sergei had shipped...in January 1915 from Buenos Aires. He received his first surprise.

The German language documents, signed by Nevsky the sender and Moguer the recipient, had not been completed in the compulsive Swiss style. Under "Item(s) shipped" Nevsky's hand had penned "Valuables." Nothing more.

What valuables?

Aboard the Moscow plane the Attorney randomly checked the handful of bills of lading he had transferred to his briefcase. All listed "Valuables," but nothing else! He cursed under his breath.

Had his master run afoul of *two* confidence men? Harsky and now Koswig?

Yet there was still hope. Moguer had re-shipped what Nevsky had sent him. He chose from the Swiss's shipping records. He found pages of entries. All were completely filled out! He read the first that caught his eye. Under "Item(s) shipped" he saw "Fifteen papier-mâché clowns. Weight: 20 kilo. 24 cloisonné vases, .5-meter diameter. Weight: 55 kilo. 35 Egyptian camel seats. Weight: 240 kilos..."

And so on. It seemed every odd thing under the sun had been shipped. All of them to...

His heart sank. He put away the cardboard folder box. Though there were many more such boxes sent through bundled with his luggage, he had seen enough for now.

He was not looking forward to meeting Detrovna.

As planned, he found him at Petrouchka, a new private Moscow club where wealthy politicians gathered to drink, eat, and be entertained, as most Russians would never be. Detrovna had a private table. The adjoining ones were empty. He nodded at the chair opposite his. "Sit. Tell me what my ten thousand Swiss francs have bought."

There was no easy way for the Attorney to put a good light on his findings. He had to use the lavatory and his spoon just to tell his tale, seeing the frown on his master's face deepening like gathering thunderclouds.

Before Detrovna could reply, he said, "I have a theory about all this shipping and transshipping, Boris Petrovich."

Detrovna cocked his head and pursed his lips. He said nothing.

"All red herrings. Everything," the Attorney blurted. "Sergei Nevsky sent nothing, or he sent empty boxes. The things Moguer shipped, clowns, vases, museum pieces, were calculated to deceive, to pose an meaningless riddle." Seeing Detrovna's scowl subside somewhat, he rushed on. "Sergei carried everything back with him after every trip! He hid *everything* somewhere at his Great Meadow estate."

Detrovna shrugged, sighed, and closed his eyes. He said, "Another possibility: Moguer completely falsified the bills of lading. What were listed as mere vases, for example, were Chinese Ming Dynasty, and so-called 'small inlaid cabinets' once held the dishes of French kings. And so on. So altogether the multitude of items shipped amounted to the Romanov Cache."

The Attorney nodded, glad to be nearly out of the hot spotlight of his master's anger. "That, too, is conceivable," he said.

"Even so, we *must* get our hands on what was shipped. After all, our unfortunate little accountant was able to find some of the items and photograph them."

The Attorney played a card of competence. "I took a few hours to search through the records of shipments," he said. "I found *three*—not one—suits of armor! So at least we have something more for our rubles: what Harsky brought to us was very likely listed in the Swiss shipments." He stepped a bit out on a limb. "So can't we assume that Harsky found the cache, whether he knew it or not?"

Detrovna scowled. "It all doesn't come together neatly enough for my taste." His expression lightened. "Just the same..." A ghost of a smile haunted his face. The Attorney knew his master enjoyed thinking that the road to treasure might be a short one.

Detrovna waved to a waiter and demanded American Wild Turkey bourbon. After they both drank, he said, "Tell me the bad news, then, Gennady Efimovich. Does the shipping address for the bulk of the items match the longitude and latitude on Harsky's map?"

"It does well enough," the Attorney said gloomily. "The United States of America. Near the city Pittsburgh." Again he had the feeling that the timid accountant had, after all, swindled them. To his surprise Detrovna refilled his glass. He had more to say.

"There is another, possibly important side to this entire affair, my friend." Detrovna pressed a thick hand firmly against the table in emphasis. "You remember the name of the czarist landowner provided by Harsky?"

"Of course. Sergei Nevsky," the Attorney said.

Detrovna nodded. "My sources have been in touch. They tell me his grandson lives in that Pittsburgh. I am given to understand this Yuri Vladimirovich, an odd man of no special merit, might possess information useful to us."

The Attorney nodded. His master's words, framed by whiskey and cocaine, helped him shake off the gloom he was coming to attach to the pursuit of the Romanov Cache. Detrovna might yet soar high enough on wings of old Imperial gold to settle on the high crag of total leadership of the new Russia.

10

The Monastery of St. John the Baptist, northeast of Moscow

Above the trees Alessya Harsky saw the onion domes of the monastery church on high ground more than two kilometers distant. She guided the Toyota into the parking area. Signs warned that no "unauthorized transportation" was allowed beyond this point.

Visitors had two options: walk or ride the mule carts. The latter was a concession granted when the monastery had been founded five hundred years ago and recently re-established. Carts and pedestrians shared the same rough track. She imagined it muddy in spring and fall, dusty in summer, and decorated with mule droppings year round.

It was late spring; the ground was firm. The walk would give her time to discover whether or not she was going to weep again right now. As she moved she drew gazes from passersby, though nothing in her dress was unusual. She wore a loose light blue blouse, ordinary khaki slacks, and woven leather sandals. Her heavy black hair was held up by a rolled red babushka. Her height—more than one-point-seven-five meters—and the determination of her steps singled her out. Her face showed a compelling mix of Tatar and European Russian blood. Her brown, liquid eyes had the slightest almond angling, their lashes thick, their brows heavy. High-set delicate cheeks, bony reminders of invading ancestors, promised passion and unpredictability. Her mouth was large, her teeth wide and very sharp.

She resented how hard it had been to arrange a meeting with the man called only Korchevko. His city handlers had probed her motives and of course she could not reveal them. She suspected it was her naked passion to devote herself to his ascendancy, rather than her evasive words, that in the end led to her appointment. She was told it was to last "no more than ten minutes."

Within the monastery a novice led her to a small meeting cell containing a three-legged table and two chairs. She knelt before the ikon and blessed herself. Shortly Korchevko arrived. She had never seen the man or any image of him, so hadn't expected the tall dancer's figure, the fine white shoulder-length hair, the white peasant tunic and trousers, the unhurried graceful bow to the ikon. Nor had she anticipated the look of peaceful determination in genuflection. She was embarrassed to admit it had occurred to her that Korchevko's well-publicized wish to live for a while in this place was an act largely designed more for public consumption than pious contemplation.

A look at his Arctic ice blue pupils further proved her earlier thinking wrong. She had not made a mistake coming to him with her cry for vengeance—and a heart and soul to commit to it.

Sitting at his order, she sensed the strength of his personality. Its force was so great that she was certain he was marked by destiny to guide Russia to the heights she deserved.

She swallowed and, grateful for her few years stage experience, set her voice firmly. "I am Alessya Harsky. I've come to serve you. To help you defeat your rival."

"Which rival?" Korchevko's smile was gentle.

"Boris Detrovna!" Despite herself, her voice cracked. Fresh tears burned behind her eyes.

"You must explain," he said.

She told him everything. She began with how she had become Detrovna's mistress. She plunged ahead, no matter a face flaming with shame. She described his wealth and how he had imagined it would substitute for his regular presence in her life. How their days turned sour! So it was with mixed feelings two weeks ago that she heard him order her away. The tears that welled at that command were born at least in part in genuine relief.

On the heels of that upheaval came worse. While crossing the Leningradsky Prospekt her father Josef was accidentally struck by a hit-and-run truck. He was killed.

Two days later Mikhail Ludinov, her father's neighbor and presumed friend, interrupted her grieving. Mikhail was a short, hairy heavy drinker in his mid-forties. He would have been handsome, save for pendulous lips that a heavy goatee and moustache failed to hide. He gave her a large office envelope. Her father had told him to do so in the event he suffered an unnatural death.

She read the pages written in her father's hand. She learned everything about the deal he made with Detrovna. Her face whitened as her intuition told her that the criminal politician had seen to her father's murder. Rage roiled up bringing fresh grief. She and Detrovna had shared love! She had seen affection in his eyes, heard it on his lips, and felt it to her core in the bedroom.

Now she understood well how little weight he gave his love—or her. On the scale of his heart both were far overbalanced by greed and ambition. Their feelings for one another had not slowed him one whit in the assassination of her father! While Ludinov looked on in amazement, she wailed and tore at her hair. She felt filthy, naive, and hopelessly soiled. She could not have been betrayed more vilely! She threw herself to the floor to kick and froth like an epileptic. At first she wanted to kill herself.

After a short while she came to want revenge.

Calm at least for the moment, she re-read her father's documents. He wrote that she now knew all he did about the Romanov Cache. She was to take the papers, especially the map, to a man named Korchevko whom he believed offered Russia "her best hope for the future."

She found no map. She had received the envelope unsealed. She stared at Ludinov. "Where's the map?" she asked.

"I have it," he said.

"Give it to me."

"I read what you have there. It's all nonsense!" he said. "Those who believe something will come of all that are fools!"

"Then give me the map so that I can stand equally among other fools," Alessya said with a smile. She held out her hand.

He moved to her side. "You can have it *and* my silence." She felt the touch of his pendulous lips on her neck. For a moment she stood unmoving, shocked. His hand moved to her blouse, slipped between its buttons as fast as a ferret. She heard him gasp with pleasure at the size of what he found. She shoved him away. "Enough! My father thought you were his friend."

"I can be *your* friend, too." He wasn't to be discouraged. He grabbed her around the waist. The vodka on his breath nearly watered her eyes. He jabbed the edge of his palm into her crotch and shifted his arm over her shoulder to draw her closer.

Detrovna had given her many delicate, sweet-smelling gifts. In Afghanistan he had beheld the fate of some less lucky women. So he had also given her what together they called the Needle. It was a thin Czech blade folded into a bone handle. A powerful spring snapped it out for instant use.

She tore a hand free and slipped the Needle from her pocket. She thumbed the blade into position and stuck its tip a centimeter into Ludinov's neck.

With a howl he stumbled backward, away from her. He touched his skin where the blood poured from a shallow wound.

They faced each other panting. She waved the Needle back and forth in front of her as Detrovna had taught her.

He touched his neck again. "Then you will pay for the map with rubles!" he said.

Eyes still on him, she sidled to a cabinet. From it she dragged a bundle of bills, the last remaining from Detrovna's generosity. She tossed it to him. He rifled it with blood-smeared fingers and raised his eyes to hers. "Half-enough, Alessya. Have the rest here tomorrow."

She had no more money of course. In any case the next day Mikhail didn't return. Later she learned that he had gone on a binge, the vodka paid for with her rubles, and been fallen upon on a dark street by hooligans who beat him to death and robbed him. She searched the wretched rooms he shared with two other men. She found no map. Undoubtedly he had been carrying it. His attackers, finding it meaningless and without value, had likely destroyed it or saved it for use in one of the city's inadequately supplied lavatories.

Alessya drew a deep breath to steady herself and looked into Korchevko's tranquil eyes. "So instead of the map, I bring you myself and all that my father shared with me. I want to work for you and toward Boris Detrovna's destruction!" She couldn't keep the passion from her voice. "To destroy his hopes of finding the treasure. And if possible to destroy his political career as well!" Her determination burned through her welling tears. She dared not confess to this upright spiritual soul that she also intended to kill Detrovna if she ever had that chance.

Korchevko nodded. "I understand, daughter. But have care. You must know that the Greeks wrote that one who plans to seek revenge must first dig two graves."

"I don't care! I'm not afraid!"

Korchevko nodded. He rose and paced the narrow cell, hands behind him. Long minutes passed. Alessya waited, looking at the back of his peasant blouse, white trousers, and the heels of his sandaled feet.

He turned back to her, that benign smile returned to his handsome face. "Alessya Josefiya, do you like to travel?"

She frowned. "I—I suppose."

"How are your powers of persuasion?"

Her frown faded into a look of determination. "I know how to get what I want!"

His eyes covered her, hair to heel. He nodded. "Yes, of course."

Korchevko moved forward. He lightly held her hands. His skin was cool. His eyes were increasingly magical. "We will arrange your itinerary and other details," he said. "Prepare yourself to leave at once."

"Where am I going?"

"To America."

11

Latrobe, near Pittsburgh,

Thanks to an excellent Exxon road map Sasha the Swiss had made quick time along the roads from the Greater Pittsburgh International Airport. It was time for a rest and a bite to eat. He checked his Piaget: an hour to spare. He pulled off into a diner parking lot. He liked American diners, all of them curiously run by Greeks. Their menus were large. And though the coffee was ordinary, there was plenty of it. After he ordered in what he always liked to think was perfect English, he drew a deep breath and relaxed in his booth. It was his first moment of peace in forty-eight hours.

How quickly the Raptor had moved after the telephone call from America! While he kept its source and nature to himself, the speed with which he laid out Sasha's assignments spoke of the call's importance. It was the Swiss's guess that those others who sought the czar's treasure had been more aggressive than expected. Rapid action was now necessary.

Once again he unfolded the photocopy sheets of the peasant Lyubov's unsent letter to his master. It was the frame on which the whirligig of Sasha's recent rushing about had been erected. It had come as memorabilia into the hands of Parisians of Russian descent. Their heirs had learned of the Raptor's recent interest in the Family Nevsky. From their fingers to his proved a short distance indeed. The letter, in an envelope bearing Sergei Nevsky's name but no address, had been found after the peasant's unexplained disappearance in late May of 1922. It had been overlooked by those who ransacked his tiny cottage in Sazilly south of Tours where he had been living since early 1917.

Sasha's eyes again scanned the lumpish Russian script.

January 4, 1917

To my honored master, Sergei Ivanovich Nevsky —
I write to apologize. I failed in one small part to completely follow your orders. That failure nags me. So I must tell you that good I did do. Knowing the best, you may thus forgive the worst.
The journey went well enough. The freight sled and team of eight were the best I ever drove. I found the town and its harbor hard by the Gulf of Finland. The men you named were ready. I saw your covered cargo safely

stowed. *As you ordered, I made sure our destination was St. Pierre en Port on the north coast of France.*

Even now I must curse the seas and all the idiots who sail upon them! Men were given legs, not fins, for a reason. The Petrel *was not ten minutes from land when I began to grow ill. The captain and his mate, an oily duo, laughed at my sickness. They told me it would pass "in a day or a week, who knows?"*

For hours I hung over the side spewing. And freezing half to death! The captain gave me a rough bunk down in the dark cargo hold. I could no more sleep walled in than jump to the moon. Even deep swallows from the first of my four vodka bottles did nothing to make me feel better.

I stumbled up on deck in the middle of the first night. The sea tried to wring out my already empty stomach. Afterward, I found shelter in the lifeboat. I was away from the spray but not the icy breeze without which I would have died. There I dozed—and woke with ice under my nose.

The days at sea passed slowly. I grew well enough to try the mate's wretched stew—and spat it out. Vodka would do me until my boots again felt God's hard earth where they belonged. At last I learned I had to endure only one more night of pitching, tossing, and icy decks. We would dock the next evening.

I awoke in my lifeboat in a night darker than the inside of a priest's pocket. The ocean was quiet, the air bitter cold. I heard captain's and mate's voices. The mate said he had slipped away from me and "got a peep at it." He had loosened the lashing that held the canvas to your cargo, master. He said he saw a box with no opening. "Riveted metal stretching on," he said.

The captain said it seemed he had been wasting his time. The mate said no, he had seen something painted on the metal. Some words he couldn't make out—and the Romanov double eagle! I made the sign of the cross three times, master. To think that I was doing the business of Matiushka *and* Batiushka!

The captain grew excited. There were men in St. Pierre en Port who were savage enemies of the great czar, supporters of the coming revolution. They would pay well to have whatever lay within the box. The two villains began to make plans...

Dusk had fallen when we sailed into port. The harbormaster and customs man had been bribed. The first pointed out a shadowy pier by low stone warehouses.

Master, no sooner were the Petrel's *ropes made fast than a large flat bed wagon pulled by eight matched dray horses came from the deepest shadows! It drew up alongside the vessel. It bore no writing or numbers. I saw its driver wore a black hood cut with small eyeholes.*

The time had come for me to earn my passage. When the captain jumped to the deck to go to the wagon, I slipped behind the mate. The captain told the driver that the vessel's winch was damaged. He couldn't unload his cargo that night. The driver should come back tomorrow. By then the czar's box would be in the hands of his enemies. Not quite so fast, I thought.

I freed a short iron pin from its frosted hole in the railing. I swung. Down went the mate. I hurried below and took from my duffle the weapon you know I love well. That one I pleased myself to use shooting wolves to earn my name, Lyubov the Wolfkiller. Yes, my heavy short barrel scatter gun. With its cold metal against the captain's neck I ordered him to unload your cargo, master. The mate needed to be awakened to do the job.

As they worked I carried out the next-to-last of your orders. From around my waist I pulled your gift, the eel-skin money belt. As you insisted I wait until I reached French soil, I hadn't opened it. I did then. Master, so many gold pieces! A small fortune as sure as I am a believer. I thank you a thousand times!

Your note amid the coins, though, quickly brought me back to earth. I never expected you to order me never to return to the Motherland! That I was to live out my days in France for my safety and that of the czar. That I would never see my nagging Olga and our four brats again!

Then I understood why Mitya's purse-mouthed French tutor had been sent to afflict me for the last three months. The man was at me for hours every day like a fox after a chicken. No rest. And always with the verbs—the infernal verbs! And pronunciation. A honking language French, all snorted through the nose instead of spoken in the throat like decent Russian. Well, I learned enough, despite myself. But I had never dreamed why.

Understand then, master, I was already in a foul mood when the mate made a foolish move below decks. The captain, too, leaped at me with a knife, thinking two at a time would give them success and yet a chance at the czar's box.

Their mistake.

My knots were far clumsier than their sailors' ones would have been when I fastened their dead legs to heavy bits of iron. But my rope work was good enough to draw the pair down deep into the dark water. Good riddance!

I should have sunk their stinking ship as well!

When I climbed on deck and looked toward the pier, the wagon was gone!

I thought then of your final order, repeated at least six times: Do not pursue the cargo. Start a new life instead.

At that moment I failed you, master. The Devil reached me in the guise of curiosity. Instead of turning my back and walking away, I hurried up the quay. There was a public house. Outside horses had been tied. I chose a decent mare, cut her reins, and was off over the cobblestones.

I caught up with the wagon at the first turning, then in cunning fell far enough behind not to be seen. I told myself that if I was to spend the rest of my life in France, I could begin it as I chose. Hear how the Devil spoke!

I reached inside my jacket for the last bottle of vodka. I took a swallow deep enough to wash the reek of the sea forever out of my gullet. It was a pleasant enough night for a ride. December in France was as warm as May at Great Meadow.

Very soon the driver grabbed the neck of the hood and pulled it off. A toss of the head spilled down a mane of thick red hair. A woman was at the reins! No matter. She managed the team for many kilometers along roads far better than the Motherland's, but none too good at that.

Four days later I was still in the saddle in the middle of nowhere. The names of French towns meant nothing to me. The most recent was Gien. That was still in my mind when I saw the wagon pause by an iron delivery gate in a long high stone wall. The gate opened. The wagon entered. In time the gate closed and all was as before. I waited an hour then rode slowly past. An iron plaque had been set in stone by the entrance. It read: Château de Sollonier.

Master, not content with disobeying you, I then went further and played the Tempter's imp. My infernal curiosity! At the local café I tamed the snake of my new French well enough to speak to the waiter. I asked him about the château and who lived there. Count Jacques Sollonier, I was told. A diplomat, he was seldom at home. His wife was a beautiful red-haired Russe with an equally beautiful daughter Sybille of nine years.

So I satisfied myself, saying nothing you had planned had been bothered by my doings. But since then I haven't shaken the feeling that I failed you.

When I have the courage or brother vodka gives it to me, I will find out where you are and post this to you.

I throw myself at your feet and beg for your forgiveness.
Your man who believes in Jesus Christ our Redeemer,
Lyubov the Wolfkiller

Sasha folded the letter and slipped it back into his pocket.

The Raptor's French friends were high in the ranks of police and security. It did not take them long to identify the Château Sollonier south of Gien. Nor was much time needed for Ostrovsky to bark out orders.

Expectations rising, Sasha had flown to Paris and driven the more than two hours south following the faxed marked map.

He rang the bell set into the wrought iron fence that angled around the elegant château and its stunning grounds.

A Japanese servant answered the bell.

He worked for an Osaka banker who had bought the château some years ago. "Respect for history" had prevented the multi-millionaire from changing its name or appearance. Sasha turned away dejected. Thorough clandestine search of the entire grounds and sprawling structure, though possible, would be too time-consuming.

No matter. Another route to the riches still lay open.

Ostrovsky's growing political importance encouraged his like-minded French friends to dig through archives. Those efforts proved worthwhile. Information about the Sollonier family was uncovered. Natalia disappeared in June of 1922—as had Sergei Nevsky. Jacques died a hero in World War II under the Cross of Lorraine. Sybille was accused of wartime collaboration. She renounced French citizenship, fled to America, and became a naturalized citizen.

Her United States address was on a number of documents for anyone to see.

Sasha made an international call. He contacted the telephone company's information service. The Raptor was in luck! Sybille Sollonier still lived at the documents' address. He phoned and reached a woman who called herself "Mademoiselle Sollonier's companion." Sasha said he would like to arrange a meeting. "Call from this country—if you ever get here," the companion snapped and hung up.

Sasha now was here. He had called earlier that morning. The companion had asked him general questions about his reasons for wanting to meet Sybille. He felt his lies about being a journalist assembling reminiscences of World War II satisfied her. They set the time for him to meet the nonagenarian.

He glanced at his watch, rose, and paid his bill. The cashier gave him directions to the Sollonier address. Less than twenty minutes later he was climbing a walk edged with carefully husbanded roses. At its end was a tidy but aging farmhouse. His heart beat more hungrily. Why not?

Sergei Nevsky and Natalia Sollonier had conducted some business related to the Romanov Cache.

Both had disappeared about the same time in 1922.

More important. The brutish lackey Lyubov had seen to it that a certain sealed metal box had reached the Sollonier estate. What else could it have contained but the czar's treasure?

Sybille might well know about all these things.

A woman in her sixties opened the door. Fine gray hair clung to her scalp. Above her ears it darted out in little curving wings. "Are you Alexander Sorokin who called?" she asked.

He said he was and tried to edge by her. She didn't move. "Mademoiselle Sollonier isn't here," she said.

"What?"

"She left this morning immediately after your call."

Sasha was baffled. "Why? Where is she?"

The companion went ahead ignoring his questions. "Sybille has lived a long life. There are some years about which she doesn't speak to anyone. Those times left her with an expectation that one day she might be contacted by those with whom she *could* talk, could...empty herself before she died."

"Who's to say I'm not among those she's waiting for?" Sasha asked.

The woman rolled her small dark eyes. "Haven't I heard enough about who *they* are! She hopes her visitors will be connected with a man of an earlier age living in a place called Great Meadow. Connected with Sergei Nevsky."

Nevsky! Damn that name! Sasha thought. The one tangled into this whole affair as completely as fishing line snarled on the reel. Ostrovsky, who knew more than Sasha, now linked that name to a curse every time he uttered it. "Where is Sybille Sollonier?" Sasha didn't try to hide the edge in his voice. He didn't intend to suffer a second frustration.

The woman's pointed nose wriggled. Her angular chin's pores were spread and dappled by the years. She met his eyes with awesome indifference and said nothing.

Sasha's hand touched her forearm. It was so lightly fleshed he could feel the separation between the two bones. "Tell me where she is!"

Silence. Her eyes were bright, thin-lipped smile hostile.

He lowered his hand into the pocket where his garrote lay neatly coiled. More than once he had held its custom-shaped handles and worked the wire into human flesh. He looked at the companion's chicken neck somehow shocking in its pale vulnerability. How long would she stay silent with the wire a centimeter into her?

He lifted his gaze to her curiously indifferent eyes. The Swiss, a traveler through the world, had become a shrewd judge of humanity. His fingers caressed the shaped handles lightly, weighing what he read in her face's indifference against the dreadful potential of the garrote.

In time he withdrew his hand. He was facing a rare woman, one who had walled off fear from her mind. Even at the edge of death he sensed she would remain silent.

He bowed and offered regrets at having missed Sybille. Possibly at another, better time... He clicked his heels, bowed, and smiled before he turned away.

After all, there were many roads to royal riches. Ways that unfortunately would have to involve the living Nevsky.

At his car he looked back. He saw the woman motionless in the doorway she had so successfully guarded. For the first time it occurred to him that she might have been both lying *and* bluffing. Maybe the Sollonier woman had been within all along.

Had he suffered a small defeat? His lingering look back told him nothing.

The companion stood silent, knowing, and like her mistress, infinitely patient...

12

Pittsburgh, Pennsylvania

More than a week had passed since Grushkin's disappearance. Nevsky learned nothing about him from his Russian Slope sources. He hated to admit it, but the bearded one had snookered him. The guy had paid the cheap admission of a few glib lies and heard much at Father Ruslan's bedside. Whether or not the information was useful in the search for the treasure, Nevsky couldn't guess. For all the drama and emotion surrounding the long ago exhumation of the silvery box, after all it had been empty.

What ate at Nevsky had nothing to do with treasure. Grushkin had come to St Basil's rectory because he knew Father Ruslan had valuable information. How did he learn that? Maybe he followed the two priests all the way from Russia, maybe all the way to the rectory. But he couldn't have known exactly what they were about until he talked to the only man on the continent, beside Nevsky, who knew.

Father Alexei!

So it had been Grushkin who tortured and murdered the priest!

Now Grushkin had disappeared and Nevsky felt a fool. Hadn't he set himself on a mini-quest to find the gentle priest's killer? Like a hero from some mythic tale who gallops off to vanquish evil and returns years later to find that all along it had been scuttling in disguise by his own hearth, he too had missed the swift route to good.

He guessed it would be a long, dangerous while before he had a second chance—if it ever came.

Despite Lyudmila's threats over his making an immediate decision about joining their cause or losing the chance, she phoned him daily to press her case. Daily he put her off. He owed her and Shmelev something to compensate for his reluctance. He owed her alone for his practice of that cruelest art, bedroom brinksmanship. So he arranged for them to be invited to a private party at the Imperial Court high on Russian Slope.

From the Imperial Court's floor-to-ceiling windows one could glimpse the distant towers of the Golden Triangle. The windows were about the only things that hadn't changed over the years. Management had taken the place from ethnic enclave to supper spot, to musical dinner theater, and to comedy club in search of continued solvency. Lately, though, the owners were all smiles. After half a century things Russian were fashionable again! The Cossack doorman was back! Bring on the gypsies and balalaikas! "Authentic Russian artists touring from Moscow..." cried the small marquee.

The party raged. The vodka flowed. Shmelev led the toasting. *"Do dna!"*—Down the hatch! His jutting cheeks gleamed with pleasure and the heat of drink. Lyudmila in her snaky black dress drew the admiration of middle-aged men for whom an unattached woman of a certain age was a welcome rarity. For the evening she had cut and styled her hair. Her gray eyes flashed with energy, though she had dampered her usual look of determined commitment. For a few hours at least, Korchevko wasn't the center of her life.

I was in bed with her, Nevsky thought. And let her get away. Which had whispered in his ear, wisdom or stupidity? And would he ever know?

A hand touched Nevsky's shoulder. He turned. Butch Hanson! He was an old pal from Nevsky's long-gone government investigator days. He worked for one of those agencies doing necessary dirty work, some of it nasty. "Nevsky! I heard you might be here," Butch said. "Talked my way in. Got a minute?" Butch's blonde hair had thinned. His face was turning jowly. But he still had the wide football neck that seemingly plunked his head directly onto ox-wide shoulders, and hands wide as small manholes. He led Nevsky to a corner table stacked with dirty dishes. "You still find out things for people?" he said.

"Butch, I'm semi-retired."

"I want to hire the unretired part of you."

Nevsky sighed. Butch was an old, good friend. It was bad luck to say no to old friends. Anyway, he needed a change of pace. Lately he had been feeling like the Wehrmacht retreating from Stalingrad: too many Russians in his life.

So he listened to Butch's story. His father lived about thirty miles northeast of Pittsburgh, along the Allegheny River, up past Godfrey and Johnetta. He was long-pensioned. He amused himself by working a little vegetable farm on a small part of the fifty acres he owned, some of which fronted on Lake Nagle. A few days ago men in suits representing an outfit called Triangle Associates came with real estate papers and cash. They offered him three times what the place was worth and promised to pay on the spot. All he had to do was sign the sell agreement and a few other documents—and move out fast.

He asked them what an old man would do with all that money. They said he could think of something. After some give and take the suits realized he didn't want to sell. They raised the price to four times market value, "final offer." He said no.

The suits went away. In the evening two different men came. They threatened him. Sell and keep quiet, or else. Decide! He decided not to sell.

"So you know what they did?" Butch asked Nevsky. "To a seventy-eight-year-old man? They broke one of his arms!"

Nevsky winced. "Then what happened?"

"He signed. They left the cash on the kitchen counter." Butch drew a deep breath. "My father had to go to the hospital to get his arm set. I went, too. Something went wrong. He died there!" He made a loose fist and studied the nails of his right hand. "I looked at the papers and tried to find *anybody* from Triangle Associates. I went to all the local motels. Six guys had listed Triangle as their business organization, but they had all checked out. I tried to reach them at the business addresses they gave in New York. All phony." He shook his head. "I was very determined, very angry. It didn't help. I still ended up frustrated. I didn't want to drop it. I tried to think of something. I came up with you, Nevsky."

"What do you want me to do, Butch?" Nevsky asked.

"Find out the names of the two guys. Maybe their addresses."

"So you can call the law?"

A grim grin cracked Butch's square face. "Didn't you read *The Godfather?* The Hansons handle family problems themselves."

Nevsky took another look at Butch's shoulders, the arms knotted with muscle. For him the police weren't the only way.

"I'll see what I can do," he said.

"What do you charge?" Butch asked.

"I don't charge *you* anything."

Butch went to his briefcase and pulled out a copy of the sale agreement for the farm. "May be some help," he said. He also gave Nevsky his late father's clear description of the men.

A while later Nevsky surveyed the party scene. Shmelev and Lyudmila were making new friends, he by forcing passersby to share his vodka right out of the bottle, she by dancing with anyone who asked her. Everyone was still far from that old *Na pososhok*, the good-luck-goodnight toast. His mission accomplished, Nevsky paid his compliments to the host and went home.

There he scanned the Hanson sale agreement and went to the phone. It wasn't too late to call Theo Dragonian. Owner of Dragonian Properties, Theo was maybe the biggest real estate mogul in the tri-state region. Five years ago his son Theo II had left school for the bad reason of joining an anti-government militia group. Theo asked Nevsky to find him. He did, and talked the boy into leaving—not easy. Then he had to deal with "the commander" and his cronies who looked at Theo II as a future source of funds for their revolution. It was dicey for a while. Glocks were fired in anger, but no one was seriously injured. Since then Theo I had felt himself in Nevsky's debt. "What can I do for you?" he said every time they met. "*What can I do for you?*"

Theo was home. When he heard Nevsky's voice, he said, "Yuri, what can I do for you?"

Nevsky read him the key information from the agreement. He told him he wanted to find out more about this Triangle outfit that was buying up properties around Lake Nagle northeast of the city. "Call you back tomorrow morning," Dragonian said.

At ten the next morning the phone rang. Dragonian said the man involved was Mark Malanger, Allegheny Realty. He gave Nevsky Malanger's business address. "He'll meet you at noon, his office."

Nevsky started to thank Dragonian who interrupted. "One thing, Yuri, he doesn't want to talk to you."

"So why is he?"

"He owes me—big."

Allegheny Realty took up two storefronts in a strip mall outside of Johnetta. The receptionist was a girl of twenty with bad skin and good legs. She led him to Malanger's office. Its walls hung with Rotary and chamber of commerce plaques. On the desk stood family photos in Lucite mounts, the wife, the son and daughter. Malanger was looking out the window, smoking a Swisher Sweet. The odor invaded Nevsky's nose like a Hun.

Malanger turned toward his visitor. His horse face showed both anxiety and resentment. His handshake was brief, all fingers. He didn't offer coffee or sit down. He said, "I'd like to ask you a favor, Mr. Nevsky."

"What?"

"I want you to leave—now. Tell Dragonian I met with you, as he asked."

Nevsky shook his head. "What I need to know is no big deal. Whoever you're afraid of doesn't have to know we talked."

"*Please.* Go away!"

Nevsky ignored him. He pulled out his copy of the Hanson sale agreement. "Here's all I want to know. Tell me where I'd find the two guys who persuaded old man Hanson to sell his farm and—oopsy!—broke his arm doing it."

Malanger's face whitened. "I—didn't know anything about *that,*" he said. "They didn't tell me."

"Who's 'they?'"

"Triangle Associates."

Nevsky pointed at two of the signatures, buyer and witness. Peter Ivanovich and Dominick Voysovich. "These guys work for Triangle?"

"I suppose so. I never met them." Malanger was trying to be cool, studying the damp end of his little cigar.

"I want to find them," Nevsky said pointedly.

"Good luck. Everybody from Triangle was from out of town. New York, I was given to understand. If they finally got Hanson's property, they probably went home. It was the only one they didn't score right out of the chute."

"Why don't you tell me about it? The whole deal, I mean."

Malanger's little black eyes darted around like a couple of mice dodging the cat. "I'd rather not," he said. He added quickly, "Everything I did was honest."

"What *did* you do?" Nevsky said. "What did you get out of it?"

Malanger gave his head a little shake. "Not that much."

"*What?*" Nevsky was getting annoyed.

"I don't want to tell you anything!"

Nevsky sat on the desk and worked up a nasty little smile. "You have a real estate license?"

"Of course!"

"And you want to keep it. So you probably wouldn't want me going to the *Allegheny Valley Herald* and WLVT-TV with my story."

Malanger raised his Swisher Sweet to his lips. His hands were shaking. "What story?" he asked.

"The one about how you worked hand in hand with men who broke an old man's arm to force him to sell a piece of property. I heard his son Butch is crazy to go on TV and tell everybody what happened."

"Don't!"

"So, talk to me and you won't have to talk to any reporters," Nevsky said.

Malanger made fists. "Christ!" He tore the cigar from his mouth, threw it on the floor and stared at it. "I *swore* to the Triangle people I wouldn't say anything!" He looked at Nevsky with something like pleading in his eyes. "They came in smooth and tough, man. They didn't threaten me, not directly at least. But I could read them, and imagine the fist in the velvet glove. They had a—a *mob* style, but they weren't Italians. When they told me not to talk, they meant *don't talk!*"

"Who's gonna know?" Nevsky asked. "Be cool. I'm discreet."

Malanger's tone turned whiney. "I thought you just wanted a couple names. Why do you need to know about the deal? What the hell's it to you?"

"Just curious," Nevsky said. "Talk!"

Malanger bolted for the door. Nevsky, still quick enough, grabbed the real estate agent's arm and spun him into a half nelson. He shoved his head against the wall. His skull dented the cheap wallboard. "Your choice, Malanger," Nevsky muttered into the man's lowered ear. "Either I *do* hurt you now, or Triangle *might* hurt you later."

Malanger was crying. He swept the tears away angrily with the back of his free hand. "I'm not very brave," he said. "I'm sorry."

"I won't tell a soul that, either. Let's hear it." Nevsky freed Malanger's arm. The sour smell of fear sweat mixed with the sweet stogie smoke.

There wasn't that much to it. A little more than a week ago two men representing Triangle had come to the office. They had done their homework. They had the Armstrong Country tract map for the area, the land they wanted marked in purple. They had a list of the names and addresses of the five owners. They said they wanted to buy the properties. What they wanted Malanger to do was to handle the legal details related to buying and selling property in Pennsylvania, in the county. His cut: ten percent of the selling prices and a five thousand dollar bonus if the paperwork was ready in less than fourteen days.

Four owners were quick to sell at such high prices—even though they had to sign a paper saying they would be off their properties in two weeks. What did they care? Two lived in ratty split-levels, the other two in falling down farmhouses. With what they got from Triangle they could live on the water in Naples, Florida.

Nevsky frowned. "Why does Triangle want the land?"

A deep breath heaved away the last of Malanger's tears. He relaxed. "They said they were going to develop it. Don't know how. There is a little flat ground near a fallen down cottage. But there's an ugly big hill that runs right down into Lake Nagle. One end of the lake is shallow and swampy. Doesn't seem like prime development land to me."

Nevsky got directions to the lake from Malanger. The real estate man glared at him. "All right! I'm even with Dragonian. I've told you what I know. Why don't you get out of here!"

Triangle had done a fine job of scaring the guy, Nevsky thought. He wouldn't be surprised if Malanger left town that day on a long family vacation.

He turned his Rabbit out of town. Back roads led north of Johnetta toward the lake. He drove around, getting the lay of the land. Lake Nagle was maybe a half-mile across, roughly circular. The natural dam that held it in place was a heavily overgrown hillside that ran down to the south shore of the Allegheny. A wide stream ran out of the spring-fed lake and disappeared down the steep slope.

Turning toward the level land on the other side of the high hill, Nevsky found the dirt road blocked with a heap of newly cut brush. A man with a holster on his hip appeared at the driver's side door. Another angled in from a thicket.

Nevsky rolled down his window.

"Private property!" the closer man said.

Nevsky looked up at him. "Since when?"

"Since I said so."

The second man was standing with a shoe sole against the VW's front bumper. The message: not one more inch forward.

Nevsky took a second look at the two men and compared them with what he remembered of Hanson's description. One with his hair worked into a plait, the other pale as a wraith. No doubt. They were Peter Ivanovich and Dominick Voysovich!

Well, well, Nevsky thought. Mission accomplished!

With his blandest smile and most sincere apology he put the car in reverse. As he moved backward, he heard Ivanovich say to Voysovich, "We better hurry putting up the signs."

He said it in Russian.

13

Pittsburgh, Pennsylvania

Lately when returning to 138 Morlande Nevsky hoped to find Charity Day's luggage on the porch. Her weepy phone call suggested she might soon return. But she wasn't there after his trip to Johnetta either. He went to the answering machine and found a message. It wasn't Charity's voice. His stomach did a little disappointed flip. The caller spoke with a crisp English accent. He asked Nevsky to call a number about "a quite important matter."

Important or not, Butch Hanson was first. Nevsky called him and reported what had happened around Johnetta. He told him Ivanovich and Voysovich were armed and mean. They looked like big trouble from any angle, maybe were some heavy hitters from New York. After Butch thanked him Nevsky asked him what he was going to do. "Reconnoiter," his old friend said.

"Stay in touch then, OK?" Nevsky said.

"Will do."

When he returned the answering machine call, the English-accented voice said that a General Sviatoslav Slavkovich Ostrovsky would like to speak with him. He was staying at the Holiday Inn on the Parkway East near Edgewood.

"What would he like to talk about?"

"Certain events centering on your grandfather's activities."

"I see. I'll be there."

Ostrovsky? A new name! Nevsky imagined the rich dazzle of the Romanov treasure shimmering in the air like a mirage. He guessed here was another contender squirming over his hot sands to reach it.

General Ostrovsky had a suite of top floor rooms. Nevsky stepped off the elevator to face a rod-spined man about six-three. Two like him stood guard between the elevator and the room at the end of the corridor. He sensed all of them were or had been soldiers. He wanted to say, "At ease." Instead he said in Russian, "I'm here to see General Ostrovsky."

"Da!" Rod-spine pointed at the distant suite door.

The man in front of it spoke a password. A fourth soldier opened the door. Nevsky noticed their every hair and clothing crease was in perfectly neat order, by the book. Discipline thrived. He wanted to laugh, but didn't. He knew discipline could achieve much.

A man who introduced himself in English as Alexander—call me "Sasha"—ran a metal detector over Nevsky's body. His was the voice that had left the answering machine message. Now he switched to fluent Russian. "The general has waited a long time to meet you. He has much to talk to you about."

When Nevsky entered his suite, Ostrovsky jumped to his feet. The general was just short of six feet. He had thinning hair and wore a goatee. Here was another disciplined rod-spine. Determination set his face and guided every movement.

Not a guy with whom to fool around was Nevsky's snap judgment.

He embraced the American. His arms were wiry. He was about fifty and in good shape. As he turned toward the chair positioned for him Nevsky noticed the room was a chambermaid's delight. Nothing was out of place. The bed was made. There was no trash in the baskets. Clothing was aligned on hangers in the closet. Take away the bottle of Russian mineral water on the desk and the suite was ready for the next occupant.

Ostrovsky's voice was low as the best Bolshoi Opera basso. "It's an honor to meet the grandson of the genius Sergei Nevsky!" he boomed.

Nevsky smiled and shrugged. "Thanks."

"You have the American shell on you, I see," Ostrovsky observed. "What is it, the 'oh, shucks' way, like these old James Stewart films?" He snapped a shrewd gaze at Nevsky. "The question is: how thick the shell? How deep do we go to find the Russian?"

"I don't know," Nevsky said. "A lot of my life seems to have involved trying to find that out."

"The larger affair before us will settle that question, I think." Ostrovsky's speech was rapid, pointed. "Listen to me, and then we'll talk."

The bass voice boomed. Nevsky was surprised that Ostrovsky had traveled all the way from St. Petersburg to meet him. He was astonished to understand that the general's family had kept the Sons of Continuity alive for ninety years. But it came as no surprise at all to hear that Ostrovsky fully intended to ride the streamlined organization fueled by the Romanov treasure to the top of the heap—total leadership of Russia. Nevsky's intuition had spoken well: here was yet another who wanted to be czar.

Nevsky thought he'd play the Devil's advocate. "What about the five dozen Romanovs hanging around all over the world, still adding to the family tree even as we speak? Why don't you give them the treasure, if you find it?"

The general waved a dismissive palm. "Their time has passed. Their blood is thin as piss poured onto the sand of insignificance."

The man's audacity! It was easy to call him a loony, except that many called such had beaten the odds and triumphed. Nevsky contrasted the general with the impressions he had of Korchevko, another would-be maximum leader. Korchevko seemed a man of principle, compromise, and morality. Not Ostrovsky. Here was a stiff shot of killer ego force, hold the mixer.

"So much for the past," the general said. "To the present." His wide gray eyes met Nevsky's. "All from here forward would go better if you felt yourself, by blood, a Son of Continuity."

Nevsky shook his head. "My father... Some chose not to forget. He chose the other route. Accept brutal loss and ugly change, and then put it aside and go ahead. Anyway, I was too young for him to pound any monarchist rhetoric into my head. Sorry about that."

Ostrovsky's thin lips twitched. "What ever goes easily?" he asked, half to himself. "I ask you then to join us, to become a Son of Continuity."

Nevsky thought a moment. First the Force for Leadership wanted him marching in their ranks, now the Sons. He shook his head. "I'm not a joiner," he said. "I go solo. Another American trait, I suppose."

Ostrovsky nodded curtly. "Another American illusion," he muttered. He rose from his chair, put his hands behind him. "I sense your grandfather's diary has prejudiced you against the Sons."

"The diary?" Nevsky said.

"Of course!" Ostrovsky snapped. "The diary brought to you by Korchevko's people. The one stolen from us!"

How did the man know that? It seemed Ostrovsky wasn't a guy with whom to play dumb. Nevsky sensed he was starting a dangerous balancing act, like the juggler on the wire whose assistant tosses up more and more flat rings. Or in his case, sooner or later tosses up maybe one too many rings. "How do you know I saw the diary?" he asked.

Ostrovsky snorted. "He who would rule must first intrigue." He tossed his head and Nevsky understood he would get no more answer to his question. "If the diary left you with a bad impression of us, I suggest you revise it. Treat us with the respect we deserve. *Bargain* with us as we deserve." The general's voice boomed persuasively.

"My grandfather's incompetent, dilettante Sons are gone?" Nevsky asked. "A new breed stands before me, one might say?"

"You understand! Precisely the case." Ostrovsky paced. "You would do well to deal with us. You surely know you have information we want. As well we plan to ask you to do something important for us." Ostrovsky turned a palm held wide in a gesture of reasonableness. "We don't expect charity. What must we give you to bring you into our camp—even on a provisional basis?"

"A priest was murdered here a couple weeks ago. A Father Alexei from Moscow. I think a man named Grushkin did it. I want to see justice done, rough or otherwise." Nevsky went on to say that the death was somehow connected to the treasure, but provided no revealing details.

Ostrovsky swore he didn't know Grushkin. He frowned. "Yuri Vladimirovich, I had expected your desires to run along a more material plane."

"They don't. Not everything American has rubbed off."

Ostrovsky saw no impasse. Such men never did. That was why they succeeded. "My friend, let me make a prediction. As we draw closer to the treasure—and so we shall!—our rivals will have to be overcome. As this happens, all the actors in the drama will reveal themselves. Then you very likely will find your priest-murderer Grushkin. This assumes that you cooperate with us."

"I hear you." Nevsky hesitated. Could he work with both Korchevko *and* Ostrovsky? He could for a while, he supposed. That would be playing this dangerous game a little crazy—the only way he had figured would work.

He had done some thinking about the search for the treasure, and drawn at least one conclusion: there was a lot more to learn before anyone put their hands on a single ruble's worth of what was hidden. As it was, he was bogged down with his little hoard of information. He had no way to get more. Unless... He was thinking of—and like—his grandfather. He looked up at Ostrovsky. "Let's keep materialism on vacation," he said. "And try a different approach."

"Of course!" Ostrovsky said. "Which one?"

"For now, I propose an exchange of information of roughly equal value."

That slowed Ostrovsky's straight-ahead style for a long moment. Nevsky prompted him. "I assume you have more to offer than the diary."

"Yes. Yes..." The general frowned. "But...I must ask how do you feel about my ambition, the ultimate goal of the new Sons of Continuity?"

"About your becoming a czar with that name or another? It's none of my business," Nevsky said. "If you want the impossible job of running a riddle like Russia, and get it, more power to you."

Ostrovsky wasn't satisfied. "Still, there are other considerations. Are you trustworthy? Will you betray us?"

"Turn it around, general. Should I trust *you?* You find out what you want from me—then what? One of your stiff spines puts a couple rounds in the base of my neck?"

"That is not our intention."

"All right. Treachery isn't my intention either."

Ostrovsky paced, finally whirled and boomed, "We will try this!"

He summoned Sasha who had traded his metal detector for a voice-activated dictation unit and a spiral notebook. "How shall we begin, then, Yuri Vladimirovich?" Ostrovsky asked.

Neither he nor Ostrovsky were fools, Nevsky thought. Today's promises of honesty and straight dealings could become tomorrow's quaint recollections. He and the Sons one day could cause each other no end of trouble. Both men knew it. They also knew there was no way to tell how the whole business would ultimately unfold. Well, they had one thing in common. They weren't afraid to take a risk.

"Let me go first," Nevsky said. "After I'm finished, you can reply in kind. In equal value. I have a story to tell you about a big silvery cube in the desert."

Nevsky caught the expression darting across the general's face. Was it disappointment? If so, that suggested that Nevsky, without intending such, was going to get something for nothing.

And Ostrovsky dared not confess it.

14

On a road east of St. Petersburg, Russia

Such haste at getting out of Peter! The false priest Archangel giggled, the sound a guttural chugging in his thick throat. How often he had come and gone in wild rush at the bidding of the priest now in the driver's seat.

A priest like no other.

Father Fyodor of Kolyma!

As had happened more than once, Bishop Paulos had sought Fyodor. This time for at least a week. Also as before, Fyodor could not be found. Even the Archangel couldn't find him.

A fine time he picked to appear! Nearly five hours ago, just after midnight. When the bud of one of those revels so much to the Archangel's taste had been about to unfold into a riot of fleshy petals. Still the stink of stale wine clung to his black beard, along with the thin perfumed scent of the first of the little flowers. How the three, scant months from their dolls, had danced! How the eyeless gypsy had fiddled! The rag around his eyes flamed red as gore. His booted foot, heavy as the Devil's tread, thumped the floor.

The Archangel had taken the first little flower onto his lap. She well saw the condition of the giant thing beneath her, touched it, and made a lewd joke. For, no matter their meager years, all three of the girls were whores. Likely clean, always expensive. Already they had the thirsts of their grown sisters. This one, crowned with a shock of curly red hair, bore breasts like hard little figs. She needed both small hands to manage her tumbler of wine.

So the Archangel had waited for the momentary arrival of his Heat. Only when it overcame him did he lust—or kill.

Then in rushed Fyodor, coat collar up, hat brim down to shadow his hatchet face. He tossed a bundle of rubles into the air. The bills fluttered down among the dancers' naked ankles. They dove and scrambled for them like starving birds after grain, forgetting about the giant they entertained. In moments the Archangel was in Fyodor's car, privates exposed to draft, and robes loose.

He asked Fyodor what they were about this time. The priest didn't reply. The Archangel asked him if he knew that Bishop

Paulos had been trying to find him for the last week. At this he nodded. He said, "Have I not often been a man with many masters, Archangel?"

The giant chuckled heavily. "But God is your greatest master, is He not?"

"He's chosen to show me the dark side of His world. Can I follow Him with less zeal for it?"

The two shared sharp, arid laughter.

They drove on unspeaking, but not in silence. It pleased Fyodor to carry with him a lengthy string of Greek ceramic beads. His long fingers played over them continually, bringing forth a dry rattling sound. It had always seemed to the Archangel's wildly looping mind to be the chatter of the restless bones of the dead.

From time to time Fyodor pulled over. With a strong hand lantern he checked the road map. Each time he folded it with a satisfied grunt. The car plunged back into the darkness. The beads clicked and clicked.

The Archangel sat back and closed his eyes. These doings were no less strange than many in which they had played a part over the years. The God Fyodor served was demanding and savage. Often the Archangel had found the priest's normally hard brown eyes pooled with tears. Each drop was a lament over what had been done to him and what he had to do in return. The Archangel saw the narrow face contorted with anguish. He saw the priest's long fingers twisting in sorrow through his tight curly hair like worms after rain. He beheld, over the long march of monstrous acts, the retreat of a true priest's faith followed by the advance of the Devil. Knowing this and being a man, Fyodor suffered torment.

The Archangel knew he, who shared everything with the priest, was a brute, so felt nothing.

At Fyodor's bidding he had laid his heavy hands on commissar, apparatchik, and turncoat cleric alike. Those he maimed and murdered quickly faded like ghosts into his conveniently spotty memory. Like the priest the Archangel had known torture. He had lived to satisfactorily reckon accounts—by rending bones with an implacable grip and tearing tissue with his teeth.

Fyodor broke the silence. "I was sent...elsewhere at the command of one of my masters. There I was told of something hidden where we're headed. Something that interested the master. I find that *I* want to see it first."

The Archangel chuckled. Who could guess which way the wind would blow Fyodor's desires. "What is it?" he asked.

"A box that holds something of great value. Holds it too cleverly for ignorant ex-soldiers and a half-mad priest to find." He nodded forward. "Up ahead we'll find the man who hides it."

"What if he doesn't want to tell you where it is?"

Fyodor's grin was visible in the faint light of approaching dawn. His teeth were white and narrow, like his face. "Then I will thank God again for having given me my Archangel."

Now the car made frequent turnings onto poor roads then mere tracks. Fyodor used the powerful hand lantern to search out scanty ill-written road markers.

It was mid-morning when their long journey finally ended. A weathered and broken sign angling up from a ditch told the Archangel they had reached what had once been the Red Banner Collective Farm.

Hinges had failed on the metal tube gate. It had been shoved aside to rust in the grass. Ahead on both sides of the road lay immobile farm equipment—tractors, tillers, combines, and trucks. The Archangel knew well they did not operate for want of fuel, technical skill, or parts. Likely they had not moved for decades.

A few izbas lay scattered along the road, thin smoke rising from their daub chimneys. A handful of farmers stood by the doorways smoking a morning pipe and staring after the car. The dusty track turned and rose. It passed through an older, far better made gate, this one of crafted stone assembled by skilled masons. Though abused by men and weather, it survived. As did certain large foundations once supporting structures long destroyed through acts of vandalism, revenge, or ignorance. The Archangel knew they were on land once part of a great estate.

Ahead lay concrete barracks like dormitories. Some had fallen down: inferior materials and workmanship. The survivors were occupied. Greased paper replaced broken window glass. Patches lay on the concrete like so many scabs.

Whatever water system had existed had evidently failed. A pump and trough stood in an open area between the two largest dormitories. It was there that Fyodor stopped the car. The two men got out.

The priest beckoned to a young girl playing near the pump. "Find your mother," he ordered. "She may welcome a blessing."

Shortly seven women stood close by. Some were babushkas. Too old for the Archangel's taste that ran to the freshly corrupted innocent. He joined Fyodor in making the cross on their foreheads. The blessing of a false priest was better than none at all.

The men of course hung back. The Archangel saw more then one spit before his boot and rub the white smear into the earth.

Fyodor had prepared an impressive lie: a man who might well live here and whose forbearer had been called Gregory had been left an inheritance through the Church. He had only to come forward and be identified to live the rest of his life in decent comfort.

This set the women to chattering. The Archangel heard more than once "Gregory the Odd." Yet no one came forward with information. The group of women broke up, moving toward their crumbling concrete apartments without meeting the two men's eyes.

The Archangel guessed it wasn't who they were that had put the women off. What had they seen except two priests, albeit one of them over two meters tall weighing 124 kilos with a heavy crucifix around his neck? He guessed they had been told to say nothing to strangers, be they paupers or princes.

The two men strolled about, trying to start conversations. They met little more than chilly politeness. The Archangel whispered that it was time to do some arm-twisting.

"Patience, my beast," Fyodor said.

The best they could do was two cups of hot tea brought out to them by a young boy at the bidding of some hidden adult. They stood in the weak early morning sunlight with the cheap glasses warming their hands. For an hour they hung about, trying to draw anyone into conversation. Failing, Fyodor ordered the Archangel back to the car for a conference.

They discovered that a boy had hidden himself on the floor before the back seat. He sat up as they climbed in. He had a bowl-shaped head of flaxen hair and a cast to his left eye. Within his pinched mouth a sea creature's sharp teeth were set in a heavy jaw. Seeing him, the Archangel had a single thought: young brother!

"Will you pay me to take you to Gregory the Odd?" he asked.

A forty-minute tramp across fields and finally into the forest brought them to a log hut built up against a fall of boulders by a swirling stream.

The boy was sent scurrying away with a handful of rubles. The two men stood before the hut's only entrance. Fyodor hailed loudly. Two men emerged.

No mistaking which was the Odd. His pale, forty-ish body had the look of having been stretched on the rack, its limbs like long poles. His head too seemed drawn out, brow high and smooth below a soft down of white hair. His appearance disturbed the Archangel. Often the giant suffered from hideous nightmares in which the forces of the Devil met those of heaven at Armageddon. The Odd had the look of one of God's warrior angels.

The other was made of coarser stuff—squat, powerful, thick of brow. He called himself Mitya of Great Meadow.

The four exchanged greetings. The two from the hut didn't ask for blessings.

"We have come on Church business," Fyodor began. "The archbishop of Moscow wants to resolve an old matter. Valuables belonging to the Church were hidden in a box sent here some fifty years ago." The priest made a shrewd guess. "Sent to your father."

The Odd nodded. "I am Gregory's son. His name is mine." His voice was light, airy—angelic to the Archangel's riotous hearing.

"The box came to him from the Kirgiz Steppe. You know it?" Fyodor's gaze was as piercing as a hawk's, alert for the smallest bounding rabbit of deceit.

The Odd turned his back and began to walk toward his hut. Mitya stood unmoving. Fyodor called out and tried to hurry past the squat man. He got a hard shove that sent him stumbling backward. "Leave!" the squat one ordered. "Gregory has no business with you."

"We have business with him!" Fyodor insisted.

The Archangel, blood quickly warming, strode toward Mitya. He reached out to grab him, but he was quick. He dodged away and sent a solid kick into the giant's right kidney. Pain turned the Archangel's bowel watery. He hissed in pain.

"Enough for you?" Mitya said.

With a guttural howl the Archangel rushed at him again. For his trouble he got a second kick that stretched the cords holding his left knee together and a third that nearly landed flush on his stones. He had been injured!

Now the Heat flooded into him. He was a man aswim on his own serene sea of violence. From his neck he tore the crucifix. Its gilt covered heavy steel. The arms of the cross were sharpened to points. At the foot of its long upright, the figures of Mary Magdalene and the Mother of God were cunningly cast to form a handle. So armed, he swung at the squat one, grazing his skull.

Still he dodged away, shaking his thick head to clear it. The issue was far from settled until Fyodor stuck out a tripping foot. Down went Mitya onto his back. Before he could scramble up, the Archangel was upon him. Down came our Lord in His Passion.

The way to the hut was open.

The Archangel dragged out the earthbound angel and gave him a look at his dead comrade.

To business went Fyodor. "Where is the box?"

Silence. Gregory's serene gaze bit the Archangel like the tip of a holy lance.

"Again: *where is the box?*"

No reply.

"Your tongue can be loosened!" Fyodor shouted. "Archangel!"

The giant put a palm on each side of the angel's head and lifted him. He applied pressure. The angel didn't struggle—not that it would have made any difference. Nor did he fly away, to the Archangel's incredible relief.

"Where is the box?" Fyodor said again.

The Archangel welcomed the silence. It gave him permission to squeeze the sanctity out of the man. To *squeeze...*

Hard.

15

Pittsburgh, Pennsylvania

Ostrovsky sat back as Nevsky finished his story about Father Ruslan and the mysterious cube. He nodded, frowning. "Interesting. But not...conclusive by any means. The more we learn, the less we understand, Yuri Vladimirovich."

Nevsky had hoped for a more enthusiastic reception for his information. Again he had the feeling that somehow the general had made a bad bargain with him. He took another sip of mineral water. Talking had been dry work. "I never said what I knew would lead you to the treasure," he said.

Ostrovsky nodded in agreement. "Nor did I expect it." He smiled thinly. "One hopes nonetheless."

Nevsky got up and stretched. "Your turn," he said.

Ostrovsky hesitated, in reverie. He awoke. "Sasha, the translations!" he said. "Have Kanig join us."

When Sasha left, Ostrovsky explained that Helmut Kanig was one of the most reliable Sons. His family had fled the October Revolution from Kiev and gone to the Ruhr region. His arrival in Russia a year ago brought to Ostrovsky's cause an enviable ruthlessness and German precise thinking.

The man following Sasha into the room was tall, blonde, and handsome. He wore wide metal-rimmed glasses of a shape that gave his face a hard edge. He carried a briefcase. He thrust his free hand toward Ostrovsky at shoulder level, making a fist.

"Mother Russia will be great again!" he said.

Out went Ostrovsky's arm in the same gesture. "If her Sons dare make her so!" Nevsky could tell the ritual reply gave the leader satisfaction. He smothered his urge to ridicule. Somehow ritual fit these men. No mistaking, they made up a serious group of treasure contenders. He was introduced to Kanig.

In precise phrases the German explained the history of the documents that had come into the Sons' hands. By late 1941 the Germans occupied much of Ukraine and the Crimean peninsula. A broad piece of Ukrainian border territory, including the city of Odessa, was transferred to Romania and called the Province of Transnistria. Under its leader, the brutal Reichskommisar Erich Koch, the Nazis were quick to implement their agendas. Among them was the well-documented transportation and extermination of whole classes of people, among them Jews and gypsies. Less publicized was their appropriation for transfer west of artistic and historical valuables from the occupied lands. Here even German obsessive concern with organization fell afoul of greed. Despite Hitler's direct designation of an agency to uncover and control the treasures, the SS Ahnenerbe and even the Wehrmacht vigorously contested the spoils.

During the retreat of 1943 military columns and railways were subject to partisan attacks. In one of these a portion of the official SS records and files was seized. While such material was generally destroyed at once, circumstances this time didn't allow it. The railroad car containing the hundreds of cartons was shunted from place to place and eventually forgotten.

The records lay neglected on a rusted track spur that became heavily overgrown. Decades passed. When the documents were discovered, they fell not into the hands of the Party, but into those of a new generation of rightists. Instead of looking on the records as obscenities they saw them as testimony to an enviable efficiency and a way of thinking with much to recommend it. Very cautiously word of the find was spread to the like-minded.

After the events of the early '90s that altered Russian society, historians who maintained a certain political perspective studied the records. One such academic happened to meet Ostrovsky at a political rally shortly after Sergei Nevsky's diary came into his hands. Ostrovsky recalled that the landowner had written about sending his daughter to Ukraine on the eve of the Revolution. On a whim he asked the historian if by chance there was any mention made of an Anya Sergeyevna Nevsky in the SS documents. The historian said he would check. He reported back that, to his great surprise, events were recorded in which she played a part.

Curious events.

Kanig opened his briefcase. His glasses seemed wider than before. The glow of the desk lamp gave him the look of a predator. He pulled out a thin sheaf of documents. "These pages alone concern us, Nevsky. I have winnowed them out of the thousands and translated them into Russian for our use."

"What do we have here?" Nevsky asked.

"First, official correspondence from Waffen SS Division 'Viking' to an SS Sturmbannführer Professor Herbert Jankuhn," Kanig said. "This Jankuhn, I gather, was in charge of plundering Russia's southwestern archeological sites and museums—and anything else that came before his covetous gazing. The correspondent in all cases was Colonel Karl Rosser of the Viking

Division. This memo should be read first." Kanig straightened in his chair. Clearly he had enjoyed developing this presentation, its debut for Ostrovsky, encored now for Nevsky. The American found his heart speeding. He was hoping for a big piece of the puzzle, though Ostrovsky's tempered response to his own recent disclosures still hovered in the air like an incubus.

Kanig offered the first memo.

FILE COPY
[File record numbers and document IDs omitted by translator.]
Memo
STATUS: Confidential
Odessa, Transnistria   January 8, 1942
From: Colonel Karl Rosser, Viking Division
To: S.P. Herbert Jankuhn
Re: A possible major acquisition

Heil Hitler!

First, let me thank you for the kind words of appreciation you forwarded from Reichsführer-SS Himmler concerning the five oil paintings we shipped to Wewelsburg. I sensed they would be to our leader's taste. That they are to hang on *his* walls gives me a great sense of satisfaction and accomplishment.

That art was a lucky find, I must confess. The Ostland is strange, filled with *untermenschen* of all types, yet worthwhile items can appear at the turn of a corner.

For example, the subject of this memo came to my attention in a roundabout fashion. Some background is necessary. During the course of our successful Ukrainian campaign I made the acquaintance of Major Manfred von Teilmann zum Sonnenmann, a first-rate military man. Though not a Party member, he shares our enthusiasm for ultimate victory. His is one of Germany's oldest families. Its members are accustomed to serving the Fatherland.

When Odessa fell to the Wehrmacht in October, we appropriated properties useful to us. Among them was a villa close to the sea. I took charge and found the site wholly delightful. I have heard the Führer expects to place Aryan settlements here. I understand his thinking: the climate is a delight! For that reason I invited my brother Dieter and Teilmann here for the year-end holidays.

Dieter was assigned to France on the staff of Reichsleiter Rosenberg who, as you know, was granted overall authority for the preservation of cultural riches in all occupied lands. Making the journey east with Dieter was a French art restorer, an attractive redhead named Sybille Sollonier.

Teilmann brought to the villa a Russian woman of indeterminate years who appeared to be his mistress. An enemy of the Communists, she fled to Ukraine as a young woman. Wisely she cast her lot with the Thousand Year Reich. Her name was Anya Nevsky.

When the two women were introduced, Sybille lost color. She asked if Anya's father was a Sergei Nevsky. When she said yes, Sybille began to cry.

Dieter asked her wasn't "Nevsky" the name she had mentioned in connection with what she thought was "the czar's treasure?"

My attention at once picked up, Herbert, you may be sure. I posed some tactful questions to Sybille. What and where was this treasure? Her reaction was to burst into wild weeping and flee the room. Dieter could throw little light on the matter. Once after an atypical drinking bout she had hinted at a girlhood tragedy. She said she had seen the "czar's gold, diamonds, and fabulous jewelry." Sergei Nevsky and her mother Natalia had been involved. Past that she had been most vague. Whatever happened had been so severely traumatic that she never told the whole tale to anyone, not even him.

I then turned my questions to this Anya who said she knew nothing of any treasure whatever and, in any case, doubted her father's involvement.

I sensed she was dissembling. I began to press her harder. Only the intervention of Teilmann spared her from an informal interrogation. He reminded me that she was, after all, a guest in my house as well as his companion. That night I couldn't sleep. Should not Romanov treasure of whatever kind become the property of the Reich? I planned to question Sybille in the morning, her tears be damned!

I awoke from a short doze to find she had left the villa. Efforts to find her were unsuccessful. Only later did I learn she spoke Russian fluently. She had undoubtedly fled with the help of other *untermenshen*.

My efforts to question Anya were stymied by Teilmann whose archaic gallantry on the behalf of his whore I began to find tiresome. After a day they cut short their visit.

I was left with nothing but questions.

In addition to informing you of these potentially significant events, I wish you to note that *this* department was first to get wind of the Romanov gold and jewels. *Any* subsequent action on *any* front concerning the treasure *must be cleared through me.*

` I wish you the happiest 1942 and promise you further word on the czar's horde.

May we meet in an occupied Stalingrad before the year is out!

K R.

Nevsky put down the sheets and stared at Kanig for a long moment. Sybille Sollonier! She was the daughter of Natalia, Sergei Nevsky's very good friend. Couldn't Natalia Sollonier be the "Countess S." whom Korchevko's French allies were trying to trace? Was it possible that the whole vast puzzle had boundaries after all? Could there be a beginning and an end to it, not just an endless accumulation of unrelated riddles? He said, "*Was* there a Romanov treasure as so many of you think?"

The German handed him another sheet, grinning like a sage. "Read on, Nevsky."

Nevsky read.

FILE COPY
[File record numbers and document IDs omitted by translator.]
Memo
STATUS: Confidential
Odessa, Transnistria   January 27, 1942
From: Colonel Karl Rosser, Viking Division
To: S.P. Herbert Jankuhn
Re: The Romanov Treasure

Heil Hitler!

My efforts to find out more about the treasure—if it exists—have been frustrated for the time being. Even though I requested that the Gestapo help us track down the Sollonier woman, so far we have had no luck. She melted away, either here or after returning to France.

Consequently I turned my attention back to Anya Nevsky, Teilmann's woman. First I went to visit her socially. Though I asked to speak with her privately, she arranged for Teilmann to be there. Blinded with emotion, he took her side. He said that if she said she knew nothing of her father's involvement with czarist wealth, then that was the truth. He believed her. I did not.

I returned twice more to her home near Uman. Not an easy journey there, I might add, as partisans opposed to the Reich's policies in the occupied lands have sprung up and done damage in lightly patrolled areas. I met with no success. Both times she agreed to rendezvous. Both times she failed to appear.

Losing patience, I ordered her arrested. My subordinates returned saying it was not possible to do so. She was now on Teilmann's staff performing tasks "vital to the welfare of the Reich!"

So for the moment I am frustrated.

But not defeated.

When you next hear from me, it will be with word of my success.

K.R.

Kanig took the sheet from Nevsky's hand and replaced it with another.

FILE COPY
[File record numbers and document IDs omitted by translator.]
<u>Memo</u>
STATUS: Confidential
Odessa, Transnistria   February 15, 1942
From: Colonel Karl Rosser, Viking Division
To: S.P. Herbert Jankuhn
Re: The Romanov Treasure

Heil Hitler!

Gott mit Uns! I just received word that Teilmann and his woman were part of a small reconnaissance column ambushed by partisans. The swine were driven off, but not before Teilmann died of a massive neck wound. Anya Nevsky was also wounded, but survived.

I have just arranged her transfer to one of our hospitals. You may be sure I saw to it that our most expert physicians were assigned to her case.

I do not think it will be long before we get to the bottom of this little Romanov mystery.

You will be the first to hear of our success!

K.R.

16

The former Red Banner Collective Farm

Lyubov had seen them climb out of the car. The two ravens! The big one with more the look of a vulture, forget his robes. Lyubov had a nose. It told him these two bore watching.

So he kept them in view. He circled behind the crumbling buildings, the shoddy apartments, the half-dozen izbas and garages housing the few serviceable machines. He saw the ravens give blessings, walk around, drink tea, and search for conversation.

Though priests, they had the way of the commissars. Behold the strutting about, the false face of friendliness, the sharp barb of curiosity masked by the soft worm of politeness. He had seen their style in the Party men, as had his father before him. Not his grandfather, though. He had departed in service to the old family and had the good luck never to return to see what had become of Great Meadow, never mind Mother Russia herself. Party men, priests, or jackals, Lyubov knew they were looking for someone.

He guessed he knew whom. They searched for the one who had said dreamily that those who hadn't come to see his father would come to see him.

Lyubov had hoped the two ravens were going to give up and leave. Sure enough they went back to their car. He angled back behind a clump of low firs, knelt, and watched.

When he saw the head of Anatoly Two Glances rise from the back seat, he knew trouble would soon follow. That one was born a liar and a cheat. The Devil might as well have tattooed his sixes across the boy's ass.

Sure enough, off the three of them went. Two Glances knew a way to Gregory's hut. Lyubov knew another, one that ran past his kennel. Reaching it, he opened the rough cages. The eight borzois fell into a pack behind Queen Catherine, the lead bitch. He spoke to them, as he always did, like loved children. He was as proud of them as he would have been of his children, if he had any. He had bred them big—a meter at the shoulder—raised and trained them. When winter came they hunted with him. Thus he earned his way in this new Russia of suspect rubles and penurious wages.

He moved quickly up a stony track and through a wide thicket of birches. The dogs were silent behind him, their silky coats stirring in the light breeze, their pads scarcely rattling the stones.

On hands and knees he worked his way to a rock fall closely overlooking the clearing before Gregory's hut. He peered around a stony outcropping just in time to see Mitya's head crushed by a monstrous blow from the black giant's crucifix. Rage welled in Lyubov's heart.

When Gregory was dragged from the hut and lifted by his head like a helpless puppy, Lyubov's rage turned to action. He barked a command to his dogs.

Queen Catherine in the lead, they poured over the rocks smooth as oil, at full cry. The priests' eyes swung his way and widened. Gregory tumbled free as the giant dropped him to grab his crucifix. But even he couldn't swing his forearm with two seventy-five kilo dogs hanging from it. Nor could the shorter priest brandish the knife he pulled from his robes. Queen Catherine's teeth, clamped his wrist like a finger in a door hinge. Blood ran. His hand went numb, Lyubov knew. The raven's bones were about to snap! A word from him and the bitch loosened her hold a bit.

Shortly both men were on the ground screaming, the dogs searching for their throats. Another command from Lyubov backed off the animals. The men hesitantly scrambled to their feet. Their faces were bloodless, their eyes wide as full moons. They were too frightened to check their seeping bites. They backed off further, then turned and ran. A word from Lyubov sent the pack in full cry after them.

He scampered to the top of the rocks. From there he could see the priests in wild flight, their skirts flying, the dogs at their heels, jaws wide, and teeth gleaming. So the ravens would flee back to their car. And be gone. He blessed himself. God had helped His believer today. Lyubov then allowed himself a barking laugh that he cut short. This was not a day to celebrate.

After so long, Gregory's assurances that "they" would come had been made good, but sourly. These two might come back, but not alone the next time. Or others even worse could appear.

It seemed the ripening time had at last come for Gregory's secrets, which had belonged first to his father and before him to priests. The things he knew no one in this random rabble of farmers, laborers, and hangers-on shared. The secrets were as unknown to Lyubov, too, as the day of his death.

He scrambled down into the clearing and raised Gregory to his feet. Bruises rose on his wide temples, but otherwise he was whole. Right away Lyubov began to talk to him about the future, about the need to make preparations to keep him alive until he told what he knew to those who were rightly destined to hear it.

17

Moscow

Detrovna stared out his suite's window at a sunny afternoon. Good weather usually improved his mood. Today it didn't. The Attorney's recent work in the United States also should have made him a happy man. Not so.

Gennady Efimovich had gone there with little more than a contact that Detrovna's source said was reliable and efficient. He was Vasily Brudikov, an émigré some years previously settled in Brooklyn, a part of New York City. The Attorney's faxes about him were ecstatic. He had such an organization!

Detrovna had faxed back: then let him do something for us with it.

So he had.

Matters had gone well. But at such cost! The Attorney had explained. The price—of course in U. S. dollars, Detrovna lamented—included the expense of total confidentiality, travel, manpower, land purchase, taxes, and commissions. Adding heavily to the financial burden was Detrovna's insistence on haste. In America, the Attorney reported, being in a hurry was costly. Even more appalling in Detrovna's eyes was the overhead his brother opportunist extorted to do his bidding.

There was no question that the outrageous costs would continue. Under the Attorney's guidance Brudikov arranged for a team of credentialed divers to explore this Lake Nagle. Used to the dangers of the deep they anticipated work in a tranquil lake to be relatively easy. So their services came cheaply enough. Treasure was not mentioned. In its place was strung up a net of persuasive lies. Should that net break, Detrovna had ordered it replaced with a few chattering automatic weapons. More divers could always be found.

Never mind their wages, Detrovna also had to pay for the guards to be housed and fed. Fencing was being erected around the entire parcel of land. More expense! Detrovna's mental adding machine threatened overload, as did his blood pressure.

The heat seemed to be creeping in through the windows. The Russian slid an index finger between shirt collar and neck. He had just finished speaking to his accountants. Not to his surprise they reported the expenses in America had eroded his resources noticeably. His immediate hopes of becoming a completely legitimate businessman would have to wait. Though he had tried to resist investing in the Romanov Cache too heavily in either rubles or emotion, he had lost that battle. Against his will the trove was looming ever larger in his life.

Only through it would he ever rule Russia.

He turned from the window and began to pace. He found himself occasionally speaking aloud, though no one was with him. His judgment told him it wasn't ever wise to back so heavily any single thing, be it racehorse, person, business, or investment—never mind an elusive treasure. Afghanistan had taught him to take risks—but only wise ones. The Romanov Cache, all his instincts were muttering, wasn't one of those. Possibly it would be smarter to pull out and cut his losses. Yes, maybe that would be the shrewd thing to do.

The phone rang. The Attorney was calling from the Pennsylvania town called Markville. He had good news.

He had finally spoken to those who years ago had purchased the properties around Lake Nagle and so recently sold them. One of the eager sellers had been a gabby old woman with knowledge of the history of the locale. She said that decades ago the lakefront property, including the high hill and some land on its other side, had been a single parcel. Everyone called it "the old Russian sailor's place." This sent the Attorney to the county recorder's office and deed books. An Igor Sodorov, who paid cash, had bought the parcel.

In 1909!

That was the year Harsky had told them Sergei Nevsky had begun his work for the Sons of Continuity. The Attorney reported that the woman said that Sodorov the sailor lived the life of a hermit, apparently without working. He built a small house, kept a garden and a large pond. He lived to be an old man, dying intestate in 1960. The state took the property and sold it off in the parcels Brudikov's men had just purchased on Detrovna's behalf.

In a flash of insight Detrovna understood what had happened. Sodorov had been Nevsky's right hand on unfamiliar soil! To him the Swiss firm had sent the many shipments that made up the treasure. Each he had then immersed in the lake. Why? Why destroy what were surely valuables?

For eight years he had been very busy so doing.

And for forty-three years he had waited in vain.

For Sergei? For the czar? Who knew how much Nevsky had told him? Very likely as little as possible. And so the poor sailor dangled on and on at the farthest end of the branch of the doomed Imperial Russian tree, like an oak leaf hanging on well into winter's storms. Then he too finally dropped down in death.

Yes, it made sense.

The excited Attorney had still more good news. The divers had already found some things amid the silt and slime. Four meter-high ceramic olive oil jars, and a half-dozen glass masks. "Boris Petrovich, listen," Gennady Efimovich said excitedly. "Those items *are on the Swiss bills of lading!* There is no longer doubt. This is the treasure site!"

Detrovna didn't know what made him snarl, "Then where are the gold and jewels, my friend?"

No sooner had he hung up than his assistant buzzed him on the intercom. A priest had asked to see him. No, not one who came with the usual pleas for rubles for restoration. His assistant reported this priest was...different.

And so he was—beardless, narrow and rapacious of face, sly of eye. His long, groomed hands were wiry. A bandage swathed his slender right wrist. Detrovna's first impressions were confirmed when this Father Fyodor said he had come to make a proposition in the name of the Church. To bulwark his authenticity he presented papers signed by a Bishop Paulos. They said the prelate had made Father Fyodor the Church's agent. He was acting for the Church and with its authority in connection with a confidential matter that he would explain. No mistake, this cleric was a smooth one. He waited patiently for Detrovna to finish reading, and then said he had come because the politician was probably the most powerful man in the country. But not yet the most wealthy. Yet he could be.

Then, to Detrovna's great astonishment, the priest began to vaguely outline a tale of czarist times based, he claimed, on persistent Church gossip—a tale that only a fool would not recognize concerned the Romanov Cache!

Now to Detrovna the suite seemed as hot as August in the Crimea. Sweat oozed forth on his brow. It was well that Father Fyodor had much to say. This allowed the big man time to compose himself.

He needed a respite because what the cleric said tallied with his own information about the cache. A reactionary landowner had gathered a treasure for the czar, a plot had failed, and the treasure had never been found. Recent massive changes in Russian society had rattled loose information about the cache's location. An American was involved. Fyodor hinted archly about his knowledge. He offered teasing details about a certain cube hidden for more than thirty years in Central Asia and then dug up thirty-five years ago...

Detrovna waved the priest into silence. "What do you want?" he asked. It took great physical effort to hold a stony face.

"An alliance between the Church and yourself, Boris Petrovich," Father Fyodor said. "We build on our information, your wealth and power. Behind you I put myself and the strength of the Church. Together we find the cache and divide it along some agreeable lines." The priest turned an appraising gaze Detrovna's way. "How does the proposition strike you— never mind the details, which can be arranged?"

Detrovna held his face with still greater effort. "Tell your bishop such doings don't interest me. I thank him for having considered me. I wish you good luck and the blessing of God in your search."

Father Fyodor's narrow face betrayed disappointment. Detrovna sensed the man was unaccustomed to that emotion. The priest raised a hand and thoughtfully touched his bandage. "I invite you to reconsider."

Detrovna shook his head.

The priest momentarily entertained persistence, and then thought better of it. He rose and extended his hand. In moments he was gone.

Detrovna rushed to the window. Far below he saw the black shadow leave his building and turn to a black limousine double-parked by the curb. Off he drove toward... Where? Detrovna imagined he knew. Toward others who would accept his proposition. And further crowd the field with players!

Though Detrovna had a confidential ear positioned in America to bring him news of those who sought the cache through other routes, he still felt rising anxiety. So far these rivals seemed to have made no progress. But they could. His people *had* to find the cache quickly. If they didn't...he imagined himself on his way overseas to save the situation. Entertaining that possibility brought forth a sensation of ill-defined foreboding.

In seconds he was on the phone to America again, tumbling the Attorney out of bed. His words to his underling were many. Not so their direction.

Haste! More haste!

TATIANA NIKOLAYEVNA

Inwardly he cursed. *And more expense!*

18

Pittsburgh, Pennsylvania

Kanig adjusted his large spectacles and took SS Colonel Karl Rosser's memo from Nevsky's hands. Into them he put a half dozen other sheets. "Read on, Nevsky," he urged, expressionless.

Nevsky touched Kanig's forearm. "Did the Nazis find the cache? *Was* there a cache?" he asked.

"Better to read their words than hear my interpretation, Yuri Vladimirovich," the German said. "The cost is only a few more moments of your time."

Nevsky's eyes found the fresh pages.

[Excerpts from a logbook of the SS "Viking" Division]
February 27, 1942, 1800 Hours

The care of our expert doctors and a strong constitution brought Anya Nevsky back to acceptable health quicker than expected. For reasons outlined in earlier documents Colonel Rosser requested permission to lead her interrogation. It was granted.

Questioning began shortly after 0800 hours at our headquarters annex. The subject reiterated her certainty that her father played no role in gathering treasure for Czar Nicholas II. The tone and directness of her replies left no doubt about her positive feelings for the Reich in light of its opposition to Communism in all its guises. Her relationship with the late Major Teilmann undoubtedly played a part in forming these feelings. Sensing our reaction to her sincerity, she expected to be released. This was about 1100 hours.

In fact, questioning had scarcely begun—as became apparent to her as the hours passed. She stood by her statements, irritation—even anger—beginning to surface. The same ground was covered repeatedly. Her responses were much the same. Shortly after 1700 hours the interrogation was ended for the day. The subject was told to reassess her obstinacy overnight. Tomorrow's questioning would be more robust.

Log Officer: Karl Rosser [Signature]

February 28, 1942, 2100 Hours

Interrogation of Anya Nevsky began at 0500 hours. Two teams of interrogators were used. Food and rest were withheld from the subject. Despite the advisability of revealing her secrets, she grew stubborn and uncooperative. Toward 1800 hours she fell totally silent. She was warned about this intransigence, but paid no heed. At this point Colonel Rosser chose to continue questioning around the clock.

Log Officer: Karl Rosser [Signature]

March 1, 1942, 2100 Hours

The Nevsky interrogation has continued for nearly twenty-four uninterrupted hours. The subject's failure to cooperate has become intolerable. Team members remarked that the Slavic race is remarkable for its intractable stubbornness and hopeless resistance in lost situations. So it was explained to her that unless she spoke with total openness, physical force would be used. Her response was to spit at Lieutenant Stultzman. She will rue that act.

Log Officer: Karl Rosser [Signature]

March 5, 1942, 1900 Hours

The Nevsky woman has been broken! Her senseless resistance lasting nearly a week was matched only by her foolishness. Had she spoken earlier, she would have saved herself much pain and ultimately disfigurement. As it was, the vital information when revealed did not at first appear significant. For that reason the interrogation was continued well past the necessary point. Colonel Rosser has accepted full responsibility for this oversight.

There came a time late in the interrogation when the subject's resistance had finally been destroyed. The landscape of her life lay open and unprotected. She hid nothing. Yet, *she still claimed to know nothing of any Romanov wealth.* Nor did she acknowledge any role for her father in the matter. The interrogators, all grown weary, feared that she had been telling the truth from the beginning. Possibly the Reich's time had been wasted.

Questioning moved over even the most intimate aspects of her life. *None* of her revelations bore on the czar's treasure. In time the interrogators came to the hours before her final departure from the family estate she called Great Meadow—and passed over the details of her narrative as commonplaces. Only much later were they returned to. In fact in all she said, only these few moments spent with her father, Sergei Nevsky, promised the Reich *anything*.

The brief meeting went as follows. She was summoned to her father's study in the late summer of 1917 and told she was being sent to Ukraine where he imagined the power of the Bolsheviks was unlikely to quickly take root. He gave her his blessing and a custom-printed Bible with heavy metal embossed covers. He told her, as one would tell a child of seven: "Should you be called on to serve czar, God, and the Motherland, first read here carefully. Then pray at my grave." Though most uncertain about his meaning, she asked him where he had chosen to be buried. He said: "In the St. Mikhail Cemetery on a hill in Odessa."

Naturally these florid displays of Christian piety were not considered significant by the interrogators. Furthermore, the subject reported that she had heard that forces of a regional soviet had overrun the family estate. Her father fled for his life, leaving Russia forever. He would not have had the luxury of enjoying that burial spot.

Were we not occupying Odessa, it was most unlikely anyone would have made the effort to travel to St. Mikhail's Cemetery. As it was, Lieutenant Hausholtz was dispatched there—and found Sergei Nevsky's grave!

What else was found has been detailed to appropriate channels according to standard operating procedure. The required documents have been written and filed.

Let this log report only that the whole matter seems to have come to the happiest conclusion!

Log Officer: Karl Rosser [Signature]

FILE COPY
[File record numbers and document IDs omitted by translator]
Memo
STATUS: Confidential
Odessa, Transnistria   March 7, 1942
From: Colonel Karl Rosser, Viking Division
To: S. P. Herbert Jankuhn
Re: The Romanov Treasure
    Heil Hitler!

I invite you to an "opening." I can assure you this event will lack nothing when compared to the more traditional opening in which a famed artist presents his work to the public.

Here are the facts behind the upcoming event. From Sergei Nevsky's daughter we learned the location of what she did not believe to be his grave. Nonetheless, a large plot in an Odessa cemetery was so marked with a marble slab bearing plausible dates.

Over the protests of the cemetery manager I ordered a forced labor crew to begin to dig. I intended to open Nevsky's coffin. I hoped the Russian had included the key to the treasure's location with his remains.

At the expected depth shovels struck unyielding material. I squinted down into the hole and, thanks to a brilliant sun, saw a gleam of metal that I assumed came from a coffin's lid. Further excavation proved me wrong—to my subsequent delight.

In search for the edges of the metal the crew widened its hole. As some dug, others cleaned the surface of what now clearly was *not* a coffin. The shining metal proved to be an early form of sheet aluminum. In time a surface nearly two-and-a-half meters square was exposed.

I ordered more workers to the site. It was becoming apparent that a large flat-sided object had been buried. I directed that digging be speeded still further. At a depth of the same two-and-half meters, the bottom of what now proved to be a cube was reached.

More digging, slings, and bent backs had to be employed before the cube could be raised. In time it stood gleaming on the grass. Only a blush of tarnish marred its metal. You can well imagine our excitement, particularly when the identical two Russian words stenciled on the cube's vertical surfaces were translated. They read: *Tatiana Nikolayevna* who I was told was the last czar's second daughter! Or grand duchess, if you like. Here we had the treasure, come through fortuitous events to the possession of the Reich!

The cube was of curious construction, in that it had no opening. A great many rivets marked its surface in regular rows, more it seemed than needed to simply hold its seams together. While awkward to move, overall it was surprisingly light. This design was chosen no doubt to permit easy transportation from the Nevsky estate to Odessa.

Despite the excitement seizing the entire Viking Division, we called a halt to the day's rewarding activities, covered the cube, and placed an armed detachment around it.

Why? So that you, Herbert, can join us when we behold "the gold and jewels" mentioned by the elusive Sollonier woman. When Herr Himmler requested that our division give your special art collection group every possible support, not even he thought it would include uncovering a treasure horde. We plan to open the cube with care on March 15. I invite you to arrange your schedule so that you can join us on that day. Your presence, Sturmbannführer, would add much to the event.

Knowing your connections with the High Command, I only suggest that you might consider inviting one of its representatives as well. I made a similar suggestion to a member of Herr Himmler's personal staff.

I await what I hope will be your acceptance.

K.R.

[Excerpts from a logbook of the SS "Viking" Division]
March 16, 1942, 1800 Hours

While the opening of the Romanov cube is detailed elsewhere, this record presents only the outline of events for the official division archives.

In the presence of Sturmbannführer Jankuhn and Dr. Christian Smits, Special Advisor to the SS General Staff, the Romanov cube was opened. It was found to contain hundreds of shallow sliding trays fastened to the aluminum shell by riveted brackets. Unhappily the trays, clearly designed to hold jewelry and other small precious items, were filled with pebbles.

The situation was an awkward one for the Viking Division. Colonel Karl Rosser issued orders to round up the cemetery staff under gunpoint. Questions about the cube were put to them. Adequate answers were not forthcoming. A woman and a man were chosen from their number and summarily shot. Cooperation of the survivors thus assured, paper records were produced giving the history of all funeral plots.

No record was found for the Nevsky parcel. Clearly an "arrangement" had been made, likely involving bribery and collusion with those now dead. However, records for other plots were analyzed. Thus it was possible to determine that the cube was buried between 1916 and 1917. It was undoubtedly authentic.

Sometime during the intervening twenty-odd years the cube evidently had been raised. The valuables were removed and for them were substituted pebbles. The cube was then reburied. All this was done without a trace or a witness.

In hopes that something of value might yet be discovered, several of the cube's trays were removed and examined, and then replaced. They were what they seemed, handcrafted aluminum padded with heavy felt and set into slides. The slides in turn were fastened into the cube walls with brackets. The entire aluminum unit was an ingenious construction.

The pebbles too were closely examined. Unhappily they were just what they seemed to be—worthless stones.

The planned celebration at the Viking Division villa was cancelled. Colonel Karl Rosser, acting with the approval of Dr. Smits, arranged for the transportation of the disfigured Anya Nevsky to the nearest concentration camp for prompt liquidation.

Colonel Rosser personally took charge of a strike squad sent to the woman's home, a rude cabin in a village on the edge of Uman. A fire was started outside its door. As villagers gathered, all the Nevsky woman's possessions were consigned to the flames. When Colonel Rosser emerged from the dwelling carrying a metal-bound Bible atop a pile of clothing, the superstitious onlookers blessed themselves. Some dropped to their knees. For understandable reasons Colonel Rosser threw the clothes and Bible into the very center of the fire. Seizing a brand from the roaring blaze he set fire to the cabin's thatching. Shortly the dwelling was a pile of ashes, as were all its contents.

Such must be the fate of all those who toy with the Waffen SS!

Log Officer: Karl Rosser [Signature]

[Excerpts from a logbook of the SS "Viking" Division]
April 17, 1942, 2300 Hours

The entire Viking Division spent the day in mourning. The early morning tragedy involving Colonel Karl Rosser has affected each of us most profoundly. All agreed that his prior behavior in no way hinted at what was to come.

Those who spoke with him at the Easter season gala held the evening of April 16 felt that he had put the events around the Nevsky "grave" behind him. The understandable brief depression that had followed the mild rebuke from Dr. Smits for "over-optimism" had passed. He even seemed to accept the inevitable well-intentioned jokes about "Russian treasure" with genuine good humor.

Major Hans Messer, one of the division members who saw Colonel Rosser at the gala, said he was very much enjoying the schnapps and Rheingau wines provided for the occasion. His mood, like that of the entire unit, was further lightened by the presence of women. While few were of German blood many, though "Swamp Dwellers," were attractive enough in a superficial sense. All were in sympathy with the Führer's objectives and confident of our eventual total victory in the East.

Major Jurgen Möll remembered Colonel Rosser on the dance floor, beaming and applauding after each waltz. He danced with many of the women, sitting out only when the music was not of German origin. Möll reported Rosser's smile growing steadily wider as the evening lengthened. His polished dancing became increasingly uninhibited. In short there was no evidence whatever of his true frame of mind.

Colonel Rosser was not alone in his high spirits. His colleagues equaled him in summoning sunshine from drink, comradeship, and hope of romantic conquest that beamed through the storm clouds of war. The festivities continued toward the wee hours

No one would have expected such revelry to be capped with tragedy.

Let this log record our admiration for Colonel Karl Rosser, note his devotion to the Führer, and his service to the German people and the Thousand Year Reich. May he stand in the grace of Providence.

Heil Hitler!

Log Officer: Sigmund Bowman [Signature]

Nevsky lowered the sheets to the table and tapped them thoughtfully. He guessed now he might have been wrong about why Ostrovsky hadn't been excited by his tale of the Kirgiz Steppe. Possibly he didn't know about that cube at all. He had had already been disappointed by the "news" from Odessa. There had been two cubes.

Neither containing any treasure.

He turned his eyes to Ostrovsky. "It sounds like the treasure was hidden and removed. Where to? By whom? When?"

"Ostrovsky shrugged. "Who can say? Not the Nazi files. Kanig has combed them for more information. Nothing!"

"What happened to Colonel Rosser?"

"A suicide, undoubtedly, after shame and humiliation." Ostrovsky smiled grimly. "It may *seem* we have reached a dead end. Not so. He rose and stood looking down at Nevsky with his hands behind him. His baldhead gleamed in the lamplight. "The question before us is how we proceed from here. Yuri Vladimirovich, do you have any more information useful to us?"

Nevsky considered that the Force for Leadership also was after the treasure. He thought he'd keep that to himself for the moment. "I guess not," he said.

Ostrovsky nodded. "We *do* have more information. So your method of equal exchange no longer will work. Nor can we give you Father Alexei's killer, the man called Grushkin."

Nevsky didn't want their little roll to stop. "You said you wanted me to do a favor for you. Maybe I could trade that for—"

Sasha spoke now. "If you did us the favor, that would give you *and* us more information. Another quid pro quo."

Nevsky's mind was racing. How far did he want to go with the Sons of Continuity? Whoever first uncovered the treasure would have incredible leverage. If he could be that person, from the others in the hunt he could pry out Grushkin's whereabouts. His ace under was that he knew better than to covet the treasure. Finding it, however, was another matter. "Let me hear what you have to say," he said.

Ostrovsky told him. Sybille Sollonier was still alive! They had found her! Nevsky understood why they were excited. According to the SS documents she had *seen* the cache, the gold and jewels they all sought. He guessed they knew even more, but weren't telling him. So he and the Sons were even on that score, too.

He was certain now that Korchevko's connections would also track down the "Countess S." mentioned in his grandfather's diary and find out her daughter's whereabouts.

Nevsky understood what to do.

Sasha told him he had tried to speak to the women, but had failed. She wanted to talk either to a Nevsky or to the relative of an obscure priest, Father Konstantine. Yuri was the only Nevsky left. As to the priest's descendent, the Gregory mentioned by Father Ruslan, he was after so many years very likely dead.

Ostrovsky sat down. "There you have it, Yuri Vladimirovich. Talk to Sybille Sollonier for yourself and for us. What do you say? Set us on the *true* trail to the cache."

Nevsky made himself hesitate, as though in thought. Finally he said, "I'll have to think about it."

The light that danced across the Raptor's eyes wasn't pleasant. "Are you toying with me?"

"I need to think."

The Raptor's face had reddened. "For how long, man? Do you think only we are after the cache? Do you think because it's been hidden for seventy years we have another seventy to find it?"

"I'll need just a few days at most."

The Raptor rose and turned his back to Nevsky. "I must return to Russia," he said. "Sasha will stay here. I give you three days, no longer."

Nevsky stood up. "If more than three days go by, what will you do? I seem to be the key to finding the cache. Will you kill me anyway?"

The Raptor's smile was icy. "Friends as well as enemies can be *made* to cooperate."

MARIA NIKOLAYEVNA

19

Pittsburgh, Pennsylvania

Nevsky sighed as a rental car pulled up in front of 138 Morlande. Sure enough it brought Lyudmila and Shmelev for a mid-morning visit. He hadn't seen them since the party at the Imperial Court. He had heard, however, that Shmelev had passed out, but not until he had amazed even the toughest-livered with his capacity. Lyudmila had flirted with many and gleaned a few earnest propositions. In the end she simply took her compatriot home. She was not an easy one to turn from her path of commitment to Korchevko. Even in Nevsky's bed it had been impossible for him to guess whether her moist murmurs bubbled from heart or head.

Hold on! They had someone with them, a tall young woman with a head of thick black hair. On the porch the couple introduced Alessya Harsky. Here was a dishy hybrid, he thought, a mix of force and hot animal. Alessya insisted on embracing him. She was soft where she ought to be. The faint scent of cinnamon hung in her heavy hair.

Like a great actress walking onto the stage of a provincial theater, she took over 138 with her story. However, she wasn't acting. Her sorrow and rage were real and harrowing. In Nevsky's world few let their emotions show as nakedly as she did while shamelessly baring her soul. Her grand honesty, demonstrated by curses, wild gestures, and showers of tears nonetheless had a match—the substance of her tale.

The details came in a rush—being Detrovna's paramour, the deal between her lover and father, the older man's betrayal, the documents in her possession sans map, and her meeting with the ascetic Korchevko. She finished with an oath of total commitment. Secondly, to him. First, to revenge!

Nevsky heard what else she was saying. Her entire presentation, though in no way calculated, was chiefly for his ears. She wanted him to understand what a monster Detrovna was.

He *had* to help Korchevko find the treasure.

A look at Shmelev and Lyudmila told him they previously hadn't heard her story. Shmelev was wiping away a tear from the angled jut of his cheek. Lyudmila sat unmoving, her face ashen.

"So, there's a big rich player in all this," Nevsky said. "It figures." He looked at Alessya. "Do you know if Detrovna's people have gone to this body of water, wherever it is, and started diving for the cache?"

"I assume so," Alessya said. "After all, it's Boris Petrovich who's driving them. He's a man who takes to things like a terrier to a rat. He shakes the life out of them with no delays or gentleness." She drew a deep breath and lifted her chin. "He is a loathsome man, but a rival to respect."

"I don't suppose you looked at the map even once, Alessya," Lyudmila said. "And can tell us where on earth the treasure has been hidden?" Her eyes glittered with hostility above the smoke curl of her ever-present cigarette.

"I told you. The swine Mikhail never gave it to me. There was no way I could have seen it. Nor do any of my father's deocuments name the treasure location." Alessya's eyes were doing a bit of smoldering themselves—and were better at it. She studied the other woman. "Have we...met before, Lyudya?"

A cold glance. "I'm certain we have not."

"You seem in some way familiar."

"We are complete strangers, I assure you," Lyudmila said.

The two ladies didn't get along. Too bad for Korchevko then, because they were both supposed to be rowing in his direction. The reason wasn't that Alessya dropped in on them like a bomb. Another, committed hand was always useful. No, some other reason. Who knew just why their backs went up? Envy? Sexual jealousy? Rivalry? Right now Nevsky didn't want to try to figure it out. He had better things to do.

Alessya laid out her father's papers on a coffee table. She turned a hot glance toward Lyudmila. "These I did read. Korchevko ordered me to do it," she said pointedly. "He asked me to draw conclusions. I have. The documents convinced me that there *is* a treasure. All of you should know my father called it 'The Romanov Cache,' as I will do."

Korchevko wasn't the only one to have doubts, Nevsky thought. All along he had been wondering about the *Maltese Falcon* Factor. Good and bad guys chasing over land and sea for something that was forever just one more journey or rendezvous away. For now he would take Alessya's word for it.

There *was* a Romanov cache.

The striking woman wasn't through. She dug into her large knitted sack purse and pulled out an index card. She put it down on the coffee table beside the papers.

Her dark eyes met Nevsky's. He felt that slap of attraction across his nervous system. Shame on you, he thought, with more than twenty years between them. His heart pounded and he knew his face was reddening. Still some fire in his furnace, he thought. His emotions had so seized him that he at first didn't hear her say, "Korchevko has sent you something: Sybille Sollonier's address!"

Ahh, Nevsky thought, here again was that connection, that boundary around the whole affair. Ostrovsky had already sent Sasha to talk to the woman, without success. He had wanted Nevsky to go to her at once. Why had he begged for time? Looking back, he saw he really didn't know why. It was as though he understood that another, solo path for him would open up, through magic.

Shmelev snatched up the card and looked at Nevsky. "Latrobe, Pennsylvania?" he said, getting the pronunciation wrong.

"Maybe forty miles from here." Yes! Nevsky pondered what seemed curious coincidences. His father came here to live at Sergey's orders. Now Sybille Sollonier was living close as well. Surely there was more to that than just chance. Right then he didn't know just what. He'd keep gnawing on it. "About time we had some action from this end," he said. He hesitated. The Sons of Continuity weren't to be trifled with. He knew that ultimately he would pay some kind of price for his unilateral actions.

He hurried to the phone. From information he got Sybille's number. He punched in the digits. A woman answered. "Sybille Sollonier?" he said.

"She is not available. May I help you?"

"Maybe. I'd like to talk to her."

There was a long pause at the other end. Finally: "About what?"

"It's—rather complicated."

"Who are you?" the woman asked.

"My name is Yuri Nevsky."

Another thoughtful pause. "Are you Alexander Sorokin, now trying to send someone else to us with a correct name?" The woman's voice now had a hostile edge to it. "If so, and you imagine that you can deceive me—"

"Pardon me, ma'am, but I've never met you. I didn't know where you lived until five minutes ago."

The woman changed her tone, but there was still aggression in it. "So you are a Nevsky? Prove it! Come at once then! Bring two photo-ID cards, one credit card. Where do you live? What's your address?"

Nevsky told her. He could tell she was writing it down.

"Bring five different envelopes with canceled stamps sent to you at that address. If you delay, I can only assume you're engaged in deception." She chattered out directions to the Sollonier home.

"All right," Nevsky said. "We're on our way."

"You will come alone," the woman said. "Make sure you're not followed. Good-bye..."

The woman waiting at the farmhouse's front door had gray hair forming little winglets over her ears. As Nevsky approached he saw she was looking behind him. He couldn't expect her to believe that over the years he had accumulated considerable experience at throwing people off his tail.

"Identification!"

He showed her what he had. She studied the documents carefully. Satisfied, she stepped aside and he entered a sparsely furnished living room.

At once he could smell age, wafts born of sluggish metabolism and elimination. The flickering flames of three small lemon-scented candles drew his eyes across the living room to the adjacent bedroom. There in a wheelchair sat a tiny woman with thick glasses. Her face was a riot of fine wrinkles.

"Bring him here, Isabel," Sybille Sollonier said. Her voice was surprisingly robust coming from such a frail body.

Nevsky moved forward. The old woman's forearms were bare and liver-spotted like color blindness diagnosis cards. She beckoned him still closer. "Bend down," she ordered. Her right hand rose and curved as softly as a fine fur around the back of his neck. "The drapes," she said.

Isabel opened them. Bright sunlight poured in. Sybille Sollonier's hand pulled his head down until his face was six inches from hers. Her smile revealed ancient dentures. "To part the mists of seventy-six years challenges the memory," she said.

"Memory of what?" Nevsky said.

"The face of your grandfather." Her Russian, like his father's, echoed aristocracy. She continued to peer intently. Her eyes, huge as an insect's behind the heavy lenses, moved without haste over his face. Her left hand rose. Dry fingertips traced his nose, cheek angles, and the shape of his lips. Her next words were to Isabel. "I think...a decided resemblance. He is whom he says. Go. Begin to prepare for our departure. Overhear nothing to save yourself possible future pain. There was no expiration date on a curse I heard long ago."

Isabel disappeared. Sybille ordered Nevsky to move her chair into a thick shaft of sunlight. He sat at the foot of the wheelchair on a footstool with a crocheted cushion.

Nevsky asked, "Curse? What was cursed? By whom?"

"Close your mouth, young man! I'll tell my story in my own way in the order I choose."

Nevsky settled back with an embarrassed grin. *"Da, da...."*

"In 1922 I was a wild, physically precocious fourteen-year-old," Sybille began. "I say again, *wild.*" Her eyes twinkled! Nevsky caught a snap glimpse of her long gone palmier days.

She told her tale, voice remaining strong as the minutes passed.

She had been away from Château Sollonier not only one night, but for the better part of two days before June 22. Returning, she knew her mother Natalia would be angry—again. Such absences she absolutely did not tolerate. Nor did she tolerate her daughter's companion of the last two days, Emil Morceaux, about whom she had already issued serious warnings. Girls barely out of pigtails shouldn't be seen with twenty-two-year-old men, or those who were lechers. In Emil's case one and the same.

Sybille found herself amused by Emil's naked randiness and love of high-speed motoring. Compared to the dullards she had met at dancing school and fêtes he was most exciting. Mother had described him as being "without family." To her that meant he had no social status. Well, as far as Sybille was concerned, his Lancia Lambda was all the status he needed.

Emil was afloat on a cloud of sensuality on the drive back to the château. Eyes half closed he hummed a passé Great War song. She asked him to turn down a dirt road that led to the back of the grounds. There stood a small gate. One key to its lock she had removed from the rack in the tool shop.

After long, moist good-bye kisses she entered the château grounds. Often she used the small gate to begin the pretense of having been in residence all along, when in fact she had been out carousing. Mother wasn't as observant as she had been, and of course she sometimes had her own lovers to occupy her. Sybille wondered if she were playing a game with herself. In the end, every time, her mother *always* knew everything she did. She often thought the woman clairvoyant—at the very least.

Her young eyes caught a glimpse of motion. Not wanting to be seen so close to the gate, she instantly dropped to her knees behind a bush. She saw a man in an unseasonable dark overcoat walking down one of the gravel paths.

He was carrying a pistol!

When he passed, Sybille scrambled off in the other direction. She found herself in the formal gardens. Ahead she heard the sound of voices speaking Russian. No one spoke Russian around the château except her and Natalia when she insisted. What was going on?

She found herself a hiding place in a corner of thick hedging. She peered through the leaves. What she saw froze her. A man whose eyebrows joined was pointing a pistol at her mother and her companion who she recognized from Natalia's description to be Sergei Nevsky.

Oh, *Mon Dieu!*

They were digging up the cube!

Sergei was sprawled on the grass face up to a hot cloudless sky. Natalia was seated on a chair beside him. Eyebrow stood over them, pistol at the ready.

The box had been properly buried. Eyebrow's men had found it necessary to remove their overcoats and strip to bare backs. They labored with shovels under the June sun. Eyebrow urged them on like a galley slave master. It was late afternoon and Sybille guessed he wanted the box out of the ground before dark.

He wouldn't allow Sergei or her mother to speak. She sat sobbing, tears seemingly without end smearing her face. In time Nevsky drew his dizzy head up and sat with his arms on his knees. Once he began to talk and caught Eyebrow's boot in his chest for his trouble. After that he was quiet.

In time the top of box was exposed, its shiny metal barely tarnished by the underground stay.

Natalia said, "You needn't dig any more. Straps were left underneath the box. You only need pull on them to raise it. It's not all that heavy."

Eyebrow frowned. "Quickly, comrades! Let us see the czar's horde."

Men had to be summoned from their guard stations to man the straps. Two straps, at each end two men. Eyebrow himself had to soil his hands.

Natalia whispered to Sergei, seemingly a call to some kind of action. He sat unmoving.

Eyebrow and his comrades heaved excitedly. Little by little the cube rose from the garden earth. It gleamed in the setting sun. Two men worked wooden planks beneath it. Six men pushed it onto solid ground.

Eyebrow stepped back and looked up. On each cube side red paint emblazoned the metal with the Romanov double eagle. Beneath each, black paint letters spelled out: *Maria Nikolayevna.*

Eyebrow chuckled at reading the name of the czar's daughter, the third grand duchess. He turned to Sergei, "This is rare, my friend! Your name for this treasure is *most* ill chosen. I had the pleasure of meeting Comrade Yakov Yurovsky of the Ural Cheka. He described to me how he had the greatest honor that could fall to a member of the proletariat—to be one of those who liquidated the czar and his brood." He jerked a thumb toward the printed name. "Your Maria had the pleasure of feeling revolutionary bullets, bayonets, acid, and fire."

Sergei surprised Sybille by chuckling. "Did you hear the tale about the monk Rasputin's sloppy death, Dishkin?" he asked. "Poison, bullets, beating, and drowning. It seems neither monarchists nor your beloved proletariat can do a job simply and cleanly. Such is Russia!"

Eyebrow snorted in disgust and pointed at two of his men. "Open the box at once, comrades!"

They rushed to the shining surface, but were repulsed. One said, "Yaroslav Mikhailovich, rivets hold it closed."

Eyebrow was beside himself. "Go, find tools, comrades! I want it open *within the hour!*"

Sybille watched them saw away the rivet heads. It was a slow process. When daylight faded, electric lights had to be jury-rigged. The lit silvery cube towered in the growing gloom like a structure from another world.

Eyebrow was everywhere giving orders, his excitement raising the tone of his gravel voice. "The czar's treasure, comrades! Saw on, blisters be damned!" He threw his weight against the smooth surface, as did his men. Still the cube wouldn't part.

One of his men cried out, "Yaroslav Mikhailovich, it's hinged! Here!"

"Lights! Move the lights in this direction!" Eyebrow ordered.

Bound by the earth on which it stood, the cube swung open grudgingly before their shoulders and spread palms. Sybille saw the scores of padded aluminum trays and the many brackets that held them. With the cube being nearly two-and-a-half meters on a side, the topmost racks of trays stood well above Eyebrow's head. He seized one at hand and slid it out.

The lights caught its contents. Refracted light darted in all directions. "Jewels, comrades," he shouted gleefully. *"Jewels!"*

He thrust his hands into the tray and raised them high, shrieking with delight. "And gold!" He held broaches, rings, bracelets, and pendants. Some escaped his fingers. They spun down in the harsh light like enchanted hailstones. *"We have the czar's riches!"*

His fellows crowded around him. Some dug hands into the padded trays drawing forth heaps of sparkling baubles. Some were speechless, others howled in amazement.

At that moment Natalia slipped away and began to run.

As though with a sixth sense Eyebrow whirled, threw down a shower of jewels, and drew his pistol.

His shot hit Natalia in the leg. She fell down screaming. "Help me! In the name of God! *Help me!*"

Sybille nearly sprang up from her hiding place. She brutally crushed the urge, knowing surrender to it meant death. She pressed her face into the loamy soil. She bit down cries with savage teeth.

When she had composed herself enough to look up, she saw her mother dragged back moaning into the circle of light and dropped beside Sergei. She whimpered. The bullet had shattered her leg.

Her hand flopped off her chest and lay palm up on the grass. It edged toward Sergei. She turned her head. Even from a distance Sybille could see her eyes were violet with agony. Their silent pleading was unmistakable.

She had told Sybille that she had loved Sergei years ago, in days when the czar still held court. But she had been headstrong and foolish. She tempted and toyed with young aristocrats and rich landowners alike. Sergei had gone ahead and married a sober, serious woman who helped him run his estate. "But he never stopped loving me!" she insisted. Who knew if that were truth or imagining?

"What about you, Mother?" Sybille asked. "Do you still love *him?*"

"Your maturing intuition will give you the answer in time, my sweet," her mother said.

Under the gaze of Eyebrow Sergei held Natalia's small hand. Eyebrow kicked their hands apart. He towered over them with his pistol pointed at the center of Sergey's forehead. "We have found your treasure, so need you no longer. Sergei Nevsky, I execute you for crimes against the people!" he growled.

Natalia screamed.

Sybille could not help but close her eyes and desperately clutch her silence like a huge doll without which she would surely die. She could not see Sergei laugh, only heard it—a chuckle that bubbled up to mirth and beyond.

To triumph!

The pistol crashed.

Sybille opened her eyes. Eyebrow turned to Natalia. They exchanged some heated but hushed words that the girl didn't catch. But her experience and ripening instincts told her that her mother had slept with that horrid man, to serve his purposes or hers she couldn't guess. In any case, he was wrought up over her. Had her enchantments showed him a side of himself he hadn't wished to expose? Had she woven some of her spells around him?

"Witch!" he screamed. He seized his pistol by the barrel and drove the butt down into Natalia's face. Sybille saw her mother's fine cheek crumble and teeth break loose from her jaw. He raised the weapon again. Her lips trembled. She wished to speak. He leaned down. To Sybille's astonishment her mother's voice was powerful, craggy even. All there heard it.

"I curse all of you who seek the czar's riches with unworthy hearts! *I curse all of you!*"

Eyebrow howled in response. The pistol rose and fell again and again like a piston in his right hand. Blood and bits of pinkish bone flew onto his shoes.

Bile rose in the back of Sybille's throat. She gagged, but stifled the sound

Eyebrow struck Natalia's features again and again. He whirled from the bloody ruin and shouted in satisfaction to his fellows, "This...*this* is the Revolution!"

When he finished he staggered upright and drew heavy breaths. He ordered the two corpses stripped. From Natalia's ears he removed two diamond ear studs. From around Nevsky's neck he tore away a thin chain from which dangled a small golden figure. He wrestled off their wedding rings. He slid open a cube tray and tossed the trinkets onto the padding where they were at once lost among grander valuables.

He ordered the bodies put into sacks. He sent his men into all the estate's buildings in search of suitable containers, boxes, chests, whatever came to hand.

Whatever could be used to pack the czar's treasure.

For hours the eight men worked transferring the contents of the many trays into the more portable containers. The emptied cube was pushed on dollies through a carriage house's high wide doors that were closed behind it.

Sybille lay shivering in the falling dew. Her discomfort was trivial before her terror.

She gathered a telephone call had been made to summon two large trucks. Before first light Eyebrow and his comrades finished loading and securing the cargo. Sybille understood that late yesterday all the servants had been locked into the wine cellar. They had seen and heard nothing.

She heard the Russians talk about the ship awaiting them on the north coast of France. In a week or so they would be in Moscow. From a touring car Eyebrow lead the convoy out of the estate gates.

Not until the sound of engines had faded in the distance did Sybille howl with fear and loss. She rose from the earth, slimed with her own dribbling. She gasped, choked, and emptied her stomach onto dew-beaded grass.

Five years ago her mother had gone away for nearly a week. When she returned, she ordered Sybille to spend the day in the west wing of the château. Even at nine years she was already disobedient. She peeked and saw priests digging a hole to hide whatever was hidden under the tarpaulin. Later she saw the cube stripped of its covering. Having seen it, she insisted all be explained to her.

Natalia surprised her. She had always been a lax disciplinarian, but now she was truly enraged that Sybille had seen the shiny cube. She was not prepared to overlook her daughter's behavior. She seized her by the shoulders so strongly that her fingernails pierced skin. "Say nothing about what you saw to anyone, foolish Sybille!" she ordered. *"Ever!* Do you *understand?"*

What the cube held, her mother explained, was something valuable belonging to "a man like a prince" who might one day come to live with them. When he did, he would open the cube and take whatever was in it.

After what Sybille had seen and heard she understood now that Sergei Nevsky had sent the lake of treasure to Château de Sollonier for the use of the czar. The czar was dead and now the Bolsheviks had reclaimed the treasure. How they had done it had convinced her of one thing:

She would *never* tell anyone what she had witnessed.

She left through her gate and walked into town where she used a cafe telephone. A call to Emil was all it took to bring him, his fast car, and restored lust. So randy was he that he failed to notice his child-lover's trembling hands and distracted state. They spent a wild three days together. She went to unusual lengths, even for her, to please him. At the end of their fleshy interlude she made him swear that he never would tell anyone that he had taken her home four days ago and picked her up again the next day. If asked, he was to say they never parted during that time.

He pressed his hand to his heart in mock seriousness. "Never fear a word will escape *my* lips."

He likely didn't mean it, but kept his word far beyond what he might have imagined. In a rainstorm three days later he ran his Lancia into an abutment and was killed instantly.

When she returned to the château, the police investigation was well underway. Her father the count unfortunately was in Brazil on state business and would be long in returning. Sybille pretended suitable puzzlement at her mother's disappearance. She said she knew nothing about the hole in the garden or the emptied cube. The servants clamored to describe the masked men who had invaded their territory, but had seen nothing that had taken place in the formal gardens. Natalia was considered "missing" through foul play. Most difficult for Sybille was masking grief over her mother's ugly death, her body disposed of in some brutish fashion.

In a way she had always been in awe of Natalia. Not because her mother lorded over her, rather because of her "powers." That she didn't always choose to confront her daughter at once with her misbehaviors had often led the girl to believe she had successfully fooled the woman. Then a week or month later, to Sybille's embarrassment, Natalia would raise the misdeed in casual conversation like a sorceress bestowing life upon the dead. As well, too often for coincidence, Natalia had foretold an event or the unpleasant consequences of one of Sybille's more notorious actions. Her mother's web of magical knowledge was cast over both past and future.

So in a way it followed that Natalia had chosen to call down a curse on all those dreadful Communists in that horrid hag's voice! Hearing it had stirred the hairs on the back of Sybille's neck like wheat in wind. That Eyebrow and his men had nonetheless marched away with the treasure failed to diminish her added awe or imagine their apparent success meaningful in any way.

All this suggested to Sybille that Natalia might have known what was going to happen to her and Sergei. Yet she hadn't avoided the situation. Had she intended for them both to perish so awfully?

If so, what did that mean?

She groaned aloud and pried her mind free of its capricious speculations.

After several days the police departed. Sybille and the servants resumed a semblance of normal life, though there was no end of gossip about madam and the strange Russian-speaking men. She learned that they were Chekists, Lenin's secret police.

Days passed well enough. It was the nights that haunted her. Sleep failed to come easily. She lay in bed shivering as she had in her dewy hiding place in the garden corner. Repeatedly her memory thrust upon her the implacable murderer chopping at her mother's face with his pistol.

She took to strolling the château's cool halls until sleep came. In robe and slippers she made the long rounds, her nerves so edgy that every harmless sound provoked a start.

One Saturday night at three o' clock she looked out toward the carriage house and gasped. She raised her fingers to her mouth and bit them.

Men wearing black clothes were busy in the drive!

A few stars provided the only light, so she could see no features, only black shapes moving quickly and efficiently.

They had loaded the empty cube on a flatbed truck. Over it they were dragging a large tarpaulin. Ropes were at the ready to tie it down snugly. She thought of sounding the alarm, and then checked herself.

These men had murdered for treasure. Why wouldn't they murder for its container?

She pressed herself into the shadows. In ten minutes the truck was gone.

She didn't go back to sleep. She dressed in one of her best outfits, then sat by a high window and waited. When dawn broke, she ordered a servant to drive her to the Orthodox Church in Gien.

She hadn't been to a service there in five years...

Nevsky saw that, though her voice was as strong as ever, Sybille had badly taxed herself. Both speech and catharsis had drained her. She leaned back in her chair. Her breath came in croaking rasps.

He rose from the footstool to stretch his legs. His mind churned in an effort to process all she had told him. He asked if he could get her anything.

She shook her head impatiently. "There...is more!" she said.

Nevsky nodded. "About the Nazis. Odessa. Colonel Karl Rosser."

Her brows shuddered in surprise that he should know. She nodded. "Yes, it's important because—" She fell silent and staring.

Nevsky stood patiently waiting. A minute passed, then several. Sybille didn't move. She was frozen. More time passed. He shouted, "Isabel!"

She came rushing in and saw Sybille's condition. She passed her hand before the unmoving face. "She's had one of her seizures. They last anywhere from a few hours to days."

"We didn't finish," Nevsky said.

"I'll call you when she returns to us—if she does."

20

Nevsky didn't take the fastest route home. He needed time to wrestle his disappointments. How many were there? Take the simplest first: secret police had taken the cache back to Moscow. Anything in their hands, be they called Cheka, K.G.B., or the Eyes of the People, fell at once behind a barrier of silence and secrecy. The valuables' fate was anyone's guess. They might have been added to the coffers of Lenin's struggling revolution. Or they evaporated piecemeal beneath the sun of Russia's legendary official corruption, never mind the era or the reigning political philosophy.

So his hopes of finding the cache and using it to lever what he wanted out of the other contenders had just hit the canvas hard. It seemed there would be no justice, rough or otherwise, for the elusive Mr. Grushkin.

His final disappointment was tougher to grip. It had to do with *dusha*, his soul. The late Father Alexei had made him turn over the flat stone of denial with which he covered those ugly squirmers of loneliness, lack of fulfillment, frustration, and potential never fully exercised, to name just the biggies. The priest also had made him ask himself where his character and emotions really dwelled. Here or in the land of black bread and kasha?

Once freed, these gross imps refused to troop obediently back under cover. He had hoped the strains, dangers, and adventures needed to resolve the puzzle of the Romanov Cache would improve his inner imperfections before he ran out of years.

Not so far.

He parked on the Slope to get a plate of blini and a cup of tea. Maybe it was the food that got him out of his *dusha* funk. The world was looking a bit rosier. He was pouring more melted butter on the last quarter of the final little pancake when he remembered that Sybille had wanted to tell him more. More that was important. Even though she knew the treasure had gone to Moscow.

There still was too damned much he didn't understand.

So maybe there was still hope.

Walking back to his car, he stopped and stared. The Romanov Imperial Guardsman that he had thought he glimpsed earlier through his Rabbit window was ambling his way. His polished boots *klopped* solidly on the sidewalk. Passersby smiled as he strolled by. To some he spoke in growling Russian. He waved his long arms and pulled the great graying growth of his red beard.

His eyes widened in surprise as he drew close to Nevsky, who had never met the man. "Beloved of Mother Russia!" he murmured peering into Nevsky's face—and into his heart, it seemed. "The answers are in the Bible of our glorious maker, God the Almighty!"

Nevsky was released from the wild stare. The Imperial Guardsman went off down the sidewalk, leaving in his wake the unmistakable scent of drink.

Nevsky returned to the restaurant and found his waitress. She was a short round woman with cheeks plump as pears. Perspiration coated her brow; it had been a hectic morning. He asked her who the wild man was.

She said, "One of the *iurodivii*."

Iurdodivii. Fools for Christ's sake, Nevsky remembered. Deranged folk who wandered about, tolerated because of their presumed saintliness. To them it was said God spoke. Believers hung on their pronouncements and council. This one, the waitress said, fancied himself in service to Czar Nicholas II. Eight years ago he had found his way here from Russia. No one knew just how. He was an unofficial ward of the Slope. "He calls himself Major *Do Dna!*"

Major Bottoms Up! Nevsky thought. It figured. That the man drank wouldn't affect his spiritual credibility in this community—probably added to it.

Driving home, he remembered Major Bottoms Up!'s advice. "The answers are in the Bible..." There were many who wouldn't agree, but Nevsky didn't think he was one of them.

Occupied as he had been, it was a bit of a shock to get back to 138 Morlande where the trio eagerly awaited his return. The place was polluted with cigarette smoke. Empty herring containers stood on the sink counter. A few crusts were all that remained of Mogarian's heavenly rye loaf.

Lyudmila and Alessya hadn't improved their rapport. Shmelev looked relieved to see Nevsky return. Likely he had been refereeing. They all gathered and heard the story of the cache dug up on the Sollonier estate going to Moscow in secret police hands. Alessya gnawed the edge of her thumb with sharp white teeth and began to look alarmed. "How can the cache be at the bottom of a lake then?" she said.

"I guess it can't be," Nevsky said.

Lyudmila burst forth optimistically, "Korchevko has not accepted just a single road to the riches. We're to investigate all!"

Alessya's almond eyes flashed. "Detrovna, that lizard, isn't a man to make mistakes. Whatever else he is, he doesn't back losers. To the Devil with the Sollonier cube!"

"There were other cubes," Nevsky said softly.

Faces spun toward him. He hesitated for a moment, and then reminded himself that only by sharing information could he make progress toward the treasure. He told them about the two other aluminum containers marked *Olga Nikolayevna* and *Tatiana Nikolayevna* to go with Sybille Sollonier's *Maria Nikolayevna*.

Lyudmila jumped to her feet. "You have withheld information from the Force for Leadership, from Korchevko himself!" Anger brought color to her shapely face. Her gray eyes turned flinty.

Nevsky shrugged. There was no answer to such zeal. "Well, now you know," he said.

"Then you are with us?" Shmelev said.

"I'm not against you," he said.

"Do not trivialize the Force for Leadership!" This time it was Alessya indignant. She had made a commitment and sworn vengeance. Serious stuff that she didn't think mixed with Nevsky's seemingly lackadaisical cooperation. She was so young! And stunning.

To his own surprise Nevsky made a short speech. The topic turned out to be his grandfather's subtle turns of mind. They suggested, to him at least, that the cache was not only hidden geographically, but by complexity and deception, to say nothing of misdirection. Finding the trove wasn't such a straightforward affair as they might be supposing.

Into that they could stir in—count 'em!—four contenders, the Church, Detrovna, their man Korchevko and a certain disciplined rightist organization led by a charismatic general.

He chose not to answer their questions about the general's name or that of his group. Instead he told them to expect a lot more confusion and trouble before the cache came to light—if it ever did.

Lyudmila took out her frustration by making a call to Russia. She reached one of Korchevko's handlers in St. Petersburg. She blurted out all Nevsky had revealed. The conversation was a long one. During the last part she listened, saying little.

She turned from the completed call with a smug smile. "We have one less rival and an ally in our struggle for the cache."

Shmelev said, "Who?"

"The Church! The Church and Korchevko have become partners!"

"Who acts for the Church, then?" Alessya said.

"A priest Korchevko swears is like no other." Lyudmila's face rosied with excitement and hope. "One called Father Fyodor of Kolyma. He will be coming to meet with us directly."

"The more the merrier. Does he know anything we can use?" Nevsky said.

"I understand he does," Lyudmila said. She rose to leave. "We'll come back after Father Fyodor joins us."

"I will stay here," Alessya said matter-of-factly. "Yuri Vladimirovich lives like an American. In this house we could put five Russian families." Her hearty bellow of laughter came with an angled glance at him. Asking permission or showing disapproval, he couldn't tell. He tried the proverb: "'One woman in the house—heaven! Two women—hell!' I look forward to soon entering heaven."

Shmelev chuckled lewdly. Lyudmila arched her brow, but said nothing. Why should she be jealous, Nevsky asked himself? He was getting a bit long in the tooth to excite high emotions in the ladies.

Nevsky and Alessya saw the couple off. He carried her small suitcase back into the house and up the wide staircase to one of the three unused second floor bedrooms. Throughout, he was aware of her cinnamon scent, nature's or perfumer's art, he couldn't say. He found her presence charmingly disturbing.

He told her where the towels and bathrooms were. Take her choice. "You Americans are fond of bathing?" She was teasing him, as though knowing how uncertain he felt about his nationality.

"It's been said we love our bathrooms."

She strode closer to him, not a tentative cord in her long legs. "And you, Yuri Vladimirovich? Are bathrooms your love, too?"

He laid a hand on her shoulder. She was nearly as tall as he. "My loves run to the earthier, food, drink, and women."

"Women!" She chuckled. "I don't see a woman in your house! As I see vodka in a drunk's shack. I think you've trying to deceive me. You don't care for women. Maybe you're too old?"

The only answer to that was for Nevsky to grab her. He didn't care if her responses were defined by an elusive treasure, curiosity, or straight-ahead lust. It was time for him to shut down the higher-level thinking and try to celebrate the animal. So seldom had that happened in recent years!

She was still chuckling as they tumbled down on the bed. Her mouth under his was large and sweet as raspberries. Their hands busied themselves. Zippers whispered. Her skin was so white! It was made not for beaches and sunny resorts, but for a land of clouds, frost, fog, and long winters. His fingertips patrolled its poreless pearl essence, followed rise and fall, sweet curves and already tumescent protrusions. His tongue and lips gleaned hints of cinnamon.

She wasn't shy about touching him. He wallowed in it. He closed his eyes and tried to guess exactly what she was doing and how. There was no haste in the caresses that sent him sailing out on long reaches to islands of tiny, cumulative pleasures.

Under his touch she snarled and screamed repeatedly, mouth open, tongue jammed against her upper teeth. Three times her jaws snapped closed loudly like a sprung trap. She fell to trembling. Her incredible breasts shuddered on the shelf of her ribs.

He busied himself with her quivering body. He tongued tribute to her neck and flat-ended nipples. His gentle palms paraded the path to her curving belly. Tongue and fingertips dowsed the shallow well of her navel. His twisting fingers gathered ample curls from the long strands of her untrimmed pubic tangle. He twisted and tugged them gently then pressed his mouth against her. She convulsed. Her fingernails gouged his shoulders.

Over the next hours Alessya routed Nevsky's already undermanned army of inhibitions. She was a fearless natural creature seeking nothing more than to exchange pleasures—and greedy for them! Several times he thought himself completely spent. With hands, mouth, and skillful hips she proved otherwise.

Distantly he realized there never had been anything like her in his life. He smiled dreamily. It was never too late for uplifting experiences.

Eventually they both began to drift off to sleep, fingers clasped like young lovers.

Nevsky's world was suffused with cinnamon.

21

Pittsburgh, Pennsylvania

Fyodor slid into the rear seat of the taxi. A backward glance told him the Archangel had followed orders. He was staying inside their room, one of the dozen making up the characterless Motel Belle Aire on Route 8.

In his clumsy but serviceable English the priest gave the driver an address. He settled back in the seat and removed the Greek beads from an inner pocket. His fingers found the familiar spheres. He gave himself to thought.

He had already put aside his rebuff at the hands of Detrovna. His instincts told him that the politician-criminal did not feel he needed to make an arrangement to gain allies. The reason made the priest anxious. Detrovna must feel that the Romanov wealth was nearly within his grasp. That made him Fyodor's most dangerous rival. He felt the spur of haste. No time could be wasted!

His frustration at Detrovna's hands had been well compensated for by his success with Korchevko. Oh, the white-clad, icy-eyed one was a complex man, to be sure. No matter. Fyodor was adept at sniffing out the keys to men's hearts and using them to betray their owners. Quickly enough he solved him, saw the twin yokes under which the ox of his soul labored.

Piety and vanity.

The letters from that greedy old idiot Paulos smoothed his way. The carte blanche he had given Fyodor opened his field of action in every direction. He could promise anything, say anything, and do whatever was necessary to bring the Romanov treasure into the bosom of the Church. The arguments he presented to the tall ascetic were solid.

First, he urged him to consider the historical link of leader and Church. Save for the savage aberration of the Revolution, all czars took the throne with the blessing of God. All knew what had composed the historical Russia, a triumvirate of the leader, the Church, and the nation. "Autocracy, orthodoxy, and nationality!" he whispered into Korchevko's willing ear. The character of the Russian people did not change. So even today anyone who aspired to rule, no matter the title he took, would do well to enjoy the support of the Church. This support Fyodor could guarantee—along with ecclesiastical resources to use in the search for the cache. Fyodor's terms? Considering that a certain priest played a key part in Sergei Nevsky's initial plotting, he proposed a fifty-fifty split after the treasure was found. Korchevko thought seventy-thirty his way was more realistic. Fyodor was too clever to dicker. What was promised today could be washed away tomorrow by re-bargaining or treachery.

He would do *whatever* was needed to find the treasure—and quickly!

To prove his earnestness Fyodor told Korchevko much of what he knew. He guessed Detrovna thought himself closest to finding the treasure. A seemingly empty box had been found in the Kirgiz Steppe and hidden on a former estate east of St. Petersburg. Those who hid it would reveal its precise whereabouts only to a Russian-American named Yuri Nevsky.

"Through my people I'm in touch with Nevsky," Korchevko said.

"Excellent! I'm convinced the empty box somehow contains a key to the treasure," he said. "Otherwise, why was it hidden again after being exhumed? I suggest that Nevsky visit the location and examine the box." The priest hesitated. "Is Nevsky your man?"

"He has every reason to be." The tall man smiled thinly. "But I have not heard that for certain. My people are trying to persuade him. I believe you should add your voice to theirs."

Korchevko insisted that the priest go to America and join Nevsky and others of the Force for Leadership. Once there he should try to persuade the American to seek out the cube, but in any case aid him however he could.

They parted friends, both having struck a reasonable deal and learned something from the other.

Korchevko did not learn from Fyodor that weeks ago he had eavesdropped when Bishop Paulos was giving that young fool Father Alexei his assignment. Go with the ailing Father Ruslan to America, Paulos had ordered. Listen with all your attention when the priest tells his tale of murder to the victim's son, Yuri Vladimirovich Nevsky. Report every word back to me.

Mention of the Nevsky name pricked up Fyodor's ears. One person he knew had a great, abiding interest in it. So he went to that man who had already been his master more than once. He told him what he knew. Shortly he had an assignment. Should he succeed, his mother would own a small dacha near Sochia on the Black Sea. He was to follow Alexei to America and learn Father Ruslan's secrets and possibly Nevsky's as well. How he did it the master didn't care.

So sniveling Alexei had felt hot iron. Fyodor recalled the odor of his young flesh burning, an abomination to some, but an exotic perfume to him, for so God had made him, and He was without fault. Fyodor learned all the young priest knew, and then snapped his neck. Afterward he had sent Grushkin to pry...

Fyodor manipulated his beads and watched the passing suburban landscape unroll. Cars, houses, and stores everywhere! Churches seemed as rare as hen's teeth. Here they cozied up to the material, but kept God at a safe distance.

What was life without God to torture your corrupting soul?

He smiled. What delights this adventure promised! Consider how many masters he now served—first, the Church, second, that one who had first sent him here, now Korchevko and his Force for Leadership, soon Nevsky himself. Last, though to what ends he wasn't certain, he served himself! The opportunities to betray, confound, and cause misery were almost without end. The cache? What was it but an engine of the Devil to cause men to spit on the face of God and to draw souls to destruction? He chuckled loudly. The beads chattered in his fingers.

The driver dropped him off at the office of another motel, this one in Monroeville. Soon he was introducing himself to Shmelev and Lyudmila. His was a thug's stubborn commitment to Korchevko. She was more of a riddle, no matter her flagrant displays of loyalty. She excited the worm of Fyodor's curiosity. Within an hour they were in Nevsky's living room.

The woman Alessya, described in unflattering terms by Lyudmila, Fyodor found to be formidable in both beauty and purpose. Passion for vengeance marked her face as clearly as a broad scar. She was young enough to be rash and unpredictable. Possibly she was dangerous.

Fyodor had some slight hesitation before meeting Nevsky. Would the American recognize that...? He did not. As the priest had gathered, the man was not particularly bright or observant.

To such small men did capricious history assign a key role.

He asked everyone to kneel and bow in the direction of the small ikon on the bookshelf. He prayed to God his tormentor for guidance and good fortune in their search, though they were not worthy.

He opened his ears and said little. The others filled his mind with what they knew. As he had feared, Boris Detrovna, criminal and lawmaker together, had a leg up in this affair. He had a map showing the cache's location! And was likely searching for it at that moment with all deliberate speed. There were *three* cubes! The second apparently held some of the Romanov valuables. The other two seemed to have been dug up in secrecy and emptied. One was left empty, the other filled with pebbles.

"I suggest the treasure was divided into three parts," he said. "The first part was found by the Cheka. Unknown parties, likely liquidated years ago, found the others. So what's left for us?"

Shmelev said, "Sergei Nevsky's diary and Alessya's copies of her father's documents suggest all shipping went to a single location. It was named in the documents given Detrovna, but not in those given her. To this place the czar-in-exile would go for his resources." He narrowed his obsidian eyes. "Close reading of the diary hints that the landowner himself transported the cubes to Odessa and the Kirgiz Steppe. Obviously he arranged the shipment to the Sollonier estate—"

Nevsky interrupted. "I've been thinking about how the cubes were found. My grandfather scattered small clues to their locations." His glance found Lyudmila's gray eyes. "Remember, when I asked my father what he had brought here from Russia, he used to laugh and say, 'Six numbers.' And he would rattle them off—'sixty-one, fifty-two, sixteen, forty-four, eleven, and thirty-three.' When I heard Father Ruslan's story, I should have tumbled right away to what those numbers were. A couple days ago the light shined. I checked. Sure enough!"

"So, what were they?" Lyudmila asked.

"The longitude and latitude of the hiding place of the *Olga Nikolayevna* cube on the Kirgiz Steppe," Nevsky said. "I'm sure his father gave him the numbers about the same time he told his sister Anya about his 'grave'—the clue to the Odessa hiding place. The clues were vague and tiny because he didn't want his children to be aware of what they knew. Stalin's security men tortured the numbers out of my father. The SS did the same to get my aunt's information."

Alessya made fists of frustration at her sides. "How can that *be?* If they didn't understand what they knew, the cubes might never have been found. It was all left to—to chance!"

Father Fyodor's hatchet face broke into a smile showing narrow teeth. "Not to chance, daughter. The elder Nevsky was a believer. He put matters in the hands of God!"

Alessya groaned. "One can expect too much from God's hands!"

"In his day it was felt that God put the czar to reign over the people," the priest said. "God would see to it that he prospered even in exile, and also see to it that what was his came into his hands or those of his heirs."

Alessya sputtered with outrage at the unlikeliness of it all.

"There are mysteries whose workings God does not disclose to us, daughter," Fyodor said. Such as the entire landscape of evil, he said to himself, and its fascination for those of us with dark hearts. He blessed himself. The others didn't notice.

"What about the cube from which the treasure was removed? How did the Cheka find that one?" Fyodor asked. "Did Natalia Sollonier betray your grandfather, Yuri Vladimirovich?"

Nevsky's memory foraged in Sybille Sollonier's tale. "I don't think so. I think they were, despite everything, faithful soul mates. I imagine what happened was someone involved with moving the *Maria Nikolayevna* cube from Russia to France talked too much. Eventually the Cheka got wind of it. They found him or them. Out came the knout and nail pullers and..." He shrugged. "No more secret. The diary and Sybille's story lets us fill in the rest. The Cheka took over the château, held Natalia Sollonier hostage, forced her to contact my grandfather and lure him there. Not difficult, if my guess about their affections is right. Maybe this Dishkin, who led the Cheka crowd, offered to trade their lives for the cube's exact location. Maybe Natalia took him up on it, and was betrayed. If so, she more than got even for that with a convincing curse."

Shmelev's thick brow rippled into a heavy frown. "I do not like this cursing of the cache, this—*witchery!*"

"God will protect you," Fyodor said. But who knew His will, now or ever?

"Hiding the treasure and arraying the cubes would appear to have been two entirely separate operations," Lyudmila said.

"Separate, but related somehow," Nevsky said.

Alessya interrupted. "Why do you talk of these strange cubes when it's *Detrovna* who has the map and will find the cache?" Color flushed her high cheeks. "Why do we talk at all? We must *do* something before it's too late."

Lyudmila snapped, "Calm down, woman! We work with what we have. What other option is there?"

Shmelev's small eyes turned to the priest. "We were told you brought something to our meager feast, holy one. What is it?"

"It should be something much more than your blessing!" Alessya snapped.

Fyodor grinned at her. Such a woman! If his tastes ran in the direction of her sex... But they did not. Nor in the direction of the other. In that sense at least, he was a pure priest. He said, "You must control your annoyance, daughter, when I tell you I know where the Red Banner Collective Farm is, the location the Kirgiz cube." He didn't tell them he had been to the former Nevsky estate. He lied, saying sources told him where it was and that Nevsky alone would be allowed to see it. "I propose that you go there and examine it, Yuri Vladimirovich. "My feeling is there's much to be learned there."

Nevsky scowled. "I'm not sure it's worth the time. Russia isn't exactly next door."

Alessya said, "Indeed! Why bother? The treasure was taken from it. Or was there ever treasure in it?" She grimaced. "But isn't the cache to be found where Detrovna is looking? I'm so confused!"

They were all confused. Discussion gave way to arguments, then shouting matches. They cooled down with beer and sandwiches.

They returned to the living room. Fyodor knelt before the ikon and blessed himself. He turned to Nevsky first, and then extended his arm to include the others. "Yuri Vladimirovich, I beg you in the name of God and the success of our search, tell us the rest of what you know."

Nevsky scowled. "What do you mean?"

"Explain the vexing link between the cubes and the cache."

"Ever since this business started, people have thought I know more than I do," Nevsky said. "You already know what I know, father. That's all there is to it."

Fyodor shook his head. His narrow face took on a pinched, accusing twist. "Tell us about the fourth cube."

All eyes turned to the priest.

"*Fourth* cube?" Nevsky parroted.

"Of course," the priest said. "We have cubes on which the names of the three grand duchesses were painted. What of the fourth one? What of Anastasia Nikolayevna—that young woman whose distorted history was colored with so much speculation and impersonation? Should there not be a final cube bearing her name as well?"

Nevsky stared at the priest. "Interesting concept," he allowed. "There might well be a fourth cube, but *I* don't know anything about it."

Fyodor sought the others' eyes, found them. Then he turned his accusing gaze on the American, knowing the others would do the same. "This cannot be a common effort if you withhold information!"

"I told you. I don't know anything more!"

"The fourth cube may well hold the answers to the puzzle of the other three," Lyudmila said.

"Maybe it does." Sweat sheen marked the front of Nevsky's baldhead. "If there is one. But as I said, I don't know anything about it. The first I heard of the possibility was ten seconds ago."

The priest pleaded, "Yuri Vlad—"

"And that's all there is to it!" Nevsky barked.

Alessya stepped forward. "He is an honest man, I think. I believe what he says."

The others weren't convinced, but nothing was to be done at that moment. Fyodor felt his advantage dissipate. The fourth cube! Though the idea had sprung up instantly moments ago, somehow he *knew* there was a fourth cube—somewhere. He also presumed that Nevsky alone knew of it. It was the American's great weapon, to be used late at precisely the right moment. Fyodor would find the fourth cube and the answers that a God suddenly turned kind had whispered were in it. He turned to Nevsky. "My apologies. You understand time is—"

"I understand it's time for you all to leave!" Nevsky growled. "Come back another time."

"When?" Lyudmila asked.

"When you can tell *me* something about the fourth cube," Nevsky said.

Fyodor accepted a ride with Shmelev and Lyudmila. He stirred them with wild speculations about the cube very likely marked *Anastasia Nikolayevna*. Even as he spoke, his attention turned back to Nevsky.

He was certain the American possessed valuable secrets. He would be made to tell them. Fyodor had the means.

God had given him the Archangel!

If breaking Nevsky's bones and crushing his stones revealed that indeed he knew nothing, then he was superfluous. His role in seeking the cache was over. He could be liquidated. One less rival, one less with whom to quarrel over the division of the riches—if they were ever found.

He asked Shmelev to drive faster.

He was anxious to make a phone call.

And to give the Archangel his instructions.

On the motel room phone he got through to St. Petersburg. He demanded to speak to his master there. His voice came down the line. The priest wasted no time on politeness. "Listen carefully. The cube that the servant shepherded to the Sollonier estate contained treasure!...*Quite* certain. Nevsky spoke with the daughter of Natalia Sollonier...The Harsky girl brought him the address. In the summer of 1922 Sybille witnessed everything!...Of course I'm certain! Cheka men took the treasure and cube back to Moscow...No, no one here knows what happened subsequently...Nor do they know why another cube was buried in the Odessa graveyard to match the one on the Kirgiz Steppe that I told you about earlier. No one here claims to know anything. Possibly only the late Sergei Nevsky and the God in whom he trusted to guide matters to a happy ending knows...Never mind. I speculate. You can guess why I'm calling. Do you have friends among the official spies and snoops?...Of course I'm not surprised...You must have them find the records, then check them yourself. June 1922. The leader of the Cheka corps was named Dishkin.

"I have other news." He brought his master up to date with his recent activities, beginning with his vain visit to Detrovna, his success at forming an alliance with the ascetic Korchevko, and ending with the dispute over the fourth cube. His master was dismayed that a man of Detrovna's wealth and power seemed to be on the verge of finding the cache. He swore he would act quickly. His master ordered him to "work among the cubes" with all of his energy and cunning.

Fyodor agreed and said, "You will learn all that I do. Here I have other, related business to handle. I must give my Archangel instructions...About what? About persuading Yuri Nevsky to empty his most secret heart to him...You think he has further use? I don't! He is a limited man, master. If he knows more, we will find it out. If not, he's unneeded. Either way we'll bring his last day on earth to a truly agonizing end...What? Yes, of course with the help of *my* God—He who cries always for more suffering, mine foremost." Fyodor's chuckle lacked the smallest grain of humor. He hung up on his master's questions. "Archangel!" he bellowed.

22

Moscow

When his assistant said the call was from the United States, Detrovna's hand flew to the instrument and snatched it up. He was expecting word from Lake Nagle. The voice was familiar, but not the one for which he had hoped. The urgency in it delayed his impatient response. He listened in silence. He could not believe what he heard.

"The cache was *found* by the Cheka?"

"So it seems. Or some part of it. Who knows? Who really understands anything about this whole affair?" the voice said. "The monarchist Nevsky was a fiend for complications—"

Detrovna interrupted. "Those infernal cubes! I don't care about them."

"The cache is in your hands then?" the voice asked.

Detrovna bit his teeth. "Not yet. Soon."

"Hmmm. This business is more twisted than we thought."

"I feel that I'm *so* close to what we want. All evidence points to the bottom of the wretched lake."

"You're a man who prides yourself on thoroughness, no?" the voice asked.

"You know it. Why else am I patient while you waltz about with the infernal cubes?"

"It's said there are four!"

Detrovna swore loudly.

"A suggestion, Boris Petrovich, to help you find direction in all this. You have friends, influence. The Cheka records must be studied to throw light on the fate of the cache."

Detrovna's stomach sank. He did not want to believe the horde was anywhere but a few meters from where his divers were pulling more near-valuables to the surface, each vase and rotting wooden shoe tallying against the bills of lading of the Swiss transport firm.

Yet not one scrap of significant treasure had been found!

Possibly the late Harsky, seemingly a silly frightened fool, had been a master confidence man after all. Detrovna groaned at the possibility and seized his hair. Harsky had taken his motivations to the grave. Detrovna seriously regretted having ordered the man's murder. "I will do what is necessary," he muttered into the phone.

Hanging up, he touched the intercom. He ordered his secretary to call the Lake Nagle site. His supervisor Stroganov was the only man at the site who knew what the divers were in fact seeking. One did not need wagging tongues in a foreign country. The search went with enough difficulty without that. "What progress?" Not the first time Detrovna had posed that question to the man.

More of the same! Detrovna fumed. "Anything else?"

"The lake is rising," Stroganov said. "Maybe seven or eight meters already."

"What of it? It has an outlet, doesn't it?"

"A stream. It's running deep and fast."

"Is there a problem?"

"I don't think so. The stream should be able to handle the overflow. The lake's natural dam seems thick enough. We needn't worry from that angle." He hesitated. "Boris Petrovich, I don't see us being at this much longer. We're coming to the end of the pots and ceramic elephants."

Detrovna cursed. He hated to be reminded of the swamp of useless rubbish he had paid a fortune to recover—and toss aside. "I give you a week to find what I've paid you for. After that, I withdraw the promise of a bonus for you. And..." He paused, surprised at the thought that welled up so naturally. "I go there and take over your duties!"

"As you like." Stroganov was unflappable.

Detrovna hung up slowly and shook his head. Why had he said that? He didn't want to go to the United States. Yet, what choice would he have, with so much invested?

He *had* to bring the cache to the surface!

23

Pittsburgh, Pennsylvania

Nevsky's sheets were scented with cinnamon. He pressed his head between Alessya's breasts and tongued off the sweat of recent ardor. He murmured nonsense, lips pressed against her satiny softness. The bedside light filtered by a thrown towel covered her white skin with a fine golden sheen. I'm in bed with a goddess, Nevsky thought.

Her attention was elsewhere. She stirred and sat up. "Somewhere before now I saw or met Lyudmila Mogadam," she said distantly. "Possibly she knows where and isn't saying. Maybe that's why she dislikes me so much."

"And why do you dislike *her* so much?" Nevsky would have liked a little more *après amour* and maybe a rekindling. Guess not. Women bent on vengeance evidently made capricious lovers.

Alessya's smoldering eyes moved over his head and chest. "Because I smell she was in this bed before me!" She pointed at her shapely nose. "Not here I smelled." Her long finger tapped her temple. "But here! Am I right?"

"She was here, but nothing happened."

Alessya snorted and out came her heavy, fetching chuckle. "You are a man for me. Why wouldn't you be a man for her?"

"Something wasn't quite right. Then we were interrupted. We never had another chance."

"Alessya is here. For that one there will be no more chances!" She flung herself at him. Her sharp nails found his shoulders. She forced him down on his back. "I want you for my own. You are old, but patient. A patient lover is a *good* lover."

Nevsky was gloating over his incredible luck. Every tumble with this gorgeous woman was to be anticipated then squirreled away in memory's vaults. But right now she rolled away. "I *will* remember where I met dear Lyudya."

Nevsky reached for her white thigh. She flicked his hand away, as though it were a bug. "Forgive me, Yuritchka, but I can't think of anything but that pig Detrovna sniffing close to the cache. I wish to spit on him!" She grabbed a pillow and shoved it into her lap, bent over it. Her firm breasts swayed. *"But...* he cannot find the cache if it isn't there."

"What are you saying?"

"In a way I'm saying...Gari Kusnetsov."

"Who's that?"

She explained that Gari was her late father's good friend. Like him he had an interest in historical archives. Gari's taste ran toward the doings of Russia's curious secret police organizations, beginning with the *Oprichnina* set up by Ivan the Dread in the middle of the sixteenth century, through the various czarist incarnations, to Lenin's Cheka and up through the K.G.B. "Much has been made public in the last years," Alessya said. "Gari has invited himself into many of the once-sealed historical archives. He is an old man with many friends who open doors for him. So he amuses himself with what materials please him. He hasn't long to live. Cancer, I think."

"You think he might know what happened to the Chekists and the cache?" Nevsky asked.

Alessya shook her head. "No, but he might know where to find such information. I think I should phone him."

"Right away!"

After five tries she got through to Moscow and held a long conversation. "Gari is amused by the challenge," she reported. "And 'highly amused' by the thought of possible surviving czarist wealth."

"Is that good?"

She nodded. "Men near death are freed of a lifetime of self-denial. They do only as they choose."

"How long—?"

"He believes it will take him only a few days. A week at most. I'm to call him every day starting tomorrow."

Nevsky was ready for sleep. Alessya felt the need to pace the house. "Over and over I see Detrovna with the cache!" she muttered. "And I grow sick!"

He called to her, "I don't think it's going to be that easy for him, if that makes you feel any better." Then he added, "Or for us. As we're well aware, the cache might have been completely decimated long ago." He rolled over. She kept pacing. She was still at it when he drifted off.

He shot up from sleep totally awake. Some instinct like a hot coal banked over by the ashes of civilization's refinements blew hot and sparked his senses alive. Alessya slept beside him.

There was someone else in the bedroom!

A shape in the deep dimness stood tall in the middle of the rug. Now it moved toward the bed. Fear vaulted across Nevsky's nerves. He repelled it. He couldn't lie there. Charge!

He threw himself out of the covers and went at the intruder hard and low. He screamed wildly to spur himself and frighten the other.

He ran into a man as solid as a concrete piling. He tried to drive a fist into his crotch. He missed low. How low sent his heart toward his toenails. His assailant had to be seven feet tall! The man towered in the dimness like a museum statue carved too large for real life.

Nevsky's excited heart thudded like a B-movie jungle drum. He drove a decent right into the giant's kidney. That brought a Russian curse out into the darkness. No surprise. He didn't think he was up against a Sicilian. A shoe as big as a planter caught the side of his thigh and bowled him over.

He scrambled up shouting for Alessya to call the police. Oops! She spoke no English. Another kick *whoooshed* by his hip. He faked left and went right toward the door.

A phone pole arm caught him around the neck. He tried to spin free. Then he was lifted high—Lord, he couldn't believe it! And thrown!

He hit the wall with feet and arms back, so largely saved his skull.

For the moment.

He crashed to the floor, head ringing. He tried to scramble up, but the giant was on him fast. Distantly he heard Alessya screaming. The giant snatched him up again. Another throw. A different wall. This one set off bells in Nevsky's brain and loosed soft floating points of light. The second tumble down to the floor brightened those lights. Bad! He tried to scuttle along the floorboard. In his witlessness he imagined himself a roach or mouse.

He clung to consciousness with grim determination. If this guy took him out, he was as good as dead. The giant dragged him up to his feet. A wrecking ball fist slammed into his midsection turning everything there to water. He groaned. He wasn't going to get by this one. Despair taunted him from the receding edge of his consciousness.

"We have much to ask you, Nevsky." The guttural mutter sounded in the darkness like the voice of doom.

Nevsky tried slamming a palm against the giant's chin. It landed in a tangle of beard. The strength had gone out of his arm. Anyway the man had neck muscles to shame any linebacker.

Alessya the wildcat threw herself on the giant's back. Nevsky heard her nails snap as she tried to claw him. He shrugged her off. Her scream in Nevsky's shaky hearing rose and fell like a sine wave. The giant grabbed Nevsky's forearm and held it in a hand as big as a knuckleball catcher's mitt.

One more punch and Nevsky was finished. Shifting in the dimness told him the giant was ready to serve it up. He woozily waved his free arm in a feeble gesture of defense.

The lights went on! A gunshot *craaaked* like a branch in a hurricane. The bearded giant howled. His left hand flew up to his shoulder. Nevsky was free! The giant lurched off to one side. The massive crucifix around his neck swung wildly before him. Oh, my Lord! Nevsky thought. The man's a *priest!*

A woman stood by the switch, a smoking .38 in her hand.

Charity Day had come home!

She moved forward. The giant bolted for the far door. "Stop!" she shouted. She snapped off a shot, but missed. He plunged out. His footsteps thundered down the stairs. The front door crashed open and he was gone.

Alessya scrambled off the floor and rose naked to her feet. Charity lowered her pistol and eyed the younger woman top to toe. "Well, you certainly *are* carrying dangerous weapons, aren't you?" she said. "Just not the right ones for this evening's fun." The Russian didn't understand a word she said.

Nevsky was shaking. Alessya began to cry.

"Why don't you two get yourselves together," Charity said. "Then we'll chat."

They met later in the kitchen. Nevsky got out Charity's old Harvard Lamont Library chair and returned it to its customary place. He made coffee. There was no use pretending things were as they had been.

But they were close enough to make him happy.

Charity Day was still slender and white blonde, her skin as pale as fine bond. The ten years she had been away? Lines in her face whispered about that time. They had gone to work around her mouth, on her upper lip, and the corners of her eyes. Fine, fiber-like erosions served notice of mortality and trials survived. On her they looked good. She still had that generous smile beaming tonight through what Nevsky understood were her fatigue and spent emotions. "Things haven't changed much around here, have they, Yuri?" she said. "A bimbo in bed and a murderer after you."

"Alessya isn't a bimbo. You have to hear the story."

"*Dying* to," she said.

"It's been too quiet here for too many years," Nevsky said. "It's only now starting to get interesting again."

Alessya couldn't contain herself. She threw her arms around Charity and burst out in effusive thanks. Charity could guess what she was saying, and in response was cool and gracious— oh, wasn't she always!

In rapid-fire Russian Alessya wondered who had come after Nevsky, how was he connected to the cache, and what should they do to make sure it didn't happen again?

Nevsky didn't bother to translate. Charity knew nothing. It would get tangled up.

To Alessya, he said, "We can talk about that later. And we will." To Charity: "Tell me about Don and Texas."

Whether Charity knew it or not, she had been waiting for someone to ask. She poured out a story of life on the moneyed track, an existence of perpetual summer, servants, travel, and society. They spent weeks at Marco Island, the Costa del Sol, Paris's Île Saint-Louis, Thailand... She had closets filled with clothes, shoes a la Mrs. Marcos, no domestic responsibilities except to instruct the staff about daily chores and her entertainment plans. She played golf and tennis in exclusive private clubs tucked away on breathtaking patches of desert and mountain. "I lived a life any unthinking woman would kill for," she said.

Having been a thinking woman all her life, she wondered how she had so badly misjudged Don Benson, that seemingly straight ahead down home boy who just happened to own large profitable pieces of mega-ranches, oil fields, electronics and software companies. He certainly seemed to understand her and was in awe of her intelligence, even though it didn't run toward making money.

"The marriage just never *meshed*," Charity said with a puzzled frown. She had eagerly looked forward to an equal partnership in their union, but ended up an aging "show wife." Once a mother, she had anticipated being one again for Don's two sons and daughter, fruits of a failed marriage. But it was hard to be warm to two chiselers and a little liar.

The intimate side of the marriage died first. "Sex never lasts, does it, Nevsky?" she asked.

"Cooking does," he said, quoting somebody's kitchen wall plaque.

Don tried hard to make it work, but they were on hopelessly different levels. She wanted real challenges far past women's clubs and useful charity committee work. He wanted a wife who "behaved."

For a long while, the "stuff" of their lives, as Charity called the sumptuous luxury, kept their union afloat. But time—oh, that old relentless grinder at our bodies and spirits—brought mutual coldness, despite their better natures.

For Don the coldness led to other women. Charity isolated herself and failed to carry out her expected social responsibilities. There were failed reconciliations, dust-ups, repentance, and more reconciliation. They tried, but it just wouldn't work.

Charity looked at Nevsky. Tears had crept up on her. "Does it ever work, for *anybody?*"

"You're asking *me?* Because I was only divorced once? Sure, it works. But it doesn't work like in the books and movies and make-up ads. It doesn't work because of romance."

"How *could* I have gone off with Don?" Charity asked. "How *could* I have opened us both up to so much hurt? How could I have been so *blind?*"

"At least I never said, 'It's doomed before they even take the vow.'"

"Only because you never had a chance to." Charity pulled a paper towel off the roll and wiped her smeared face. She looked at Alessya who had listened in silence to a lot of gabbing in a foreign language. "Tell her she's been very kind to listen to me feel sorry for myself."

Nevsky translated. Alessya's glance burned at Charity. "Another woman from your bed?" she asked sourly.

"We were together ten years. I never slept with her. That's why we got along so well."

The Russian's almond eyes widened with astonishment. "Another one you never touched! How much nonsense do you expect me to believe?" She trotted off, head held high, like an elegant racehorse. Nevsky guessed her indignation counted much less than her awkwardness at sitting around while two old friends told long stories in a foreign tongue.

Charity visited the downstairs bathroom. She came back with her face washed and her emotions under control. "Since I talked to you on the phone that night, Yuri... I've been thinking about something I want and need. Maybe something I've wanted and needed all through the marriage."

Nevsky raised a questioning brow.

"A mystery that I can really get my teeth into!"

He laughed, "Well, have *you* come to the right place!"

The coffee pot was empty and dawn breaking behind the beeches at the corner of 138's lot by the time he finished the story of the Romanov Cache, so far. Charity hadn't been the only one in need of telling a tale.

She slid off the library chair and stretched. "And you're right in the middle of it all."

"And somehow don't really belong there."

She looked at him ruefully. The smudges of fatigue under her eyes gave her face a mask-like look. "Oh, yes you *do*, for reasons of soul—don't argue with me. I know you and your Russian-not-Russian flip-flops. *And*, there's an empirical reason why you're in the middle of it all. It came to me right in the middle of your story."

"Yes?"

"You *do* hold a key to the cache."

"Charity, I don't!"

She sniffed with a deliberately exaggerated sense of superiority. "Good thing I came back. Looks like it was *just* in time, in more ways than one." She smiled thoughtfully. "Wasn't it a good thing I'm a sentimentalist? I never threw away my key to 138. Or the .38 you made me buy and learn to use. And I brought them both back. I got out of my car and just stood on the corner and looked up at the big house I thought I'd never see again, and so happy about it. And what's waiting for me? A giant shadow is scuttling around through the bushes looking as suspicious as Don Juan in a nunnery. I opened the trunk, dug out my piece... See, there are *reasons* for things."

Nevsky snorted. "You've always made a lousy mystic, Charity Day. Stick to the facts. They were always your bread and butter."

"As I said, the *fact* is you hold a key to the cache, even though you've been too thickheaded to believe it." She raised her hands, as though to fend him off. "I know you're going to say your father didn't tell you anything more than the longitude and latitude of the Kirgiz cube. Did you ever think, even once, that the key might have been some *thing* he owned?"

Nevsky stared. In fact, never had he thought of that. But what had his father left? Old books, manuscripts, and sad, yellowing foreign émigré newspapers. But not one item was in this house. All were stored in the unused chicken coop on his Murrysville property.

Nevsky dug around in the locked metal box, formerly his mother's stash. He found the keys to the chicken coop. "I haven't seen it in twenty years," he said.

"High time," Charity said.

"Worth a shot. Might be a pearl amid the chicken do-do."

By agreement they slept three hours. When Nevsky woke, he felt that last night's giant had been tap dancing the length of his body. He ached all over. It took him several minutes to get to his feet. He tried to loosen his muscles, but it was slow going.

He limped down the hall to the phone. He called St. Basil's and asked Father Teodor if anyone there knew of a giant priest who wore a heavy crucifix. No one did. He called Shmelev at his motel. Did he know how to get in touch with Father Fyodor? Maybe he would know something useful. The Russian was embarrassed to admit that he hadn't been told anything about Fyodor's whereabouts. And his sense of Pittsburgh's geography was shaky. He apologized. Nevsky grunted in frustration. Well, he would meet Father Fyodor again. His questions would get asked eventually.

He walked down the upstairs hall to get Alessya. Charity stopped him. She whispered, "I think you've trusted too many people," she said.

"What?"

She put her hands on her hips. "Boy, are *you* getting slow in the attic. We're talking several kings' ransoms here. The thought of spying and double-dealing never entered your head?"

"Well, it has, but—"

"Everybody in this affair knows everything, Yuri. I'm guessing people you've never met know everything, too. I think it's time you did something *nobody* knows about." She inclined her head toward his bedroom. "Or are you too much in love to leave her behind?"

When he thought about it, he wasn't sure how he felt about the comely Russian. Lustful, he supposed. More? Probably. When he tried to figure that out, his head hurt almost as much as his body. He tabled the question. He called to Alessya, saying he was going out for a while. The house was hers. He turned toward the second floor door that led out onto a porch then down stairs to the driveway. "Let's go," he said.

"Thank goodness you have some sense left." Charity rolled her eyes like an actress wanting to be seen in the last row. "I returned...in the *nick* of time!"

"Do some good, Day, before you crow," he said.

24

Lake Nagle, northeast of Pittsburgh

Butch Hanson lowered his field glasses and shook his head. If he could get men to work as hard as those divers were, he could be in any business and run it up to millions. They were at it around the clock, too, with the big arc lights rigged high and what looked like halogen lamps set into their helmets. The boss must have had them on a bonus program, with some kind of top-scale wage behind it. He would like to ask them what they were paid.

He couldn't; they never left the site.

And that included Peter Ivanovich and Ivan Voysovich, the men he had come to find better than a week ago. Nevsky had told him they were security guards and about where to find them. By the time Butch got to the lake new guards had taken their places. They had been transferred to the work crews. He glimpsed the bastards from time to time through the glasses: Ivanovich who wore his hair in a plait, and Voysovich, as white-haired as an old man. Nevsky had suggested they were Russians. Who were they? Where had they come from? It didn't matter. Their time would come.

He had often scaled the chain link fence, avoided the guards, and moved in close. But there was no way he could go in among twenty men and hogtie the two he wanted. He had no choice but to come spying when he could wrestle the time from his business and family. Sooner or later the project would finish and Ivanovich and Voysovich would come out of there.

He would be waiting.

His mother, despite years, was getting over her husband's death well enough. An old friend had called from Florida and told her vegetables and flowers grew like crazy down there. Had she ever thought of coming down? And the old woman was sitting on a big pile of dough she didn't know what to do with. She'd put sunshine and dollars together before long. So Butch's need for vengeance, though as powerful as ever, was tempered with curiosity. What the hell were the crews looking for? They were pulling stuff up from the bottom of the lake, but it all looked like junk, even after close-ups through the glasses.

A few days ago by the turnoff onto the main road he waved down the catering truck after its lunch run to the site. The driver was a burly Turk with little English. He looked worriedly at Butch who asked, "What're they looking for back there? What're they fishing for in the lake?"

The Turk had brows thick as brushes. They arched impressively in puzzlement. "Don't know. Nobody say much."

"You ever ask?"

"I ask. They don't say."

"They eat pretty well?"

The Turk nodded. "Best my boss can make. Three-a-day. Pay big. Pay cash. *Goood* customer." The Turk *clunged* the van into gear. "Boss says they no talk to nobody!" Out went the clutch. Butch was left in oily exhaust from failing piston rings.

The project was a big deal for these parts. Not just because everything came in by truck and van and nobody came out. Rather because the divers were doing what they wanted with the lake. They were tearing hell out of its shores and bottom. The water level had risen. Now and then chunks of the adjacent high hill sheared off and plunged down with great splashes. Such a brass-balled attack on the lake meant the right people had been paid off, be they local officials or environmental enthusiasts.

A *very* big deal. And if Butch knew anything, a short run deal.

What were they looking for? It wasn't his business, but curiosity was making it his. When he crept close he heard many of the men speaking a language he recognized—Russian. He smiled. Nevsky's specialty. Well, Nevsky had got him out here into the middle of a puzzle. Maybe Butch could solve it as well as pay back two mean-hearted guys.

He would have to tell Yuri all about this, after his business trip to the West Coast. Maybe a week, give or take.

25

On the St. Petersburg-Moscow train

The last few days in the service of Boris Petrovich had not been pleasant, the Attorney reflected. The infernal cache had colored his master's life and so his own—for the worst. He looked into the outside window. The early evening's darkness threw back his shadowed reflection. It showed the two vertical lines that had so recently appeared where nose joined brow. Brackets now enclosed his thin mouth. The window didn't reflect the suddenly gray-streaked sideburns that he had discovered in his shaving mirror yesterday morning.

The urge to sleep welled up. To keep it at bay, as he had too often over the last week, he pulled his pillbox from a vest pocket. With practiced though shaking hands he arrayed a generous heap of cocaine on the spoon and sucked it into his right nostril. And again for the left. Let every guest enjoy the same kasha.

There had recently come bad news that sharpened the spurs dug into his leader's flanks. General Gaichev, who had the power to make the military act at the right moment, had met with the Attorney. He came at once to the point. The times were changing quickly. New players of growing importance had arisen, their power on the verge of coalescing. Some former K.G.B. men were at the fore. Even now they were nibbling at the toes of the general's authority. Gaichev leaned forward wafting vodka fumes and the scent of good smoked fish the Attorney's way. "Your man has no more than a month," he whispered.

From his American source Detrovna then heard worse news: a militant right-wing group led by a former officer was also a serious contender for the cache. At an earlier time in this infernal affair his master would have laughed off such a rival. Now, with the cache still eluding his divers and time running short, paranoia had entered the lavish suite high above Patryarshi Ponds with a leaden tread.

He ordered the Attorney to swiftly identify and locate this reactionary clique. Small wonder Rishnikov was now tired. He had spent hours in around-the-clock telephone conversations with men in special positions. He contacted media reporters. He called in favors from those who toiled in government libraries and other information centers. And of course he plundered his own memory. He had stood behind Detrovna for years in the halls of the Federation Council and remembered many representatives' political positions...

It was most unwillingly that he went back to Boris Petrovich on a recent evening with what he had learned. His master sat in his armchair under a powerful reading lamp. Standing off to the side was the rusted suit of armor raised by the Harsky diver from Lake Nagle's waters. Detrovna had ordered an armature bolted together that held the heap of rusted plates in proper order. To the Attorney, his mind too often charged with essence of coca, the red-brown tangle looked to be a skeleton or haunt hovering over their enterprise like doom itself, rather than the spur to action his master supposed.

The Attorney put his papers down on the adjacent desk and began to speak—and was interrupted.

"There are eleven such rightist organizations, you say?" Detrovna asked. *"Eleven?"*

"Looking backward politically is always easier than looking ahead, which requires imagination, Boris Petrovich."

Detrovna screwed up his face unpleasantly. "Which one, then, is our rival for the cache?"

Sweat cold as a mink's nose ran down the Attorney's sides. In a voice smaller than he had wished he said, "I cannot say."

"Well, which is led by a field marshal, general, athlete, hero, cosmonaut, or what-have-you?"

"All of them."

It was not Detrovna's rage that frightened the Attorney. He had seen the man angry before. No, not the rage.

The loss of control.

Detrovna leaped from his chair screaming. Pacing and whirling, he called down curses on the Attorney who in fact was the only truly trustworthy man in his service. That whirlwind of emotion did Rishnikov no hurt; his skin was thick.

What it did was threaten all his dreams

He had been frugal with his master's largesse. In hard currency accounts he had accumulated much of what he needed to turn his dreams into sweet realities: a dacha where palm trees grew, a pied-a-terre in Rome, and a large mansion in Kiev—to say nothing of vehicles, furnishings, clothes, and many of the finer things flooding in from the West. Capping all these, the overarching dream—complete retirement within five years.

Earlier he had enjoyed every confidence that his dreams in time would become real. Detrovna's legal and illicit businesses grew and flourished. Good judgment was multiplied by good luck. Rubles and hard currencies increasingly poured into his master's hands like a river fed with melting snows. Some of that wealth steadily dribbled down to him. Good as things were, they could be even better. The road to the leadership of Russia, though torturous and filled with risk, could realistically be traveled. Detrovna *could* become the ultimate leader—the czar!—no matter the title he took. Where the Attorney would stand when that happened took his breath away.

Now the entire array raised painstakingly over years was threatening to topple. Detrovna had taken to putting off decisions. For so long he had been a pro-active man. Now heavy preoccupation with the cache had turned him into a reluctant responder to others' cues. When possible the Attorney had acted in his master's name. This could not always be done because he lacked Detrovna's imagination and hard heart. Others had proposed *razborkas*, meetings at which urgent disputes were settled. Detrovna had refused to schedule them. The result: defections, betrayals, new competition from equally rapacious criminal organizations, and other looming problems. Nonetheless, all their enterprises still could be put back on the track.

If the cache could be found quickly.

Or proof found that it had indeed disappeared into the organs for state security seventy-five years ago. Word from America had suggested the latter. The Attorney hoped mightily that such was the case.

He wanted his old life and old dreams—not new nightmares—back again.

Boris Petrovich had no choice but to put aside his search for the rival rightist organization. And to swallow the bile poured out over the frustration of trying to unravel the secrets of eleven like-minded cadres. More bile flowed over the possibility that, despite all the evidence he had in hand, secret police had long ago devoured the cache.

Earlier in the week he had tried to find out where the Cheka archive was stored. At first he thought it a simple task requiring a few hours, even minutes. Yet this was Russia, and the crap at once floated to the surface to besmirch him once again. He was told the archive was in such and such a government building, and then found it was not. Someone else swore the material had long been declassified and turned over to a historical library of the Revolution—also not so. A third "authority" said the politically incendiary pages long ago had been plundered, bowdlerized, scattered, or destroyed.

One thing was certain: the archive had been much moved about by various edicts of the K.G.B. then by the agents of liberalization. At the end of his final telephone conversation, Detrovna slammed down the receiver with such force that the plastic case shattered, sending fragments whirling like hurt moths. "No one knows where the hell it is!" he screamed at the Attorney. "The crap! *The crap is going to bury me after all!*"

Then he gathered himself. He would yet rule Russia. He *would* become the first czar of the new millennium!

There was always a way. Some thinking gave it to him. Expensive of course. An acquaintance was a powerful figure high in the ranks of the present organs for state security. His credentials in the service of the former K.G.B. were massive. He was one of the few men Detrovna admired. He was efficient, well organized, a good planner with no bad habits. He was one-quarter Swedish. His only shortcoming, if it could be called so, was his willingness to be bribed.

For great sums of money.

So it was that the Attorney was pulled from the futile task of further analyzing right-wing groups. With the usual briefcase he was put on the train to Peter. Once there he took a cab to the rendezvous point, the Aphrodite restaurant on Nevsky Prospekt.

There the wealthy dined on superb seafood. And the underlings of important men, like him and his counterpart Yakov Storlov, met to gobble the crumbs of food and power.

Storlov, a waddling heap of flesh, was thick-browed and sloppy about his food. He inhaled it with pneumatic snorts. His napkin, though large, was inadequate to cope with the long greasy rivulets and errant gobs produced by his at-table enthusiasms. He ordered double portions of entrees and wielded knife and fork with the glassy-eyed intensity of a gourmand gone berserk.

For him food, the Attorney thought. For me, cocaine.

To business then. Behind his rolls of fat rose the shadow strength of Yakov's master, the once and future K.G.B. man. In turn the Attorney stood proxy to another of great power.

The precise-minded Attorney reviewed the agreement, as he understood it. His counterpart marked the narrative with assertive dips of his bull-like head. Rishnikov was already looking forward to dozing his way back to Moscow after a routine mission. He eyed the briefcase at his feet, anxious to empty it.

Then they struck the snag. The problem: time. Detrovna understood he would be given the location and open access to the Cheka archive in less than forty-eight hours. "This cannot be guaranteed," Yakov said.

"It's the most critical part of the transaction," the Attorney said.

Yakov waved a hand made like a cluster of sausages. "There must be some 'give' in your plans, no? Do minutes matter so much?"

The Attorney whiffed some of the crap his master despised. "Time is the *most* important factor." He saw his sweat mirrored on the jowly face of the other. How alike they were!

The Attorney despised himself for that reality. He and Yakov were in the business of fixing, greasing, arranging, expediting, and giving and receiving bribes. They were nothing but the uneasy, amoral tools of mighty men. They played the role that Russian character and history decreed should exist forever, that one inflicted on the race like Job's boils.

They argued on, each fueled by fear of his own master's displeasure. As the proverb guaranteed: *u kholopov chuby treschat.* When masters are fighting, servants' forelocks are creaking. Neither could gain an advantage. In time it was clear that the only course was compromise. Half the German marks in the Attorney's briefcase would find their way into Yakov's attaché case. The remainder would be paid when the door to the Cheka archives was opened to Detrovna.

So instead of training back to Moscow in a satisfied doze, the Attorney sweated and shifted in his seat. Detrovna would not be pleased with the arrangement. The Attorney's reasonable hope was that Yakov's master would be equally displeased. So much so that he would move himself to action. After all, there was much easy money still to come his way.

The problem was that the issue of the Cheka's disposal of the cache had to be settled quickly. Shortly Detrovna intended to take over personal supervision of the Lake Nagle treasure dive. Should the Cheka matter remained unresolved, it would hang over everything like an evil cloud, adding uncertainty and further eroding his master's character.

The Attorney turned again to the pillbox and spoon. In the rushing shift of senses he recovered hope and optimism. Matters still could right themselves.

Nonetheless, again he hoped mightily that long ago the cache had been dissolved. He was no keener to go to America than Detrovna. Both would sooner go to the Devil. Despite all his groaning instincts, follow his master he would.

Follow the man who would be czar.

26

Ecclesiastical offices, off Prospekt Mira, Moscow

For significant reasons Bishop Paulos was reviewing his use of Father Fyodor as a representative of his office. He was giving the matter most serious thought and prayer. He knew God was asking him to search his heart for moral action. He knew what he should do: end the Church's role in the search for the Romanov Cache and defrock the priest.

Until the matter arose of the Church of St. Basil the Defender.

Located in Dlugy, the town where he was born, the church had suffered its own humiliations during the reign of the commissars. First its ikons, crosses, and statuary were torn out and destroyed. The altar was toppled and thrown down a well. After that the building served as warehouse, hospital, and prison. When portions of the roof collapsed for want of repairs, the remaining structure was abandoned to local pigeon fanciers. They crammed their cages within the thick walls' anglings and did no cleaning up. Bird droppings left a thick, stinking carpet over stones joined long ago by pious masons' magic.

A letter from a childhood friend, now a town official, asked the bishop to visit and behold what had happened to the place where they had both first found God.

The Bishop did so. He could not hide his shock at the effects on the church of neglect, indifference, and defacement. So pathetic was St. Basil's that it was beyond rebuilding. A new church was needed. Nothing as grand as the original was required, but something worthy of faith.

So felt the town fathers who invited him to a dinner as grand as their poverty would allow. Of course there were many well-rehearsed toasts. Their general thrust was unmistakable. Opening the diocese's purse was an appropriate and possible task for a native son holding as high an office as he did. Only modest funds were required to purchase building materials for a new church. The townspeople's labor and love of God would do the rest. The bishop left town embarrassed to have so long neglected that place where, standing amid the pungent wisps of incense, he first heard the call to vocation.

As Dlugy did not lie within his bishopric, he had to approach his superior, Archbishop Stronsky, a younger man whose political instincts rivaled his piety. Stronsky listened in attentive silence as Paulos made his case and modest request. When he finished, the other turned to a tray bearing wine and sweet cakes. He offered them. Paulos found he had no appetite.

Stronsky began a rambling discourse on the plans for Dlugy's bishopric. Paulos found it crushing in length and detail. The man seemed to have thought out the cost of every stone to be laid, every priest dispatched, every service held, every act of charity, every crumb of incense fired for the glory of God— down to the last kopek. Each was laid against the bishopric's modest income. The phrase "all funds have been budgeted for the next three years" he repeated no less than five times. Of course a new church of St. Basil the Defender was on the planning board—targeted for five to seven years from today, ten at the latest. Likely twenty, Paulos thought, if ever.

Paulos' pleas for a shift of priorities for the benefit of Dlugy Stronsky brushed away as easily as he did the sweet cake crumbs from his beard. Commissions had been paid and staff had already been assigned. Wheels were turning. Surely he understood...

What Paulos understood came to him clearly beyond the door. Stronsky was in the vanguard of today's Church. He, Paulos, was an old warhorse put out to the pasture of unchallenging responsibilities. He was in fact without the power that would have assured the speedy granting of his modest request. Anger surged. What he had done, what he had *endured* at the hands of the Party meant nothing now. Those long, savage struggles were to the new generation increasingly irrelevant. They would say, to be sure Paulos had lived through an unfortunate time, but Russian history was gorged with them. Young churchmen wanted to get on with current business in a new Motherland.

It was now so clear that his superiors considered his talents and potential spent. Well, he wasn't finished yet! Quite naturally, to justify this position, he thought of the cache. Should he bring a portion of it into the Church, he would at first charge many hearts with awe. Subsequently he would engineer a key position for himself, one central to the distribution of the massive resources. Age had not dulled his negotiation skills honed sharp over decades against the slick stone of cloddish nomenklatura. Let them think he was drifting in a quiet tributary while the mighty river of contemporary events surged along.

They would be surprised.

And Dlugy would have a church such as its people had never dared imagine.

Thus, when the long-awaited international telephone call from Father Fyodor came, instead of telling him to desist and depart from the Church he listened with breathless attention to his agent's report. Fyodor had arranged an alliance with the Force for Leadership, Korchevko's group, and cooperation with Yuri Nevsky himself! Rough agreements had been made for division of the czar's wealth, should it come to them. All had gone forward so quickly! The bishop marveled.

The situation was complicated, Fyodor explained. To begin with, it was possible that the treasure no longer existed. If it did, Boris Detrovna seemed to be in the best position to find it. Yet there appeared to be another, truer route to the riches involving four cubes scattered around the globe. It was Fyodor's opinion that the fourth contained the major part of the true trove. How and where it was to be found was most unclear. Even so, Bishop Paulos could rest assured that, should it come to light, Fyodor would be there to represent the interests of the Church. This effort of course might require him to take "unpleasant" actions. Would the bishop condone them?

Why did he ask? Paulos, already tortured by what he had recently learned about Father Fyodor, found such a question more than simply agonizing. Like an agent of the Devil, his priest was demanding complicity—permission, even—to commit still darker crimes. It seemed he was pointing out that unworthy aspiration to possess the cache was a doorway to sin. Paulos felt his face twist with the pain of a conscience at war with itself.

Father Fyodor insisted, "I ask your permission—"

"I heard you!" Again the urge to dismiss the priest and be done with treasure hunting loomed up in the bishop like a breaching whale. Against that possibility he reviewed the indignities of his decades under the commissars' thumbs, the recent banquet in Dlugy, and the expectations of his townspeople. He saw crumbled St. Basil's carpeted with pigeon excrement. The structure stood as an abomination to believers. Across Russia similar abominations reared up as ugly as old wounds, all needing cleansing and healing. Would the spiritual hemorrhaging that had paralleled desecration of Church property also be staunched by physical improvements? He believed so. There was only one way this could happen.

The Church must have a share of the Romanov Cache!

He wet his lips. "You have my blessing, Fyodor." His voice shook.

"Excellent! Without it I wouldn't have dared entertain a certain plan."

"What plan is that?" the bishop asked.

"One that could—I can make no guarantees—leave the *entire* cache in our hands."

His heart leaped up. His *evil* heart! All. Yes, *all!* "How—?" The bishop fell silent. He did not *want* to know. To know was to further soil his already unclean soul.

"The cache must be found first," Fyodor said. "If it is, you can trust my ingenuity. Right now, all I need are your prayers for my success." The voice from America seemed to the stressed bishop to come from a darker place. "You *will* pray for our success, won't you?"

The bishop's conscience heaved like a beast in a sack. He couldn't speak.

"I need your prayers!" Father Fyodor said. "Our Church needs your prayers. I say again: will you pray for us?"

"Yes," the bishop breathed.

"Excellent!" Laughter rolled down the line, and then the connection was broken.

Bishop Paulos sat motionless at his desk for a long moment staring ahead. He lowered his gaze to the papers before him, then to one in particular.

The one that had cried for him to end the Church's search for the cache and dismiss Fyodor.

It was a memorandum from Archbishop Stronsky circulated to all bishops. It described a fatal incident at the former Red Banner Collective Farm east of St. Petersburg. It asked if the priests responsible could be identified through the descriptions attached: one a hatchet-faced cleric of normal size, the other more than two meters tall.

Bishop Paulos had heard tell of a giant false priest. Rumor found him with gypsies, whores, and drunks—and more than once in the company of Father Fyodor.

Bishop Paulos knew the evildoers. To his everlasting shame he would remain silent.

He sank from his chair onto his knees and so crept toward his personal ikon in the corner of his office. Tears sprang from his eyes. When had he last wept? He had thought the Party men had long since drained him of his last drop of true emotion.

He pressed his forehead to the carpet, never mind his protesting spine. He prayed to a God he knew forgave the worst festering in the dark human heart. He didn't pray for success in finding the cache, or for Father Fyodor the murderer.

He prayed for his own sick soul.

27

Murrysville, Pennsylvania, east of Pittsburgh

On the drive out to Nevsky's Murrysville property Charity started to sniffle. Seeing it made Nevsky ache. He reached out with his right arm and gave her shoulders a light hug. "Hey..." he said. She sniffled all the louder.

Nevsky the psychologist! He was sadly amazed to find his longtime friend vulnerable to the emotions she had held in check so well during the years they had shared 138 Morlande. Her control had been born in the accidental death of her entire family. Now further loss and bitter disappointment had cracked her shell.

A new Charity had come home.

But still the same old smart one. She wiped away her tears and said, "I told you how glad I am to have something beside myself to think about, didn't I? Well, I've *been* thinking. First thing I thought is that your father might not have *known* what he had that linked him, and now you, to the cache. And by the way, Yuri, by now something about the whole puzzle *must* have occurred to you."

"What?"

"Your grandfather made sure no one except he understood all its pieces. That includes all the clues and misdirection."

"Between his faith in God working His will and his own cunning it'll be a wonder if anyone finds what he hid," Nevsky said. "And maybe...that's for the best."

Charity turned a sharp gaze his way. "Meaning?"

"Unworthy cache chasers were cursed."

"Do you *believe* that?"

Nevsky drove on in silence. Then he said, "Let's say it makes me nervous, and let it go at that."

"Let it go is *right,*" practical Charity snorted.

Last night Nevsky's bruisings had kept him from sleeping well. As he stared up into the darkness revelations came to him. Today he was grateful to be able to share them with Charity. He reminded her why at first he had allowed himself to get involved in the search for the cache. For clear reasons: to find out who killed Father Alexei, and to try to straighten out who Yuri Nevsky was. Now, after several weeks of growing entanglement, nothing about the cache had proved straightforward. His petty motivations appeared childish, even simpleminded, because he at least was finding the cache shrouded in deepening mystery, like a Grail or Nordic Ring.

He couldn't put exact words to what he meant. "It's more than just a heap of wealth for me, Charity," he tried lamely. "It's my past. It's Russia's past, too. If Korchevko or Detrovna end up with it and start ruling Russia, the cache will be part of her future as well." He frowned. "Do you begin to see what I'm trying to say?"

"Vaguely. I'm not much help with that sort of stuff," Charity said offhandedly. "I leave the unseen to you, remember? Not my forte." She shrugged off that topic and squirmed upright in her seat. She was anxious to talk—about *her* topics. "I've drawn one conclusion I like." She turned to him eagerly. "It's about the cubes. Those strange cubes. The one in Odessa filled with pebbles. The one in the desert empty. Some people think they once had treasure in them that was taken out. I don't."

"Why not?"

"I think the cubes are markers, road signs, what have you— to the treasure. And in your grandfather's style, they invite misinterpretation."

"The French one was loaded with treasure," Nevsky said.

"Was that all of it?"

Nevsky had wondered about that. Indeed, maybe Detrovna was diving for a lesser part of the horde, or a greater. "And the fourth cube—if there is one?" he asked.

Charity drew in a slow hissing breath. She was going out on a limb. "I think...the three somehow point the way to the fourth."

She went on to say she was working with some other ideas, but wasn't ready to share them.

Nevsky was involved with some thoughts of his own. When the affair started quietly enough with a visit from a humble priest, his instincts had warned him of deep dangers ahead. But even intuition had fallen short of unfolding reality. The search had sucked in more and more contenders like a hurricane feeding on warm waters. All sailed those dangerous seas in small boats, no matter their arrogance, wills, or wealth. Shape events? Could men plan history?

He couldn't sort out where he was among priests and bishops, ascetics, demagogues, politicians, charismatics, generals, and criminals. It seemed he had allies. Yet they could turn to enemies at the first flash of cache gold. His initial motivations had been trivialized, but that did not excuse him from the quest, even though the abuse he had suffered last night at the hands of the giant priest could well be warning of worse to come. A young passionate woman was sharing his bed. Whether or not she belonged there was further clouded by her passion for revenge.

The cache overshadowed all their lives.

He recalled his poker dictum also dating from what seemed a simpler time: play crazy. He saw the need to amend that behavior in light of immense complexities. So he did.

Play crazy—like his grandfather!

Nevsky's parents had bought the acreage and one-floor farmhouse back in the late '40's. They spent summers there. When they grew older, they rented it. Now, like 138 Morlande, it was Nevsky's.

He pulled the VW around the back of the house where the drive ended. On foot he and Charity negotiated the fifty yards of flourishing sumac and knee-high grass to reach the chicken coop. Its lock was rusty, but yielded to a couple squirts of WD-40 and some energetic key work. Inside was a single long low room. Even though the last chicken had gone to Sunday dinner forty years ago, the wood was still gripped by faint acid stink.

He looked around the debris of his father's past. He recognized items he hadn't seen for many years: the metallurgical treatises, the bundled Paris-published émigré newspapers, and crumbling leather-bound editions of Russian classics. The now antique Vari-Typer composing machine that printed in Russian and English crouched in a corner, furred with dust. The tables and chairs piled to the ceiling had come to his parents with 138 Morlande. They still carried the featureless black finish of turn-of-the-century furniture styles.

"Uh oh," Charity said.

"What?"

"Rodents have been at work."

So they had, gnawing at book spines and pages for their glue. Charity picked up a hardbound book, shook it by its covers to produce a shower of confetti and mouse droppings. "Yuk!"

"So, wise one, what are we looking for?" Nevsky asked.

"We are looking at *everything* in here," she said.

They found correspondence, much of it from émigrés washed up by the storm of the Revolution in places like the Tyrol, Mexico City, and Nanking... Nevsky read or scanned every piece, found nothing bearing on their search. There were pencils, dried up pens, old paperweights, even a green eyeshade his father had used while pounding out technical translations on the Vari-Typer.

He found piles of cancelled checks bundled together, and checkbooks emptied of all but stubs. A few yellowed photographs fell out of books. Émigrés on American and European beaches shared the cautious grins of those spared the dark fates of kin and friends, but not yet completely relaxed.

Some religious items were in a wooden shoeshine box: a hand painted wooden ikon, some prayer cards, and a metal-bound Bible. His father hadn't been much for religion. Nevsky had never seen him open this Bible or any other. He picked it up. He rubbed off some of the dust and ran his fingers over the worked covers, felt the faces of saints and Christ hand-worked into the metal. He thumbed through it, riffled parchment pages that showed little mouse damage. Nothing fell out. He put it down.

Charity was most methodical. Nothing in the chicken coop was going to be missed. She took every item in hand, however small, and checked it carefully. She gave Nevsky any with Russian text. Each time she riveted him with a demanding glance. Each time he translated, pondered, and shook his head. When daylight faded, she turned to the two heavy-duty hand lanterns she had carried along in a grocery bag.

The final Russian items dwindled down with shakes of his head. When he dismissed the last, she stamped her foot and shouted, "Yuri Nevsky, will you *help* me, for God's sake?" She was angry. She thought he wasn't trying.

For God's sake...

God. The Bible. There had been something about Bibles... Nevsky screwed up his face in an effort to remember. He went back to the shoeshine box and picked up the Bible again. He swung open the worked metal cover. He saw a dedication. The writing had to be his grandfather's. Sergei had given this Bible to his son Vladimir and another to his daughter Anya when life at Great Meadow tottered before the abyss of the Revolution. The words written here were the same as those noted by the SS during Anya's torture. "Should you be called on to serve czar, God, and the Motherland, first read here carefully."

"Well?" Charity said. "Or should I ask *what?*"

Nevsky held the Bible. "Something..." he said, not knowing how to continue. As he stood unspeaking, his memory conjured up a voice saying, "The answers are in the Bible." It was uniformed Major Bottoms Up!, the fool for Christ's sake, who had spoken ambiguously to him on a Russian Slope street. Hmmmm... Wait. The Bible was the word of God. Then he remembered! The numbers Sergei had given his father that proved to be longitude and latitude had been amended. "And the word of God," he had told his son. Why couldn't that mean the Bible his father had given him? *This* Bible. "I don't *know* what about it, Charity," he said. "But it's important. It goes back with us."

On the ride back to 138 Charity was a bit peeved that Nevsky couldn't pinpoint what it was about the Bible that should interest them. Patience wasn't her long suit. Even so, she intended to hide it among her possessions until they could study it. "Less likely to be stolen that way," she said matter-of-factly, as though the house was crawling with thieves.

In bed that night Alessya questioned Nevsky about the errand that had taken nearly the whole day. Had he found out anything? He reached out. Her pearly skin gleamed in the dimness as though with its own light. He touched her warm shoulder, held it and drew her toward him. Her breasts overflowed his cupped hands like tender fruits.

"Did you find anything?" she said again.

Charity's suspiciousness infected him like a virus. "I found nothing that I know of," he whispered.

Her large tongue traveled his face like a cat's. She knew he found it arousing. Like a softened burr it went its wet way. Forehead, close attention to eyebrows, cheeks... She paused in her thorough work to murmur, "Then you would have done better to stay home with your Alessya." She shoved him gently down and cleared his pajamas away.

Her tongue resumed its rampage...

Nevsky and Charity had planned to examine the Bible in the morning. A call from Isabel, Sybille Sollonier's companion, changed their plans. Sybille had recovered from her seizure. She wanted to talk to him.

At once.

Arriving at the farmhouse, Nevsky noticed a rental van parked by the rear entrance. A young man was loading it with boxes and furniture. A Toyota Tercel waited behind the truck.

Isabel explained hastily that she and Sybille intended to leave the area the moment she finished her story. She had said to Isabel, "My mother's curse follows my knowledge."

Nevsky went to Sybille's bedroom. The attack had left the old woman with less energy. Her movements were subdued, but her eyes still glittered. Again she motioned him closer. She pointed to the low stool with the crocheted cushion. As before, he sat. "You want to know what more happened in Odessa?" she said, voice frail but firm.

"Yes."

"Then I will tell you..."

When she fled Colonel Karl Rosser's questions, she found it impossible to immediately leave the city. Enemies of the invaders who knew only that she fled for her life hid her. Weeks passed. During this time she learned what horrors the Nazis were inflicting on the population. She saw trucks and train cars loaded with poor souls destined for slavery or worse. She regretted her fraternization with Dieter Rosser, though he wasn't a wicked man. Then word reached her of Anya Nevsky's fate at the hands of the SS. After that she came to hate all Germans.

One night she had a visitor. He was an Orthodox priest, old, gray, and possibly half mad. His name was Father Konstantine. He explained he had served the religious needs of Sergei Nevsky, his family, and all those others who lived at Great Meadow. He also evoked the name of her mother Natalia. He mentioned her decades-long love affair with the landowner.

To Sybille's astonishment he knew much that had happened in the garden of their château twenty years ago. Nothing could bring Natalia and Sergei back, he said. But their "work" could continue. Sybille could be of the greatest assistance, if she had nerve and no love of Germans...

His lengthy explanations led to her great soul searching— and to decisions.

So it happened that she appeared as a guest mid-way through the SS 1942 Easter revel. With hair cut short and dyed black, and make-up heavy, she took on the identity of a German-speaking Ukrainian. As instructed, she put herself in the way of Colonel Rosser. Her principal fear was that despite her disguise he would remember her. She needn't have worried. He had been drinking heavily. She led him on. They danced. She encouraged his nibbles and gropes.

When the revel was winding down in the small hours, she invited him to "her apartment." She leered and made herself touch him suggestively. She made sure they departed unseen. She led Rosser into the room chosen by Father Konstantine. The German officer staggered forward and toppled onto the bed. Sybille had not settled with herself to what lengths she would go with a man she loathed. Again, she need not have troubled herself. He commanded her to expose her breasts, feebly tweaked their nipples, and then fell into a slumber roaring with snores.

Silently Father Konstantine entered. With him he brought a shotgun. He didn't wake the German. "He must be sober for us," he said. He sat on the edge of the bed. He and Sybille traded stares and curt phrases for better than four hours. Time allowed her to study the priest. His long beard was a tight white tangle. His eyes gleamed. His breath came in heavy wheezes. Armies of thoughts warred within him, generating wild expressions that rolled across his face like waves at the water's edge. She sensed illness and torment had eroded a once massive frame.

They had not eroded his purpose.

The moment Rosser stirred, Father Konstantine shoved the shotgun barrel under the German's chin. His free hand clamped the cloth of his collar. In Russian he said, "Tell him if he struggles, he dies!"

Sybille did so. Rosser's eyes rolled in rage. He began some arrogant bluster. The priest jabbed the shotgun up, making him cough. He swallowed and fell silent. As rehearsed, Sybille brought the room's telephone to the bedside table.

Father Konstantine gave Rosser his instructions, she doing the interpreting. He was to call the rail dispatcher and identify himself. He was to say his call had to do with top priority SS matters. In the Odessa rail yard a flatcar held an empty cube covered with canvas and marked as SS property. This car was to be coupled to a locomotive that was to follow a certain route northwest, toward the front. The priest pulled a sheet torn from a larger German rail map and held it under Rosser's wide eyes. The route had been marked. The locomotive and flatcar would be switched toward the small town of Drinya, beyond the front. On a spur by the Drinya station the flatcar was to be uncoupled. The engineer was to put the locomotive into reverse and return. He would not be interfered with going either way.

"I will not do this!" Rosser shouted. Drink and disorientation robbed his voice of authority.

The priest looked at Sybille. "Tell him: he will do it or die!"

At her words Rosser struggled weakly and tried to break away. The priest held him down without difficulty. The German shouted for help with all his strength.

Father Konstantine said to Sybille, "It's been arranged that there's no one to hear him. Tell him I will not ask again."

She did so. Rosser's eyes darted about the small room…and found no escape. He held out his hand for the telephone.

Father Konstantine said, "Tell him one word more or less than we've told him to say will mean death."

Rosser's shifting eyes told her that he indeed had planned to ask for help in some way. The priest shoved the gun barrel hard into the German's neck. "Enough delay!" he said.

In the end Rosser followed instructions perfectly. Sybille guessed he intended to have the one-car train stopped later. How Father Konstantine intended to prevent that she didn't know.

Until a few minutes had passed.

The priest shoved the German back on the bed and centered the gun barrel under his jaw. He said to Sybille, "Translate. When he meets the Devil, tell him to send us *more* of his Germans."

As she spoke the priest transferred the shotgun to his left hand. With his right he blessed himself and said, "For God, czar, and Mother Russia!"

He pulled the trigger.

It took only moments to arrange things to suggest suicide.

Father Konstantine made her swear on an ikon never to reveal what had just happened until she knew the right time had come. His connections cleared the way for her to leave Odessa immediately for Paris via indirect but safe routes. Before her departure he told her that Sergei Nevsky's farsightedness had made a haven in America. She could use it, if it became necessary. He told her where to find the landowner's agent in a town outside of Pittsburgh, Pennsylvania. There she would be given modest resources and, more importantly, safety. One day strangers with questions might contact her. God would tell her what to do.

"So when I was accused of collaboration after the war, I dared not defend myself with my role as Rosser's co-murderer," Sybille said. "I chose the life of an expatriate and came here. I found Sergei Nevsky's agent and accepted a large loan. I used some of it to buy this house. The rest I invested wisely. I've never moved."

Nevsky drew a heavy breath. "Through all of that, did Father Konstantine tell you what it was all about?"

She shook her head. "Not really."

He wanted to question her further. But she was anxious to leave; the rental truck was filled. He knew better than to ask her where she was going to spend the unburdened days left to her. He thanked her with enthusiasm.

She replied, "Are you wise to be grateful to one who has brought my mother's curse now to *your* side?"

On the way home Nevsky's attention turned to both Sybille and his father ending up in near Pittsburgh. And what was that about Sergey's "agent" also somewhere nearby seventy or eighty years ago? None were here by coincidence, all by the actions of his grandfather. What of it? He didn't know. He needed to think more about all that.

Father Konstantine... Why had he embraced a murderous violence that ran totally against his religious vows to send the Odessa cube west? What had Charity called the cubes? "Signposts to the treasure." Nevsky sensed he had all the pieces, but couldn't put the puzzle together. He forced his level of concentration higher. The cubes...

He remembered the cube that had cost his father his life on the Kirgiz Steppe had been returned to Great Meadow. Therefore, wasn't it possible that the final destination of the Odessa cube was the same?

He ran through his memory of the aftermath of Sybille's horrid night of gold, jewels, and murder in 1922. He snatched a thought out of the air, one as elusive as a housefly. But there it was now in the grip of his mind. Those who came several nights later to take the plundered cube from the château weren't Chekists.

They were Orthodox priests acting under Father Konstantine's orders!

The cube's final destination? Where else but Great Meadow where time, destiny—or God, if one liked—had in the end placed all three? Not abandoned there, but put under human care.

As his grandfather had designed.

But *why?* Possibly Charity was right. The riches found in the château cache were but a small part of the horde. The three cubes were now arrayed to point the way to the fourth where the greater part of the treasure rested—in the one marked *Anastasia Nikolayevna.*

Nevsky liked the overall concept. He'd have to tell Charity what he had built on her foundation and see what she thought.

But when he walked in the door, Alessya rushed up and gently pushed him back onto the relative privacy of the porch. "I spoke on the phone with Gari Kusnetsov's wife. She said he was taken to the hospital! But before he left he ordered her to call me."

"Did he find the Cheka files on the treasure cube?" Nevsky said.

"She didn't know."

"Why did she call, then?"

"To tell us Gari wants to talk to us in person."

"Why—"

"Because he has little time left." Alessya's liquid eyes were wide. "And trusts not a living soul. We have to leave at once!"

28

Beyond the northern outskirts of Moscow

The Raptor was displeased.

First with this sinkhole of a road! Though it was summer, boggy stretches still slowed his three-car caravan to a crawl. Incredibly, some rough pushing had been required. All this while haste was paramount! When the springboard of the czar's riches vaulted him to power, he would make improving Russian roads a high priority. His recently ended visit to America had shown him highways of which a Russian motorist could only dream. Such know-how could be bought and shared. He would arrange it. He anticipated flowing rivers of asphalt and concrete, legible road signs everywhere required...

The Raptor's further displeasure came from Nevsky having disappointed him. While not precisely betraying the Sons, he had come close enough to spark the general's wrath. Others had given the American Sybille Sollonier's address. Primed by the Sons, who had pointed out her importance, he had rushed to visit her—and not reported to Ostrovsky what she revealed! When the two men met again, the general would make it plain that Nevsky's deliberate oversight had badly damaged their relationship. There would be punishment.

He could not bring himself to hate Yuri Nevsky. There was something simpatico in the man. Possibly the general's hard edge had been dulled by the American being the grandson of the *maître* Sergei Nevsky, the sole genius among the original Sons. More likely the Raptor was extending his forbearance because word of all that Nevsky did reached him through a reliable source, and was useful. It was unfortunate that Sybille was stricken before her tale was done.

He turned to Sasha who shared the rear seat of the middle car. "Use the radio," he ordered. "Find out what's going on up front! We're not sightseeing."

His source had shared other, alarming information. Boris Detrovna, that master demagogue and criminal, appeared to have the inside track on the treasure. He was in fact diving for it somewhere. Ostrovsky knew well to what use that one would put the riches. He too would be czar!

Another man as well wished to top the heap. Korchevko! The Raptor knew and admired him for his character and genuine piety. Some called him Christ-like. Russian politics was no place for Him. The Devil would do better in that forum. The general suspected Korchevko did not have the master component needed to rule Russia—sublime indifference to immoral acts, foremost his own. No matter, his Force for Leadership was well established and popular—and hell bent for as well for what he had been told was called the Romanov Cache.

The Orthodox Church, too, had high expectations of sharing the treasure. The Church!

None had been left out!

His military instincts, still sharp though it had been years since he held an official command, told him that the campaign for the cache had intensified. Once-distant contenders were drawing together. Ultimately violent engagements were inevitable.

He hoped to avoid any confrontations as long as possible. When his source revealed that it was conceivable that the entire trove had fallen into the hands of the Cheka many decades ago, he had acted quickly. He tried to get in touch with Ivan Marischenko, a man at the highest levels of the security ministry. Marischenko would find out at once where the Cheka records of the 1920's could be found, and ease the Raptor's way to their location. He was certain of this.

Marischenko had recently joined the Sons of Continuity.

As God would have it, the man was out of the country on state business. Appeals to his underlings for help in communicating with him were futile. Ostrovsky meant nothing to them, though everything to their master.

So, four precious days were lost. The Raptor's anxiety rose. It was unlikely that the other contenders would let slip a chance to pin down the loose end proving that the cache had been destroyed long ago—and so bring everything to a dissatisfying permanent halt. Unhappily his source was unable to provide him with information about how his rivals were fairing in their own searches for the records. A cool man in crises, the Raptor nonetheless felt his self-control sorely taxed.

It wasn't surprising that when the caravan's slow pace became no pace at all, he sprang cursing from the motionless car. In the end, he had to angle his own back to the bumper of a vexingly mired sedan, other Sons heaving with him.

They leaped back into the cars. The road improved. Ostrovsky sank back in his seat, content to glance at his watch as the kilometers crept by.

Their destination was a former mansion. Marischenko had told him that since the Revolution it had served a dozen functions, the current one a records center. He had provided a layout of the building. Of course the precise arrangement of the historical documents could not be predicted. This was Russia, not Germany. Marischenko had also arranged for all staff to be on vacation the day of the Sons' visit.

Consequently Ostrovsky was startled to see three empty transport vans pulled up at the rear loading dock. No one was in sight. Who knew what that meant? He spoke tersely to Sasha. "Tell the men to arm themselves. Go with them." He squeezed his elbow. "Be forceful if required. In any case, get the records!"

His six men and two women moved toward the building's main entrance, spreading out, keeping low. They had their weapons ready. They had been drilled and disciplined. Ostrovsky was proud of them. They would get the job done, even if others stood in their way. They entered the mansion without event.

Ostrovsky rolled down the window and waited. His heart began to pound as it had in times of imminent combat. He told himself the vans might mean nothing. The building could be deserted as Marischenko had promised.

Nine minutes passed. He heard a muffled burst of small arms fire. Then others! They sounded scattered through the building. My God, how many armed men were in there? The fire intensified and then tapered off. He heard muted screams and shouts.

Trouble!

Cursing, he touched a catch under the back seat. A panel opened. He snatched out the automatic rifle and two hand grenades. He sprinted to the main entrance. He loathed to be drawn into danger when his destiny was to lead Russia. Yet his Sons were under attack and honed instincts told him matters were going badly. He shoved open the heavy glass-paneled door and took cover behind a marble column.

Ahead of him stretched a wide hallway. Beyond it he saw the beginnings of a broad double staircase curving up in the fashion of bygone times.

He left the column and ran down the hallway. Ahead and above there was another clatter of small arms fire. He charged ahead, taking the stairs three at a time. At the top another hallway stretched ahead. Dusty statues of heroic workers and

Party men stood behind him on a curving marble banister. He climbed onto it, then up to the highest pedestal on which a statue of Lenin faced the hallway across the palatial stairwell.

The reports of weapons fired indoors reached his ears with concussive force. He smelled spent cartridges, heard the distant clatter of ejected brass tumbling onto stone floors. He knew the voices of some who screamed. He cursed their suffering.

He breathed deeply, gathered himself. His grin arose of itself. He was no stranger to combat. In him there was still relish for it. Enemies? They would be killed!

The skirmish was drawing closer. There was movement at the far end of the hall. He set his weapon for automatic fire and clicked off the safety.

The Sons were withdrawing down the hall in his direction. It was an orderly operation. Two faced their adversaries, their automatic rifles chattering. Two others each dragged a wounded or dead comrade. Ostrovsky muttered wordlessly in dismay and anger. He shoved the barrel of his weapon into the crook of Lenin's elbow. He had a clear view above the heads of his Sons.

The dead and disabled were dragged to the top of the stairs. While descending the curving marble staircase all would be exposed to fire from the top. Ostrovsky shouted for them to hurry. He would make sure no enemy emerged alive from the hall.

Seeing the rear guard disappear before them, six attackers unwisely rushed forward. The walls bunched them. Ostrovsky's economical burst of fire cut them down. Some sprawled dead. The wounded writhed and howled. Let them scream, Ostrovsky thought. It might discourage the others.

Seeing what had happened to their brothers, the remaining attackers advanced more slowly, slipping quickly between the doorways lining each side of the hallway. Below, Ostrovsky's Sons had reached the bottom of the staircase. He glanced back at the hallway. More men were moving up! They were huddling in doorways where he couldn't get easy shots at them. Gathering for a rush, he thought. Once they escaped the confinement of the hallway, they would spread out and chop everyone to pieces. He fired a few bursts to keep them thinking. Showers of wood splinters and marble chips filled their hallway's air.

The Raptor's emotional center was as calm as a pond on a summer day. This was his business. He would conduct it with a tradesman's equanimity.

He pulled the grenades from his belt and jumped down. He armed the first and carefully judged the distance to the front of the hallway. He arched it over the yawning stairway. It bounced ahead nicely. He emptied his clip in the same direction, then armed and threw the second grenade.

After the first detonation he turned and ran toward the staircase. Despite the crippling concussion and careening shrapnel someone still had the presence of mind to get off a few rounds that hummed by his ears like hornets. After the second detonation his flight down the stairs drew no more fire.

By the time he got outside, the Sons were back inside the cars. He hurried to join them. A door was opened and he tumbled in, his weapon clattering against the doorpost. A man and a woman had knocked the glass from the rear window of the third car. Their automatic rifles would provide cover for the retreat. Someone said there had been at least twenty who had revealed themselves to be Detrovna's men. All had been busy searching.

Ostrovsky shouted the order to move out.

"Wait!" someone shouted.

From the back of the building staggered a man. He lurched forward. His face was webbed with bloody strands. His right hand held his belly. His wild eyes found Ostrovsky. He rushed to the general's car. He stood tottering. Ostrovsky threw open the door for—Sasha!

Sasha raised his right arm to shoulder height. Its slow journey allowed Ostrovsky to see the ruined bowels his hand had held together. "Mother Russia...will be great again!" he croaked

"If her Sons dare make her so!" Ostrovsky's voice had to overcome the stone in his throat.

Sasha collapsed, dead Ostrovsky was sure. He was dragged into the car. They shot away to safety.

Sasha, his best man, was surely gone, his capabilities and efficiencies blown to dust. Such an asset to lose to the infernal cache! The Raptor gathered himself. He was a military man. Casualties were inevitable. The battle had been lost, but not the campaign.

He had learned a lesson: previously he had lost his sense of perspective. He saw now it had been a mistake coming here. Dabbling in matters only tangential to the cache was an error. Now he glimpsed with certainty the only route to victory.

He would prepare a suitable strike force. He would use it once, and only once.

He knew when that would be.

29

Moscow

When Detrovna saw the Attorney's face, his jaw dropped. Here was an ashen-faced apparition! Gennady Efimovich greeted his master, then leaned back against the garage's grimy wall and closed his eyes, briefcase dangling from a limp hand. A bullet had sliced the suit coat and pants at the hip to leave a shallow wound. Dried blood crusted the fabric. His fingers trembled steadily like leaves in low wind. *"Radi boga!"* the Attorney said. *"Radi boga!..."* For God's sake! Other, rougher men bustled in with cartons and boxes.

"So, you had your first taste of combat, Gennady Efimovich?" Detrovna asked with a veteran's knowing grin. He had received intermittent cell phone reports from the Attorney. Though panicky, they had provided the essential, unhappy information. Armed rivals had interrupted his men's search for the Cheka records. A shootout had resulted. The intruders were driven off.

The Attorney heaved breath into his thin chest. "Whoever they were, they fought like fanatics! Only a few, they seemed as many as our twenty."

Detrovna was impatient as always with excuses. "Why did it take you so long to get here with the records?"

The Attorney's eyes widened with surprise. "We had to take care of our casualties, Boris Petrovich. Seven wounded, three dead!"

Detrovna cursed softly. The location of the records had in the end been provided by his source in a tardy—but no less expensive—fashion. What had seemed victory a few hours ago now had been tainted by death. The infernal cache!—without which his hopes would die. And *with* which... Why had that alternative not seemed more hospitable of late?

"It was necessary to find doctors, the few hospitals better than butcher shops," the Attorney went on. "It took time."

"Who were these fighting devils?" Detrovna asked.

The Attorney gave an order. A woman was dragged in from the vans, arms across the shoulders of two of the men. "Our sole captive," he said. She had a nasty leg wound, a bone broken. She had to be in agony. They dropped her roughly into a chair. She didn't cry out.

"They knew the building better than we did," the Attorney said. "They were quicker to move through its stacks and hallways. And deadly shots as well. They were simply more...effective. Only our numbers prevailed."

"How many of them were there?" Detrovna asked.

The Attorney drew a breath that shuddered through his body. "Eight," he said weakly.

Detrovna growled. He sniffed the reactionary rival group he had been unable to identify. Maybe his luck in that area had changed. He tried a few questions on the wounded woman. Not surprisingly, she was silent. From under blonde bangs her green eyes revealed nothing but the shadows of pain thrown against a screen of discipline and loyalty. She was not inclined to speak. That of course could be made a temporary frame of mind. However, he had neither the time nor inclination to play inquisitor. Others could take that role. He gave orders and the woman was dragged away.

If she was a common representative of the backward-looking zealots rivaling him on the quest, they were a force to be reckoned with, one that threatened to trample his hopes.

There was a brighter side. Two victories that day! The blonde might reveal her organization's identity. More importantly, he had the Cheka records!

Since hearing that the secret police had played a heavy role around the French cube seventy-five years ago, speculation had tortured him. A central question ruined his sleep and crouched like a predator in the hallways of his days.

Had all his work in America been for nothing?

Who could guess at the Cheka disposition of the cache? Hoarded somewhere or thrown into the devouring maw of the Revolution? His heart sank to contemplate either possibility. He had already invested so heavily that to continue the quest further, into the maze of secret police doings, might ruin him financially and politically. Alternately, if the wealth fed the Revolution, well, that was an end to it.

The second possibility of course would bring peace to his soul. Imagine! The Imperial era *finally* ended, the wealth of the czar proven to be totally dissipated, and the last ruling Romanov about to be re-interred in St. Petersburg. The end. No more. Back to today's Russia and business as usual.

But business as usual, Detrovna understood clearly now, meant he would never become czar. No, he was forced to ensnare himself in the nets of the past. He had to hope—to

pray to the God whom he suspected of unspeakable duplicity—
that the cache survived.

His heart pounded. The time had come to seek certainty.
His eyes flicked over the dozens of containers. "Gennady
Efimovich, dismiss the men."

When they were alone Detrovna secured the roll-up doors
and the side entrance. No one would disturb them. Earlier that
afternoon he had ordered powerful floodlights set up. Cold
food and hot tea in insulated flasks stood on a table in a corner.
He waved toward the pond of documents. "You've taxed your
nerve and body in my service, Gennady Efimovich," he said.
"Now tax your eyes!"

The Attorney's face was still pasty. His eyes darted at the
doors, as if he wanted to be gone. "Put the day behind you!"
Detrovna growled. "The night needs you as well."

There was a seedy bathroom off the garage. After a visit
there the Attorney returned refreshed, his hair damp. He waved
at the containers, some holding neatly arranged papers, more
with tumbled piles. "We took everything we could find marked
1922," he said. "When we weren't sure, we chose to covet. It
was roughly done. We are not librarians."

Detrovna nodded. "Let us begin, then."

It was slow work through much handwritten material—
financial accounts, personnel records, memos, directives,
counter-directives, and propaganda pieces. Over all documents
was cast the shadow of Lenin. His Revolution had been
attacked from all sides like a newborn viper yet without size and
deadly venom. His response: ruthlessness, discipline, and
idealism. It worked for a while, Detrovna mused, before the
inevitable Russian crap again floated to the surface. He and the
Attorney struggled through the documents for hours.

Well after four in the morning the Attorney asked, "The
Chekist's name again, Boris Petrovich?"

"I was told it was Dishkin."

"Here is a folder with his name. *Personal Dossier—Yaroslav
Mikhailovich Dishkin.*"

Detrovna lunged toward the Attorney, eagerness painting his
face.

"It's empty!' the Attorney squawked. He snatched up
another. "This one is marked *Disciplinary Interview, Cheka Special
Unit 12—Recovery of Property of the Revolution. France, June 20-24,
1922.*"

"Surely that's it!"

"Also *empty.*"

Detrovna's howl of anger echoed from ceiling and walls. "Has a rival beaten us to what we want? Or has some K.G.B. revisionist done us the same disservice?" He remembered information provided from his American source and added half seriously, "Or do we bear the weight of the Sollonier witch's curse?"

The Attorney's response was a sidelong fearful look. "Come, look further, Boris Petrovich. If we're to be discouraged, let it be with reality, not some gypsy nonsense."

The rest of the night passed in further searching. They drank tea. They had no appetite. They sifted through the heaps of papers until ten the next morning.

Nothing!

As his hopes for certainty about the cache's location diminished, Detrovna shored up his resolve. What choice did he have but to gamble that it rested at the bottom of Lake Nagle?

He rubbed his aching eyes. In disgust he threw down a heap of memos. Enough! He glanced at his associate. A thin trickle of tears marked his sallow cheeks. Not surprising, considering the recent assaults on his body and nerves. "Cheer up, Gennady Efimovich! Shortly we'll be on our way to America."

The Attorney turned to him. Behind his pallor Detrovna glimpsed the inner rot of failing resolve. "I know of those plans," he whispered. "Why else would I weep?"

30

Iksha, north of Moscow

Nevsky and Alessya sat at a battered table in the narrow kitchen. On the oilcloth lay an envelope. He looked at it and heaved the first relaxed breath he had drawn in nearly three days.

Haste had driven them to Russia. No matter how fast they traveled, they worried that death might have been quicker to visit Gari Kusnetsov.

After customs delays at Sheremetyevo-2, "Moscow's Air Gateway," they caught the commuter rail north to Iksha where Alessya had arranged for a girlfriend named Irina to meet them with a car.

The ride to the hospital gave Nevsky a look at a small crumb of new era Russia. Like the old era Russia, he imagined—plenty of gray concrete bureaucracy-built apartment houses, lumpy streets, and ungenteel shabbiness. And an overwhelming sense of life lived with difficulty. His roots lay here. Right now he wasn't moved. He chided himself for applying Western standards. Russia had never been a Western nation.

If he needed further proof of his thesis, the former People's Hospital, Iksha Division—now the Bobikov Health Network Center—would have provided it. There was no shortage of staff, but shortages of everything else, including beds. He and Alessya were led to a couch set against the wall of a less-traveled hallway. A stone-faced nurse looked down and said, "This one is half with God" loud enough for God Himself to hear. After promising a quick return to chase the visiting couple away, she strode off.

Under a soiled sheet lay Gari Kusnetsov, an old man whose tissues had been rendered by cancer. Bones and skin were all that were left to him. Nevsky was relieved to find he wasn't drugged. No doubt there were no drugs available to ease his suffering. His large eyes and prominent nose above a fleshless face gave him the look of a permanently crippled hawk.

Alessya sank to her knees and threw her arms around him. Her mane of thick hair fell over his narrow chest. "God be merciful to you!"

"I'll take your request to Him...personally." Gari's laughter was a feeble croak. He shoved weakly at her head. She raised it and met his moist gaze. He said, "There's no time for sympathy. Listen! I knew where to look for what you wanted."

"Did you find it?" Alessya blurted.

He shook his head. "Listen, daughter. Don't talk!"

Alessya rolled her eyes. In them pity and impatience tussled.

"While amusing myself with your little investigation, my friends gossiped with me, as always," Gari croaked. "I heard that at high levels there was sudden interest in the 1922 Cheka papers. This told me something." His weak grin showed only two teeth. "One doesn't amuse oneself studying old secret police documents without fear and caution rubbing off."

Uneasiness roiled through Nevsky. He sensed the probing tentacles of Detrovna and Ostrovsky. Time! It could already be too late.

"It was for these reasons that I had to speak to you face-to-face, Alessya," Gari croaked. "One cannot yet trust Russian telephones. I own no scrambling device or fax machine." He chuckled—then choked—at the thought of new technology, as though anyone attaching any significant hope to it was mad. Recovering after a seizure of phlegmy coughing, he continued. "What I found I left with a trusted friend across town from my own apartment." A bony hand emerged from under the soiled sheet. Its index finger waggled warning. "Memorize, do not write down." He whispered an address. He followed it with two passwords, one to be used within the odd hour, the other within the even.

When they correctly whispered the information back to him, he visibly relaxed. His slightly bulging eyes closed with damp squishes.

"Gari Istvanovich, *what did the records say?*" Nevsky asked in a low but forceful voice.

The sick man nodded and began, "It was a strange—" Another burst of coughing cut off his speech. This time the seizure gripped him like a turtle beak. Crushing croupy whoops tore from his innards. He thrashed under the sheet. Nevsky tried to steady him with hands on shoulders thin as a starveling's.

"Nurse!" Alessya cried. *"Nurse!"*

"Don't call the nurse—" Nevsky bit down on a curse. The man might yet have talked! They might have *learned* after so much traveling and waiting. Then his humanity returned to renew his compassion for this suffering stick of humanity. Momentarily Nevsky had been afflicted with the corrupting power of the czar's riches. He had queued with the other "dark hearts" cursed by Natalia Sollonier. A chill ran through him. The cache's spider web! It tangled past, present, and future, and stank of impenetrable mystery, like Russia herself.

The stone-faced nurse arrived—and ordered the couple away. Alessya hesitated until Nevsky whispered, "If he talks now, she hears."

On the way back to the hospital entrance, he added, "Have your friend drop us in the middle of town. We'll find our own way."

"Irina can be trusted."

Nevsky thought of suspicious Charity Day. "*No one* can be trusted."

Better than an hour on foot took them to the address Gari had given them, another sprawling concrete apartment complex, this one with inoperable elevators. They tramped up the five flights. The apartment bell didn't work either. Alessya knocked. A woman's voice. "Who is it?" Alessya glanced at her watch and used the appropriate password.

A thin woman in a ragged cloth coat opened the door. She slammed the door behind them. Her gray hair was in a bun. Her eyes were like black darts. "What you want is on the kitchen table. I don't know what it is. I don't want to know! Gari told me to give you an order."

Alessya frowned. "What order?"

"Read, burn, and leave!" In seconds she was out the door and gone.

So now they sat looking down at the wrinkled manila envelope. Alessya pressed her palm possessively to it. She looked at Nevsky with a thoughtful smile. "If the Cheka hid the cache away and kept it secret..."

"Then?"

She patted the envelope. "Then this will show us where to find it. And only *we* will know where it is."

Nevsky studied her face closely. "And what would that mean to you, Alessya?"

She didn't hesitate. "It would mean I would see to it that Detrovna got none of it!"

"And past that?"

She made a tossing gesture. "What do I care? Give the treasure to poor Russians, if you like. It wouldn't go far among them, no matter its size."

"Maybe you'd do better for yourself to look past just vengeance," he said.

She exploded. Her gorgeous face contorted anew with the horror anchored by her father's murder. How could he presume to tell her how to feel and what to do? she screamed. Her almond eyes burned as banked rage burst into flames of resentment. Where was his passion and recklessness? Why hadn't he been moving the earth to bring the treasure to light as she and Korchevko expected? Whatever the documents on the table revealed, still *more* time would be needed to uncover the cache. How much longer were they going to give that lizard Detrovna? Before her outburst ended she was in tears.

He put his arms around her. She was so young! She still saw the world a simple place of straightforward cause and effect. The years had taught him that wasn't how it went. She saw order rimmed with chaos; he saw the opposite. And more! To him mystery shrouded all, man, beasts, bugs, and mountains. Nothing was what it seemed. She wouldn't understand. She wouldn't understand his grandfather, either, Nevsky thought. Explaining right then was a job words couldn't do. He shut his mouth and hugged her steadily until she stopped quivering.

Embarrassed now at her outburst, she tried to apologize. He cut her short. "You don't like to waste time. Neither do I. Let's see what Gari found for us."

They turned back to the kitchen table, expectation bright in their eyes.

Inside the envelope there were two sheaves of documents, each held together with a heavy-duty paper clip. One was the dossier on Yaroslav Mikhailovich Dishkin. Nevsky remembered he was the Chekist who murdered his grandfather and Natalia Sollonier and saw to it that the *Maria Nikolayevna* cube's contents were shipped to Moscow.

The couple hurried through those documents. Depending on the reader, Dishkin was either a hero of the Revolution or a monster. His was a childhood of misery and abuse that ended at an anti-government rally where a Cossack saber split his father's head. After that the lad became a revolutionary, a Bolshevik, a prisoner of the czar, a spy, and ultimately a member of the secret police. He had found his métier. He rose steadily through the hierarchy on a stairway of executions, assassinations, and betrayals. He was without the common vices. His vodka, cards, and whores were the Revolution. His reputation for efficiency and ruthlessness grew. It was not surprising that he was assigned to investigate the rumor that the czar had hidden a vast fortune for use during an exile into which he never went...

Other documents traced the rumor of the treasure. It began with the Cheka torture of a weak-minded member of the Sons of Continuity. He was vague on details but swore his group had been successful in gathering a vast treasure. After that the inquiry went nowhere for five years. It was resurrected when a French informant revealed that a certain drunken Russian peasant could be found nightly in a cafe in Sazilly south of Tours. With enough vodka in him he would tell an unlikely tale of having shepherded Nicholas II's "great cargo" to France.

Documents handwritten over Dishkin's name described what an effort it took to get this Lyubov the Wolfkiller to talk. The inquisition's methods took the peasant to death's door. But talk he did in the end, then expired in a wash of brutal curses.

Further Dishkin documents paralleled what Nevsky had learned from Sybille Sollonier. His narrative ended when the treasure reached his superiors. The tone of his final documents was one of oily expectation. Dishkin knew his efforts should be crowned with an impressive promotion. The czar's treasure now belonged to the Revolution!

The second clipped pile was a transcription of what seemed to be Dishkin's interrogation by one J. Shadoian, Senior Agent for Recovery of the People's Property. The transcriber used neither that name nor title. He preferred his *nom de guerre:* Talon.

The transcription was dated August 24, two months after Dishkin had turned over the treasure. Nevsky read the first part of the interrogation quickly. It concerned the Chekist's activities since returning from France, the birth of his daughter, Liberty, and meaningless administrative matters. The American's eye slowed when he came to...

Dishkin: I understand that a generous reward is being considered for me in view of my recent accomplishment. Vladimir Ilyich himself requested a full copy of my report on the recovery operation.

Talon: Considerations of such a reward have been...tabled, let us say.

Dishkin: But why—?

Talon: One does not question the actions of Comrade Lenin.

Dishkin: I think I'm owed an explanation.

Talon: Indeed. That is one of the reasons I summoned you. To begin with, let's consider what you brought home.

Dishkin: Yes! The Romanov treasure!

Talon: The more than seven thousand items you recovered were turned over to a large team of those with the skills to appraise them. As you can imagine, Comrade Dishkin, those at higher Party levels were in a sense continually looking over these men's shoulders.

Dishkin: Of course. We are speaking of a vast treasure.

Talon: As the appraisals continued, that interest increased. We are talking now about concern at the *very* highest levels.

Dishkin: To be sure. Lenin, Trotsky. What of it?

Talon: So when the true nature of the materials you brought to us became increasingly obvious, there was...disappointment at those levels.

Dishkin: Disappointment over *what?* You yourself said seven thousand precious items.

Talon: I said seven thousand *items.* You see, Yaroslav Mikhailovich, our appraisers—jewelers, chemists, and the like—tested every single piece you brought to us. When the first few were found to be *faux,* no one was concerned. Often the rich make mistakes or for a few rubles are able to deceive their envious friends. But as piece after piece was found to be mere costume jewelry, albeit of excellent quality, it became clear that what you brought us was *not* the Romanov treasure!

Dishkin: Talon, I had every reason to—

Talon: What you brought us was a cunning *dummy* treasure.

Dishkin: It can't be!

Talon: All seven thousand two hundred and sixty-three pieces were fakes—oh, not *quite.* Let the transcription note that from my desk drawer I am removing two diamond ear studs, two rings, and a thin golden figure on a chain. *These* are real gold and jewels. I hold Natalia Sollonier's earrings, unless I'm mistaken, and two wedding bands. Here is the inscription on one of them. "With all my love to Natalia—Jacques, June 24, 1907." We have checked. That was the Solloniers' wedding day. Sergei Nevsky's wedding ring bore no inscription. One of our chemists was a Swiss. He said this figure I'm dangling from its chain is Ulrich Zwingli, the Protestant reformer. It's a good luck charm. You took this from Nevsky, I assume?

Dishkin: I can barely find words! I only intended to further enrich the Revolution!

Talon: Instead you ought to have thought of enriching the Revolution with the *real* treasure, whatever it is, wherever it is.

Dishkin: [Gibberish]

Talon: Worse still, in your undisciplined revolutionary zeal you made a terrible error, an *unforgivable* error!

Dishkin: What?

Talon: You liquidated the only man on earth who knew the treasure's secrets! So it is lost forever to the proletariat whose blood was sucked to create it!

Dishkin: Comrade Talon, Nevsky begged pathetically for Natalia Sollonier to remain silent. He agonized when the cube was uncovered—

Talon: An act! Played for *your* benefit. You arrogant fool! Don't you understand? *Nevsky outwitted you!*

Dishkin: No! Nevsky was crawling, his wounded whore beside herself with terror—

Talon: Let the transcript show I am offering Comrade Dishkin the Zwingli figure. You should take this, Yaroslav Mikhailovich. It's supposed to bring good luck. You will need such luck now, comrade.

Dishkin: I don't understand.

Talon: Lenin himself decided your fate. Fifty years at hard labor.

Dishkin: [Wild gibberish]

Talon: You are familiar with...Sakhalin Island?

Dishkin: I—I was imprisoned there for five years by the criminal czar's secret police. I escaped—Comrade Talon, you already *know* this.

Talon: The facility has been temporarily taken over by the Revolution. What was the czar's penal colony is for now a government correctional labor camp for counter-revolutionaries, criminals, and those who have failed the people. Barrack Sixteen, Bunk Four?"

Dishkin: Once mine!

Talon: And yours once more, comrade!"

[Transcriber's Note: Comrade Dishkin jumped to his feet screaming. Talon called for assistance. Agents with experience in such situations entered hurriedly. Comrade Dishkin wildly resisted them. Unfortunately his right arm was broken. "Not enough to kill me and I curse the Devil for it!" he screamed. *"Not enough!"*]

Respectfully submitted: Svetlana P. Godor, Secretary to J. Shadoian

Alessya covered her face and sank down on her rickety kitchen chair. *"Nothing* has been hidden for just our benefit!" she cried. "The cache is as far away as ever! The lizard Detrovna will find it!"

"Only you and I know the truth about the Cheka and the cache," Nevsky said. "Let's try to keep it that way. See if we can use what we know."

He put the papers inside his shirt and took a kitchen match out of a can. He left the apartment and found the communal bathroom at the end of the hall. He burned the documents. Their dry old paper went up in a rush of flames. He flushed the ashes. Back in the apartment he said to Alessya, "Time for you to do some research for us."

She frowned. Her face had been dragged down by so many days of frustration and now fresh disappointment. Nonetheless Nevsky found her still lovely. "What research?" she asked.

"Find out where Sergei Nevsky's estate was. Find Great Meadow for us."

31

The former Red Banner Collective Farm east of St. Petersburg

The car hit another bump just past the broken gate. The vehicle had taken a beating on the roads to this remote place, never mind the four hundred miles of rude Russian road that brought them here. Nevsky told Alessya she owed her friend a suspension adjustment when they returned the car. She scowled. "You can find no one you can afford to do even such simple work. You see what a special favor Irina did us, insisting we borrow the car. You see what a good friend she is."

Nevsky slowed. The unpaved road was rutted, potholes frequent. Looking around, he had one thought: ruin. Farming equipment abandoned, fields mostly unsown, walls crumbled, newer buildings decayed, and older ones patched. He grinned sourly.

My family home...

Of course he had come here first in pursuit of the cache. Behind that, though, was his personal agenda in the whole affair: find himself. A visit to ancestral lands was a common strategy. A look around at rolling, unproductive acreage and miserable buildings all huddled under the vast Russian sky failed to spark any emotion except... Was it sorrow?

His mood wasn't improved when they descended on a cluster of state-designed concrete buildings in what had to be the center of the disintegrated collective farm. There his questions and Alessya's brightest smiles drew nothing useful from the locals. He had banked heavily on Father Fyodor's presumption that he needed only to announce himself and doors would be opened to the cubes.

His name had no effect whatever.

In fact, he had the feeling this wasn't the first time the group of ragged folk had been approached by strangers with questions. He felt stupid at not having devised some clever strategy to find out what he wanted.

As they wandered they were scrutinized by the curious, young and old alike. A lad with a walleye and small sharp teeth listened to only a few words from Nevsky's lips. He avoided the American's glance and scuttled away, dragging a leg in a cast from the knee down. A burly man with a huge borzoi at his side stared at Nevsky's face but didn't return his friendly nod.

After an hour of aimless wandering around the rough compound Alessya grew impatient. "Let's just start looking!" she said.

"Where?"

"Someone must know where the cubes are," she said.

"Who?"

She snapped an annoyed glance at him. "Don't you want to find what we came for?" she asked.

"We don't know where in the world to start."

"Well, let's just...start!" she said.

"This place reaches from horizon to horizon, Alessya. Flying off in any direction won't work." Nevsky stopped walking and turned in a slow circle. He knew eyes were on them, awaiting their departure. He thought about how much he wanted to see the cubes, how important they were. He could *taste* their significance, pieces in a puzzle that seemed to struggle with a life of its own not to be solved. He lowered his eyes.

He had no idea what to do next.

Over Alessya's complaining he decided to leave. He needed time to figure out what to do. Talk about trying to wing it... They got back in Irina's car and drove out of the main gate. A few hundred yards down the road someone stepped out of the shrubbery and flagged them down.

The burly man with the wolfhound.

He walked to the driver's side window. His cheeks and lips were thick, his black eyes quick and sharp. He stared intently into Nevsky's face. He stepped back and beckoned. "This way," he said, pointing toward a grassy track nearly hidden by a riot of unkempt bushes. A few hundred yards brought them to a stand of heavy blue spruce. The stranger beckoned them forward out of the car.

"I am Lyubov of the Dogs," he said. He pointed down at the borzoi. "This is Queen Catherine, my best animal." His voice had a sighing softness to it. Nevsky guessed he talked more to his animals than to people. "Follow me. Be quiet!"

He led them on a long walk through heavy woods that ended at a small clearing where sat his izba of square cut logs roofed by thatch. Its tiny windows carried heavy shutters. It smelled of earth and dog. He lit a kerosene lamp and closed the shutters. He pointed at a rough table beside which stood four low stools. "Sit." He brought out a bottle and put it on the table along with three thin plastic glasses. "You call yourself Yuri Nevsky, I understand." He nodded at Alessya. "This is your daughter?"

"A friend," Nevsky said.

Lyubov eyed her up and down and leered. They were both about the same age, just short of thirty. She glared at him. "What're you looking at, peasant fellow?" she asked.

"I look to see if you can be trusted, beauty."

Never patient, Alessya said, "What're you about that you should worry?"

His black eyes turned Sphinx-like with his silence. He would not be questioned. He would proceed in his own way. He opened the vodka and filled the glasses. The borzoi curled at his feet, big as a bear. He gave the first toast: *"Budem zdorovy!"* Health!

They tossed back the harsh vodka. Alessya gave the second toast: "To the help of new friends!"

Lyubov: "To old business made new!"

And off and toasting they were, Nevsky caught up in it. His intention was to get down to issues. Slowly it dawned on him that they were doing so—the Russian way. Lyubov opened the second bottle and said, "So tell me what it's like to be Yuri Nevsky, if such you are."

Nevsky attempted to describe his life. He made a decent start but abandoned the effort when a fit of remorse overcame him. He determinedly swallowed welling tears of what might have been self-pity. He talked then about his father's life, then his death linked with the cube marked *Olga Nikolayevna.*

This caused Lyubov to offer the toast. "To his memory!" And when they had drunk: "To old ways!"

Then Alessya: "To revenge!"

And Nevsky: "To the solution of puzzles!"

After more conversation and too many toasts to remember, Nevsky found himself as drunk as he had ever been, even as an undergraduate. His brain hung at that risky point between euphoria and the dizziness that for him led inevitably to nausea. His companions seemed to have better heads for liquor. Practice, undoubtedly. Lyubov proved he could still stand. He walked to a corner of the room. Under a pile of pelts and folded cardboard stood an antique chest. It was banded with steel. "This belonged to my great-grandfather, Lyubov the Wolfkiller," Lyubov said. "Kept in honor of his memory by his son, then his son, and now me." His black eyes found Nevsky. "Did you know the Wolfkiller served Sergei Nevsky?"

Nevsky shook his head. "Everybody thinks I know more than I do."

Lyubov's grin carried the cunning of an ancient race. "Then *that* is your strength, no?"

"So far."

"He sits and thinks! And waits for things to happen." Alessya glowered. "While our enemies march to victory!"

"A woman's tongue is sharper than a dog's tooth," Lyubov said.

Alessya was drunk, too. "Men are fools. Women should run the world!"

"Her visit to America has gone to her head," Nevsky said. "She imagines women have power there."

"I saw how you behaved with your Charity Day!" Alessya growled. "That wrinkled woman! So polite you were to her! So quick to let her do your thinking!"

Alessya was jealous, Nevsky realized. How could anyone be jealous over him? He said, "She saved both our lives, in case you forgot about the seven-foot priest loose in our bedroom."

Lyubov grunted loudly and stared at them. Alessya stared back. "What's bothering you, dog man?" she said.

Lyubov didn't answer. He only looked thoughtful. He opened his great-grandfather's trunk. From it he removed what looked like a square of cardboard. As he brought it closer Nevsky realized it was an image from the early days of studio photography. Lyubov slid the lamp toward the American. He compared the photograph with Nevsky's face. He tapped the card. "This is the image of my great-grandfather's master, Sergei Nevsky." His eyes moved between Nevsky's face and Sergey's. "Not exactly the same but close enough!" He dragged Nevsky to his feet and threw his arms around him.

Nevsky couldn't remember ever having embraced a man so enthusiastically. But he hugged this one reeking of dog, fish, vodka, and sweat. From the well of drink or some deeper one of heart or race his tears started to flow. Tremors of emotion shook him. He blubbered and coughed. In his tipsiness he clutched Lyubov as though he was the earth itself. Such outbursts were as strange for him as the hugging. Yet he felt no embarrassment for his smeared cheeks or the nakedness of his ill-defined emotions' outflow.

"You are Sergei Nevsky's blood, by our Savior!" Lyubov returned the hug until Nevsky's ribs clicked. He kissed his cheeks. "Know that God is in this business as well!" He shook his head. "How could He not be? So many years! So many paths that didn't lead here!" He released weeping Nevsky and hugged Alessya. She returned the embrace. "Is your nerve as sharp as your tongue, sister?" he asked. "To allow you to be with us in this search for cubes?"

"Sharper, little man!" Her face was red from drink. Loosened locks of her heavy hair curled like hooks. Nevsky's drunken thought: passion clothed in woman's flesh.

Night had come. They stepped out into the cooling air. Nevsky's head spun, and then steadied. He wiped away his tears. Displaying his emotions so brazenly made him feel exposed, like an overturned beetle. Alessya, however, was impressed. She put an arm around his waist. "You are a man with a heart, Yuritchka. A man who deserves someone to love him."

"Me, I have the love of Queen Catherine," Lyubov laughed. The sound had a near lilt, odd coming from one so bulky.

"One as ugly as you is lucky to have the love of such a beautiful creature," Alessya said.

"Inside!" Lyubov ordered. "Much yet needs to be said. We can begin with the priests ordained by the Devil himself. One of whom it seems you have already met..."

Lyubov no sooner began to tell his story about the visit of the two priests, one a giant who had to be the man who Charity shot, than Nevsky interrupted. "Describe the smaller one."

When Lyubov finished, Nevsky looked at Alessya. "Father Fyodor!" he said.

She cursed, clenched her teeth, and showed them.

Nevsky shook his head, trying to escape the vodka's effects and do some clear thinking. Fyodor and the murderous giant were a team! He recalled the long-faced priest's visit to 138 Morlande. He said he shared loyalty between Korchevko's Force for Leadership and the Orthodox Church. He had learned much on that visit. That Detrovna was diving for the treasure. That Sergei Nevsky's faith in Russia's God guided his handling of the eventuality of the czar never claiming his treasure. That there were three cubes. Father Fyodor suggested there were *four*. He then accused Nevsky of concealing information about the last.

Hold on! Before that visit he had been here in search of a cube. He couldn't have known about it unless Grushkin, the murderer, told him failing Father Ruslan's tale. He and Grushkin were allies! In time Nevsky would pry Grushkin's whereabouts out of the tainted priest. In time...

Standing under a canopy of stars the American made a shrewd guess about what had happened next. When he denied knowing anything about the cube marked *Anastasia Nikolayevna*, Father Fyodor sent his lethal giant to pay that terrifying nocturnal visit. If the monster had been successful, he would have carried Nevsky off and squeezed out of him everything he knew. Like a juiced orange, his remains would have been tossed away. What kind of "holy" man was Father Fyodor?

Lyubov told his story of the murder of Mitya of Great Meadow followed by the assault on Gregory the Odd that he ended with his wolfhounds. Nevsky's question was answered. Father Fyodor was a priest of the dark side. Who knew where he came down in all this, where his loyalties lay—if anywhere?

Alessya blessed herself. "No men of God. Two of the Devil's own."

Lyubov brought out a ragged loaf of heavy black bread then refilled the glasses. He ignored Nevsky's protests. "I will serve you as my ancestor did yours." He raised his glass. "To our forbearers! May our alliance please them!" The three drank and chewed tough chunks of the bitter bread.

Lyubov leaned forward. "Now let's talk about tomorrow..."

Tomorrow came too soon for Nevsky's aching head. His throat was raw from so much talking, or was it from the cheap vodka? A visit to the outdoor privy and a few splashes of icy water from the tub by the izba door helped some. "The walk will clear our heads," Lyubov said.

It took nearly an hour to reach Gregory the Odd's hut. Lyubov entered and Gregory came out with him. Startled Alessya whispered, "Here is a child of God!" Gregory was tall, pale, and thin. His high brow was haloed with fine white hair. He strode forward and stared into Nevsky's face. "You carry the blood of Sergei Nevsky?"

Nevsky nodded and Lyubov seconded with words about the photo.

Gregory stepped back and bowed. He blessed himself. "So God sees fit for me to at last discharge the obligation placed on my father and his father's father. He works His will and we can only marvel." He looked at Alessya. "Can you walk like a man?"

An insult reached toward her lips, but the ascetic's spell checked her tongue. "My legs are strong and my shoes good," she said. "Let's go!"

They set out into heavy scrub that soon became forest. Lyubov whispered to Nevsky, "In truth only he knows where your cubes are hidden. Until the priests came, I had no idea *what* was hidden. Some of those others living here know of the Odd One. None know his secret." He spat. "You saw the lout with the broken leg?"

Nevsky remembered the wall-eyed boy with the feral teeth. "What about him?"

"He betrayed the Odd One and cost Mitya his life. I broke his shin by way of a small lesson in behavior."

Further along Lyubov asked hesitantly. "Why do you want to see these cubes?"

"I'm not sure," Nevsky said.

Lyubov shook his head. "Such a strange business!" He eyed Nevsky with the particularly sharp vision that bright sunlight gives to the hungover. "Such a strange man I've agreed to help."

The forest grew thicker, then impenetrable with pines boughs crossing everywhere like checkpoint barriers. Behind Gregory they took to a wide waist-deep stream. Slipping and struggling through the icy water, they followed it uphill. Ahead above pine tops towered a rock face several hundred feet high. They splashed upward to a natural basin at the foot of the rock.

The stream issued from the bottom of a high tumble of boulders that completely filled a narrow V in the soaring rock. Only those with mountaineering gear could climb that height.

Where did one go now?

Gregory explained. At the basin's bottom was a wide pipe running through the rock. Were any of them unable to swim fifteen meters underwater? No? Then follow him!

The icy stream, the darkness, or danger of drowning didn't chill Nevsky's excitement. He dove and kicked hard. As he swam, he thought. He came to understand that in 1922, 1942 and 1952 a cube had been manhandled through the forest below, and then floated up the stream. Many boulders had been removed from the V in the rock. A cube was carried through. Then the boulders were replaced. Slow, repetitive work, but what drawback was that to pious priests who dwelt in this vast slow-moving land?

Surfacing, he scrambled onto a grassy bank. Patches of woodland ran up to the rock walls. Roughly centered below the towering natural barriers was a clearing.

In its center was a low stone structure with a copper roof.

Gregory, still shivering from immersion, led the three dripping figures forward. Their soaked shoes squished with every step. Nevsky saw the structure was divided into bays. Each had a heavy wooden door mounted on hand-wrought iron hinges. Gregory pointed at the doors. "The master Sergei Nevsky built this with his own hands and left it empty, or so it was told me. Then the cubes arrived, one at a time. They are well protected."

Nevsky stared and blinked. The structure had four doors. *Four doors!*

The last surely held the fourth cube marked *Anastasia Nikolayevna!*

The one that held the Romanov Cache!

Lyubov urgently touched his arm. "Listen! Queen Catherine gives the alarm!" They had left the bitch on the other side of the rock. He heard her faint frantic baying. Something was happening by the pool.

Another, much louder sound chilled Nevsky and froze him. He couldn't mistake the roaring mechanical clatter.

A helicopter was coming in fast!

32

Moscow

The phone awoke the Attorney in the middle of the night. Detrovna. Come at once! There was work to be done. He hung up and groaned.

His wife rolled over. "Go. He pays you so well!"

Margarita knew nothing about Detrovna's dark side. Behind her smooth brow and lively eyes did not sit an analytical engine. Her life sailed the sweet seas of naiveté. She was proud and happily complacent. Her husband? An attorney serving one of Russia's most prestigious political figures...

Within five minutes the Attorney had reinforced himself with two generous sniffs of cocaine. At this hellish hour, before his nose's innards began their daily swelling, the impact was instantaneous—and welcome! Within a half-hour he was a bright-eyed go-getter alarming two drowsing suite bodyguards. Detrovna ordered him admitted. Before he could sit, his master said, "A call from America! And much fast work for you!"

The Attorney raised an eyebrow.

"Nevsky is coming here! I believe he's coming to find the *Olga Nikolayevna* cube. But I can't be sure."

"The cubes, the cubes..." The Attorney's face turned sour. "What about Lake Nagle?"

Detrovna advanced and took his underling's shoulder in a hard grip. "You well know I cannot take chances around the cache. So no loose end that I know of can be ignored. We must satisfy ourselves about the meaning and purpose of the cubes. Or about what other, unknown secret business Nevsky might be about."

The Attorney had always appreciated Detrovna's thoroughness. "Then let's do so," he said.

"You might be amused to know with whom Nevsky's traveling."

"Who?"

"Alessya Harsky!" Detrovna said.

"Her? How—?"

"I was told her whole purpose in life now is to see my search for the cache defeated—and me dead. It seems she discovered we liquidated her father. She went first to the Force for Leadership, then to Nevsky, with copies of Harsky's documents. Luckily his map was destroyed before she saw it.

So neither she nor others know anything about Lake Nagle. I don't fear her. She's scarcely more than a child. But again I find myself wishing we had spared her father. He might have been able to help us further, willingly or not. Gennady Efimovich, I made an error there." Detrovna straightened his back as though to throw off the past. "My source learned of Nevsky's intentions so recently that we have little lead time. We must rely instead on your efficiency, my friend."

Still in his pajama bottoms Detrovna explained what he wanted.

A great deal. Still, the Attorney heaved a sigh of relief. The trip to America was delayed. Who knew, but permanently? Fine! An ill wind blew through his mind when contemplating that journey.

Detrovna put a heavy arm over the Attorney's narrow shoulders. He flinched. The increased weight caused his wounded hip to flash with pain. "These recent days haven't been easy on you, I know, my friend," he said. "But listen. Carry this off as I've outlined and..." His beefy face broke into a sly grin. "A bureaucrat has lost his villa to our loan sharks. Do you know where it is? Rome! I'm told its flowers bloom in profusion. The sun there makes any winter-frozen Russian's head ache with pleasure."

The Attorney's heart leaped. A big part of his dream! Here was a lucky coincidence. He steadied his voice. "What of it?"

"Yours if you don't fail."

Yes!

His master waved at the communications equipment. "Use anything you wish." He turned toward his bedroom. "Wake me only if there's a problem." He glowered. "I don't expect there will be."

The Attorney's first call was to Stroganov at Lake Nagle. He asked to speak to either Peter Ivanovich or Dominick Voysovich. In time Ivanovich was on the line.

He ordered him and his partner to race immediately to Greater Pittsburgh International Airport. He gave them the description of Nevsky provided Detrovna by his source. More importantly he described Alessya Harsky. Here was a traveler not likely to be overlooked. Ivanovich asked the Attorney what he wanted from them.

"Nevsky's coming here," he said. "I need to know when and where he's landing. If you find him, call me with the flight information. Am I understood?"

"Of course."

"Here are some things to help you. He's in a hurry. If there's a direct flight, he'll take it. If not, he'll take one with the fewest stops. We're guessing he's headed to Moscow, Peter, or Kiev. Call me any time when you know more."

His next call was to Brooklyn, New York. He needed the services of Vasily Brudikov with whom he had already enjoyed doing business in person. Brudikov, the efficient—and expensive. The Attorney explained his problem. It didn't seem a great one to the émigré.

"I doubt there are direct flights from Pittsburgh to Russian cities," Brudikov said. "Very likely Nevsky will come through JFK. I'll have men by the desks of the carriers flying into the cities you named. We'll hope he doesn't choose an indirect route. I'll check the airline schedules from Greater Pittsburgh. He *could* go through another major hub, of course."

"Let's wait and see," the Attorney said. "I'll call you again later today. About paying you—"

"Forget it!" Brudikov said. After a short pause, he went on, "I'm told it's not going all that well at Lake Nagle."

The Attorney swallowed. Trying to sound casual, he said, "We may abandon the project. It's conceivable we were misinformed. In any case work there seems to be drawing to a close."

"Then maybe you'll tell me what you were trying to find?"

"Boris Petrovich isn't yet ready to share that."

"I understand. I hope that if you're successful, you remember that I can be a great help to you in this country. I know its ways."

The Attorney tried to put himself in Detrovna's brain. In an icy voice he said, "I hope you wait to be invited to help. And aren't so rash as to take any action without invitation."

"All I ask is if there's profit, I'm invited to share it."

"I'll raise the issue with Detrovna."

"Of course."

The Attorney hung up shaking his head. Brudikov was sniffing around the edges of the thing. Damn him! So far he hadn't guessed or been told about the cache. Thank God for that. Nonetheless, time might yet allow him to find out. More pressure on Detrovna to wrap it all up. For the Attorney, another worry!

Among many.

Had the Cheka consumed the entire cache? That open question ate at his master and him. If it had escaped security's claws, why had the divers brought up nothing but ruined curiosities by the thousands—and nothing else worth more than a few kopeks?

The Attorney indulged his nostrils again. All these worries could be put to rest if Nevsky led them to the cube and some kind of clue or message was wrenched out of it. Even the flash of drug euphoria did not cast that eventuality in a likely light. His mind spun away toward divers, confounding cubes, and an aristocratic witch's curse...

Instinct whispered again that it was all too much, even for Detrovna.

They should abandon the search for the cache.

But would not.

He paced before his master's expanse of windows overlooking the Moscow sprawl as dawn crept into the late June morning. Here he could enjoy the pleasure of ordering by telephone a breakfast with good coffee. But his appetite had left him.

Where was the call from Pittsburgh?

Nearly two hours had passed since he talked to Ivanovich. New bodyguards presented themselves. He curtly nodded welcome and they replaced the night men. He waited.

The phone rang!

Ivanovich. Success! Nevsky and Alessya Harsky had boarded the 12:10 Delta Airlines flight to New York's JFK. The Attorney praised their good work and hung up. A small victory. He needed a string of them to own the Roman villa. His hands poured sweat.

He called Brudikov with the information. "Excellent! They suspect nothing, so they're taking the fastest, most direct route. Their time of arrival and the schedules suggest they'll be on the Aeroflot 3:00 PM flight to Moscow. A direct one. It arrives at Sheremetyevo at 8:20 AM tomorrow. You'll hear from me again. If you're in a hurry to act, you can do so on a reasonable assumption..."

By midday the Attorney had gathered a reliable cadre. Among them was rotund Raskov, the electronics specialist. He described the two travelers for his men, but didn't name them. They were to be followed without realizing it. *Without realizing it!* The exits from Sheremetyevo would all be covered. Raskov was to see to the hand-held radios, more reliable than the city's capricious cell phone systems. The Attorney would be on hand to personally supervise the surveillance.

When the others were leaving, he asked Raskov to stay behind. "Bring your best portable equipment with you," he ordered. "I mean listening devices, night vision glasses, homing beacons. Whatever you have that might help us avoid losing the two of them. Understand?"

Raskov nodded. He seldom spoke. But his eyes, turned small and piggish by impossibly thick glasses, missed nothing.

When Detrovna awoke, the Attorney briefed him. He nodded agreeably. "Excellent so far." He added, "If Nevsky leads you to the cube, we must seize it. I want to be there for that. Arrange it. I'll be busy these next few days, but available."

The Attorney sweated afresh. Once more he hurried to the phone...

When Nevsky and Alessya boarded the commuter train heading north, the Attorney, Raskov, and two thick-shouldered men scrambled aboard the car behind them. The more nondescript of the two went ahead to Nevsky's car to maintain visual contact.

The Attorney was uneasy. There were too many ways the couple could slip away from them once they left the train. He would have to think and act quickly.

They detrained at the Iksha station, the quartet behind them strung out to be less noticeable. Outside the building the Attorney was unhappy to see the couple get into a car driven by a woman who had obviously been waiting for them.

His men looked to him for direction. He ran toward an idling Mercedes, waving his men after him. He jerked open the door and shoved a roll of U.S. twenty-dollar bills under the driver's nose. "These for you now! The same under the seat when we're finished with the car. To pay for your inconvenience." The man hesitated, sputtering. The Attorney motioned to his largest agent. He dragged the driver out onto the sidewalk and jumped behind the wheel. In moments the Attorney and the others had tumbled in and were in pursuit of Nevsky's car.

The Attorney called to his driver. "Stay as far behind as practical. We must *not* be seen."

How to continue not to be seen occupied the Attorney's thoughts until his quarry reached its destination, a medical center in the northern suburbs. Nevsky and Alessya rushed inside. The woman waited in the car.

The Attorney ordered a man to follow the couple and to use the radio if they went out a different exit.

Now was the time to seize the instant, the Attorney thought. There could be no hesitation. Nevsky could return at any moment. He climbed out of the Mercedes and knocked on the driver's side window of the woman's car. He peered in, smiling.

She was short of thirty. In her long face were set covetous blue eyes with unusually wide pupils. Her hands carried no rings. She wore no earrings either. Her clothes were plain. She wasn't a beneficiary of the skewed new prosperity. She leaned toward him, but didn't open the window. "What?"

There was no time for stylish maneuvers. He held up another roll of twenties. "These are yours for answers to a few questions."

The covetous eyes widened. She rolled down the window a handbreadth. "The money first!" she said.

Ahh, the Attorney thought. Here was a transparent soul indeed! Speaking quickly, he asked her why Nevsky and Alessya had come to this clinic. She said she didn't know. Nor did she know where they were going next. Alessya was a casual friend; she, Irina, was doing her a favor. No, she hadn't thought about how long that favor would continue.

The Attorney charged ahead. "Let it continue as long as they like," he said.

Irina sniffled lightly, brushed her nose with the back of her hand. "How can I? I need my car. And who are you anyway, and what do you really want?"

The Attorney smiled afresh. "I want to make sure you're well compensated for allowing Alessya to continue to use this car."

Her brow furrowed. "Why? And who—"

"Compensated as well for not asking questions."

"Are you going to...hurt her?"

"Your final question, Irina! The answer is no," the Attorney said. A lie? Who could guess? He knew only that Detrovna wanted information, not blood. He pulled out his last roll of twenties and shoved it through the opening.

She took it. She sniffled again and brushed her nose. Her wide eyes met the Attorney's with a whore's frankness. "Thank you, but that's not enough."

"Irina..."

"I don't know who you are or why you want her to use this car, but it must be very important to you to throw me American

money as you do. Important enough for you to pay me more."
She sniffed again.

The Attorney's thoughts lunged this way and that like a
frightened aquarium fish. So damned much was riding on these
unanticipated negotiations. The Roman villa... As he hesitated
Irina rubbed her nose again.

Then he knew. The nose! The eyes! His smile widened to a
beaming grin. Luck was with him this day.

He and she were as alike as two kasha grains.

He whispered, "In my car, in my briefcase, I have seventy-
five grams of Colombian cocaine. It's yours if you do as I wish."

Her first smile! She had good teeth, a nice mouth—and a
habit like his! "I would do far worse for so much drug," she
said. "Get it!"

On the way to the Mercedes he spoke with Raskov. The
heavy man hurried to hide a homing device beneath the car.
The Attorney let out a long breath. Some pressure was off.
They would not lose Nevsky. Nor would he see them.

He carried the unlatched briefcase back to Irina. He slid
into the front seat, opened the case, and unzipped a
compartment. He removed a glassine bag and gave it to her.

'Radi boga! I can't believe this!" She snatched the bag,
noticed that it had already been opened. She moistened her
fingertip and took up a sugaring of drug. She tasted it. Her
smile widened. She closed the bag and slid it under her seat.
"I'll do as you wish," she said.

The Attorney closed the briefcase. "You will be most
persuasive in offering your car, Irina. But not overly so."

"What will happen if they don't need it or won't take it?"
Anxiety filled her voice. She had guessed the kind of men with
whom she dealt.

"Nothing," the Attorney said. In saying that, he said
everything. He doubted she would dare to fail.

His man hurried out of the clinic. In the car he said, "They
were visiting a sick man, nothing more. He gave them nothing."

Matters then went forward smoothly. After a short ride
Nevsky and Alessya left the car and began to walk. The
Attorney followed them to an apartment house, and then sent a
man up after them. He reported the couple stayed in a unit for
about twenty minutes after a woman left it empty-handed.
Nevsky used the bathroom. Nothing more. Again, they left
with nothing in hand.

Alessya then made a phone call from a public stand a few blocks away. Shortly Irina appeared with the car. She got out, the couple got in, and off they drove. The Attorney beamed. The woman had done her work well! He settled back in the seat as the leisurely pursuit continued.

The roads Nevsky chose carried them north.

The couple drove until well after dark, then pulled into a lay by and slept. The Attorney consulted his maps. He had done some research on the location of Nevsky's ancestral estate. He guessed Detrovna was right. The American was headed toward it. Somewhere there the cube was hidden. He ordered only two men to sleep at a time. The others were to see to the homing receiver and maintain visual contact with Nevsky's car through a screen of trees.

Before he dozed—when had he last truly slept?—he radioed Detrovna's headquarters. He asked for six more men, these to bring a variety of small arms. They were to leave immediately and join him here. He then spoke with Detrovna himself and explained what tomorrow might bring. He should be ready.

It took the better part of the next day to complete the drive. When the couple arrived at the estate, Raskov watched their wanderings through a powerful telescope from nearby high ground.

Similarly, night vision glasses were used to make sure the couple and the man with the dog remained in the izba.

Reinforcements arrived before dawn. The Attorney ordered their silence. Their car was hidden.

When the three emerged from the cottage and prepared to set out, the Attorney used the radio. His transmission was expected at the military base on the Moscow outskirts where his master's influence was substantial. They knew what he wanted: it was time to fetch the man.

He phoned his master, briefed him, and told him to be ready. By the time he was airborne the Attorney promised they would be closing in on the cube. He would be in radio contact with the helicopter pilot. Nevsky, Alessya, and the peasant marched off, a dog at their heels. The Attorney thanked God that the breeze was in their face. The animal wouldn't smell them. In respect for that possibility, he kept his men farther behind than normal.

At a hovel in the deep forest the trio met another man: their guide. They took a long hike across increasingly inhospitable terrain. They pressed on, the Attorney and his men trailing safely behind them.

So it was that when they came up to the pool at the foot of the towering cliff, the Attorney's heart sank.

The three had completely disappeared!

His innards twisted. Above all, he had battled not to lose Nevsky. And now... He thought of the villa and the speeded retirement it meant now borne away on the dark wings of a magical disappearance.

Then he saw the dog fussing by the water's edge. Seeing them, it began to bark. Before long the mystery was solved. He sent four men into the water first. An underwater tunnel went forward, they reported. He ordered them into it. One man returned to say the swim wasn't difficult. There was a wide meadow beyond the mountain of stone.

The Attorney contacted the helicopter and described the terrain, told the pilot to put down in the mountain bowl. Though not fond of cold water he plunged into it. His breath left him at the shock. Mountain streams be damned! He floundered to the far rock face, heaved in a half dozen deep breaths, and then held the last. He did an awkward surface dive that carried him down to the tunnel's entrance.

He kicked and stroked. His efforts were too weak to keep him in the pipe's center. He was borne upward. His head thudded against cement. He saw stars. He lost half his air. Panic touched him with fiery fingers. With each frantic swimming kick his wounded hip screamed with pain.

He clenched his teeth to better hold onto himself. Then he swam wildly. He bent back one of his fingernails on the rough metal. Now his shoes were soaked and dragged down his legs. Still there was no end to the pipe.

His swimming became mad thrashing. His lungs were on fire.

He wasn't going to make it!

Then the big hand of one of his men caught his pants at the hip—his wounded one. He screamed. Water flooded his mouth, filled his throat! He would certainly have drowned, except that the man pulled him to the surface.

Coughing and vomiting, he allowed himself to be half dragged onto the soft grass.

With smeared vision he saw Nevsky, Alessya, the peasant, and their guide surrounded by his knife-wielding men. Then he heard the helicopter! Thank God! He had done his job well. Detrovna would be pleased.

His Roman dream was still alive!

33

Detrovna shouted to his soldiers over the helicopter's roar. He was in command. Follow him! He leaped out, legs made younger by confidence in the coming cache breakthrough.

He saw Alessya Harsky with others, all ringed by his men. She looked more beautiful than he remembered. Having had her moaning under him made overlooking her beauty easier. He saw a burly peasant and a gaunt, disturbing man with a halo of fine white hair. The bald one about Detrovna's age had to be Nevsky.

He ordered his men to lower their weapons, but keep them ready.

He beckoned Nevsky forward. When he approached, Detrovna apologized for the physical threats. He studied the American's face, trying to read his feelings. He introduced himself and offered his hand. To his satisfaction Nevsky took it, though his expression was totally neutral. Detrovna had been told the American was cooperating with both the Force for Leadership and the Church. Conceivably he was also hand in hand with the rightist clique that energetic interrogation of the captured woman before she expired had revealed was called the Sons of Continuity. The man was everyone's ally. And it seemed not Detrovna's enemy. However, what he meant to the search for the cache was not so transparent. Detrovna made a guess.

Catalyst and key both.

"I'm very pleased to meet you," Detrovna said.

"I know who you are and what you want," Nevsky said.

"I can say the same," Detrovna replied.

"No, you can't."

Detrovna frowned. He wondered if the American, in addition to being a hard man to read, was wholly right in the head. He ordered his soldiers to search him and his companions for weapons.

His eyes turned to the structure with the four doors. He asked Nevsky what he knew about it.

He told him his grandfather had built it with his own hands. "Four doors." He added, "Behind them maybe four cubes."

Detrovna's heart pounded. Was the treasure at last within easy reach, no matter all his efforts at the Lake Nagle site? Nevsky volunteered his belief that the cubes had been brought through the V in the mountain over the decades with the help of determined priests.

"Why all four cubes?" Detrovna asked. "Why not just the one with the treasure?"

"I haven't figured out the cubes yet," Nevsky said. "Neither has anybody else. Maybe this is our chance." He grinned. "Then again, maybe it isn't."

Detrovna found this air of ambiguity and lightheartedness distasteful, even unpleasant. Such did not sit well with him. Men of action like him needed a clear field in which to operate. One could not play chess with half the board smothered in fog.

"Open the doors!" he shouted to his soldiers. He followed on their heels, ordering Nevsky and his companions after him.

The solid oak doors weren't locked, just latched. All were nicely designed to hang balanced from heavy handcrafted hinges. The first swung open at the touch of a soldier's hands so smoothly and silently that it seemed a daily event. The cubical bay presented a square surface of slightly tarnished aluminum. Its black letters below the red double eagle might have been painted yesterday.

Olga Nikolayevna!

The second bay opened. *Tatiana Nikolayevna!*

The third. *Maria Nikolayevna!*

Here were czarist doings, no doubt! Past times. Past ways. And wealth possessed on a scale to dwarf present greed. Detrovna's heart busied itself in his chest. He drew in a heavy breath. He hurried to stand before the final bay. Behind it lay the elusive last cube.

The one marked *Anastasia Nikolayevna!*

In it lay all or some of the Romanov Cache.

The final door swung open as smoothly as the others.

The bay was empty!

"Where is the last cube?" he bellowed at Nevsky and the others. For his trouble he received blank stares.

Shortly he held a conference—he, the Attorney, Nevsky, and his cronies. They stood in the empty bay. The others were ordered out of earshot.

Alessya shook her fist at Detrovna. "You'll get nothing like help from me, murderer!" she shouted. "Nevsky and the pale one are fools enough in themselves. You won't find me being a third!"

Detrovna faced her raging with unblinking eyes. "I made a mistake with your father for which I'm very sorry—"

She howled and spat in his direction, a trace of the warm spray touching his face. His own rage flared. How did she dare! Hosts had died by his orders. One woman more would scarcely matter. Many deaths were a necessary byproduct of Russian political success. And yet... He stayed the words that would have slaughtered her. Alessya Harsky was *not* the matter now concerning him. He heaved a heavy breath and turned his back on her for a moment to recover perspective and temper. When he turned back it was to glare at Nevsky. "If she's yours now, control her!"

"The first is unlikely. The second, impossible," Nevsky said. Nonetheless he turned to the girl. "Be quiet or you'll end up meat for Lyubov's borzois."

She growled but said nothing more.

Detrovna soon learned that the one more apparition than man had been custodian of the cubes for most of his life. He was inclined not to speak. Only the encouragement of the burly peasant could squeeze a few words from the ascetic's lips like meager drops from a dry lemon.

"God put three cubes here before my time," Gregory the Odd said. "The final space was never filled."

Detrovna made an impatient gesture. *"Where is the fourth cube?"* He glowered up at the serene face atop the pole-like body.

The pale blue eyes returned his glance with sublime indifference. Gregory's silence spoke eloquently of total ignorance about the fourth cube.

"You *must* know something more—"

"He doesn't," interrupted the peasant.

Detrovna swallowed his annoyance. Instinct told him not to torment the ascetic. He turned to Nevsky in something like desperation. "What do *you* know of the fourth cube, Yuri Vladimirovich?"

The American's persistent smile still irritated Detrovna. "I know enough of my grandfather's thinking to tell you one certain thing."

"So? Tell it."

"Just because there's this space for a cube doesn't mean the fourth cube would fit it—or that there *is* a fourth cube."

"You talk nonsense!"

"I'm talking the way Sergei Ivanovich thought. Nothing in this whole treasure hunt has been what it seemed." Nevsky turned a peculiarly intense gaze on Detrovna. He waved his hand to include everything in the clearing. "Anyway, none of this matters. The cache is gone. The Cheka got it in 1922."

Detrovna was a master at hiding his feelings. Thus he didn't betray his innards' downward swooping.

"How do you know this?" the Attorney asked in a tight voice.

"I read the Cheka files about the cube hidden in France." He pointed to the third bay. "That one, *Maria Nikolayevna*." He explained how the documents had reached his hands.

Like Detrovna the Attorney well remembered the two titled but empty file folders, the pitiful fruit of the death of three men and the wounding of seven others. He drew closer to Nevsky. "Describe the files!"

"Two piles. One a dossier on Dishkin," Nevsky said. "The other a transcription of his interview by a man called Talon. Talon had heavy responsibilities in 'the recovery of the property of the Revolution.'"

"What happened to the cache?" Detrovna said, his voice snagging like cat claws in velvet.

"It was 'made the property of the people,'" Nevsky said. "What else? Food for the hungry Revolution."

"Why was Dishkin's interview a disciplinary one?" Detrovna asked.

"He had dipped in before he turned over the bulk of the treasure."

So... There was no doubt Nevsky had seen the missing documents. Detrovna's glance caught the eagerness to believe in his Attorney's eyes. Possibly it was mirrored in his own. Belief meant the end of their quest. It meant a kind of peace. Even so, he was moved to skepticism. He took an automatic rifle from the nearest soldier. He thumbed off the safety and jacked a round into the chamber. He put the barrel against the side of Nevsky's head.

There was a long moment of human stillness. Detrovna heard insect buzz and the cries of birds. He could smell rich soil and sun-warmed grass. "I fear you're lying," he said softly. "You're trying to end our efforts while you continue on to the treasure."

"No," Nevsky said. "From the start, I never wanted to find it."

Detrovna chuckled hollowly. "To be sure."

"I don't think you should want to find it either," Nevsky went on. "You or any of the others."

Detrovna frowned. What kind of conversation was this? Possibly this man was a lunatic after all. "Speak clearly. Make sense!"

"The cache is too much for any of us. You could say none of us are 'worthy' of possession, as Countess Sollonier said—while cursing Dishkin and all of us who come after."

Detrovna chuckled. "And who would judge who is worthy and who isn't? Sollonier's ghost? Some celestial power? An angelic tribunal?"

"Who knows?" Nevsky said. His grin was infuriating. "Maybe Mother Russia herself."

Detrovna was certain the American was crazed. How else could he explain his fearless eyes so unlike those of other men against whose skulls the Russian had pressed cold steel. Fearless, even as he chatted—was it philosophy, mysticism, or outright nonsense? Whatever, Detrovna had no time for such musings. He nudged Nevsky's head with the weapon. "I don't believe you're being honest with me. Listen, my good friend. I'm going to kill you unless I hear the truth. The *absolute truth!* I will count to three..."

Detrovna deepened his study of the American's eyes. What he saw there made him understand he had made an error. Nevsky was prepared to die to put the stamp of truth on what the Russian suspected was a lie.

And in death raise the lie to the edge of truth.

So that all who continued after the cache would be hobbled with the crippling doubt: it no longer existed!

Possibly there was even more to the man's suicidal intransigence. It was this: that if he, the key and catalyst, died prematurely as his grandfather had, the cache would never be uncovered. The "unworthy" would be defeated. The younger Nevsky had donned his grandfather's mantle—gatekeeper of the treasure.

Detrovna wrenched inwardly. It seemed everything to do with the Imperial horde twisted and turned back on him like an ill-pinned viper. He glanced around quickly. His men and Nevsky's trio were frozen for the moment in witness to his next move.

Retract his threat? All would see him as a weak old woman. Kill Nevsky? He sensed that would be an insurmountable error, too. Even so... He began, *"One...two..."* And took up the trigger's slack.

Alessya's shriek bit into his ears. *"Stop!* He's lying!" She rushed toward him. "He's gone crazy! Don't believe anything he says. I was with him. I read the documents, too. The Cheka found a treasure. But it was fake!"

So... Emotions thrashed in Detrovna's chest. He lowered his weapon. The infernal Nevsky's eyes showed not one crumb of relief. Madman!

Thus distracted Detrovna didn't see the Needle flash high in Alessya's hand. "Die, murderer!" she shrieked. Too sudden to be stopped, the dagger dived down toward his chest.

And merely pricked it.

The swift-footed peasant's iron grip on Alessya's forearm checked the blow. She howled in frustration as Lyubov twisted the Needle out of her grip. "He dies, we all die, sister," the peasant said. "Lyubov of the Dogs isn't yet curious about the grave." Alessya lunged and squirmed in rage. The peasant had to wrap a thick arm around her waist and raise her off the ground. She spat at Detrovna and clawed the air. Her heavy breasts heaved. Between them his searcher for weapons hadn't dared grope.

"You were lucky that time, Detrovna," Nevsky said. "Keep after the cache and see if your luck holds."

Detrovna backed away, staggering slightly. To his soldiers he said, "Guard them. Shoot if they so much as scowl." Sweat poured down his face. He beckoned to the Attorney. They stood apart. His underling began expressions of relief at his master's narrow escape. Detrovna cut him short with a curt wave. "Gennady Efimovich, what do you make of this business of the fourth cube, likely marked *Anastasia Nikolayevna?*"

"I believe the snow-haired hermit. He's never seen it."

"Where do you think it is?"

The Attorney did a poor job is masking his sigh. "America, after all," he said in a near whisper.

Detrovna nodded agreement. At least that, of all recent goings-on, made some sense.

He ordered his soldiers to load the three cubes into the cargo helicopter. They would go to America with him and the Attorney. There he hoped secrets could be lured from their aluminum maze.

He returned to the Attorney's side and studied him closely for the first time since landing. He was pale with the pain of his wound and shaking, his clothes sodden. A snail track of mucous eased from his nose. Detrovna nodded toward the foreign quartet. "What should we do with them, Gennady Efimovich?"

The Attorney drew his finger across his throat.

Detrovna pondered. Nevsky's passive resistance seemed to have mesmerized him. His imagination had been sparked for the worst, he decided. Phantoms and fears had sprung up like toadstools. Enough nonsense! They must be shot. He spoke hurriedly to the four soldiers. At some distance from the captives, so as not to alarm them, they prepared their weapons. They slowly advanced. He moved behind them.

Nevsky, Lyubov, and Alessya looked toward them warily, like grazing antelopes scenting lion. The ascetic Gregory wandered with eyes raised to the white puffy clouds scudding like celestial ships across the blue sea of the sky.

The soldiers raised their weapons and the three froze, the ascetic oblivious.

Alessya took a step forward, pulled her arms back and thrust her chest forward. She shrieked, "Go ahead, you scum! Shoot straight, if you can!" Her eyes flashed. She was like a young soldier, not afraid to kill or die. Despite his recent burst of aggression, vague regrets once again assaulted Detrovna.

Nevsky stared at Detrovna who now had even less liking for his gaze than he had moments earlier. Having their lives in his hands gave him no sense of either power or pleasure. What was wrong?

The Attorney, his voice a nervous rasp, told the soldiers to take aim.

Detrovna's eyes moved back to Alessya. Her hair had in part unbound and snaked down over her shoulder like a heavy jet rope. He remembered it spread like a fan on the bed sheets of their short-lived love nest. She had given him much pleasure. Gave it honestly, without guile. As she now howled defiance in the face of death her gaping mouth exposed inner lips and the pink tool of her uninhibited tongue...

Abruptly an ugly image rushed forward from Detrovna's past—that of his love Fatima lying in a Kabul street with her leg blown off. Dying.

Was he now a murderer of woman, too?

And of peasants like this queer Lyubov?

And Nevsky. Detrovna had murdered Aleyssa's father and now mightily regretted it. Was he about to make the same—or a worse—mistake now? His mind flung itself around all he knew of the Romanov Cache. His intuition, with scant evidence to support it, made a declaration.

Sergei Nevsky, the wizard, had woven his unborn grandson into the web of misdirection and concealment. After everything was said, Yuri Nevsky was the key to the treasure and the ultimate triumph that would follow its possession. He had to live until he and Detrovna met again. After that...well, he would see.

"Put up your weapons!" he shouted.

After a brief whirlwind of activity he, his soldiers, the cubes, and the Attorney were back in the helicopter hurtling over the landscape. Seating put Gennady face to face with him. His expression was that of one whose lifeboat is found to have a large hole.

Detrovna knew what had overwhelmed him. Betrayal!

At the hands of his master's unexpected compassion.

He feared that Detrovna, long ruthless and without either pity or remorse, was being made into a toothless old woman by the cursed cache.

Who could say that he wasn't right?

MARIA NIKOLAYEVNA

ANASTASIA NIKOLAYEVNA

34

Pittsburgh, Pennsylvania

The flights from Moscow to New York then Greater Pittsburgh were the most peculiar of Nevsky's life. Not due to mechanical problems or storms, rather to the hours being shared between the rollercoaster of Alessya's careening emotions and his own long periods of deep thought.

She was quick to demand to know why he had risked his life for the sake of a lie. She was indignant when he couldn't provide a precise explanation. His attempt to do so was as much for his sake as hers. He tried different approaches, like a child trying to fit shaped blocks through matching holes in a container.

At first he said he simply didn't want Detrovna to find the cache. He wanted him to believe it was gone, make him abandon the quest. She scoffed. "Was that a fair trade for your *life?*" she asked. "Old and bald as you are, you have some years left."

Possibly closer to his true motivations—if in fact he had consciously conceived any at all—was a cloud of foreboding hanging over all the treasure hunters. He had told Detrovna he wasn't worthy. He truly meant that the Russian fell among those cursed by Countess Sollonier seventy-six years ago. Weapon in hand, Detrovna had scoffed. Alessya now did the same.

Digging deeper still, he ventured out on the branch where reality waned and wizards and witches walked. He turned his head toward Alessya and whispered, "I was a tool of my grandfather."

The young woman erupted in a rattle of abuse, finishing with, "I think you *are* crazy," she said.

Then there were the hours when she slept or kept to her own thoughts. Nevsky had time to dwell once again on the three cubes now in Detrovna's possession. He remembered Charity saying they were signposts to the fourth. He turned that idea over and over and looked at it from every angle, like a shell collector with a prize specimen. To his surprise he drew some conclusions based on few facts and great inspiration. He suspected the cubes carried two messages. The first was the location of the cache. The second was its nature, what made up the treasure.

Everyone had been obsessed with location, including him. He hadn't spent five minutes thinking past "gold and jewels." As Europe and the North Atlantic slowly fell behind he focused on the contents of the three cubes. Had they all been empty, intuition told him they would then be only locators. But two had contents.

One held pebbles, one a false cache. And of course one was empty.

Knowing his grandfather better the longer the quest continued, he understood that there was a reason for that arrangement. He entertained possibilities, but none struck him with the energy of his concept itself, that the cubes were in part keys to content.

Then Alessya was awake again, now after him about his immediate plans. How did he expect to stop Detrovna "who now holds all the cards?" He said he didn't know. He'd figure something out. That annoyed her. She wasn't any more patient than Charity. Telling her he needed to talk to Charity only upset her further.

He changed the subject. He asked her why with her dagger and recklessness she had proven herself willing to throw away her own life in exchange for Detrovna's. "You have a lot more years left, as you're fond of telling me, my sweet," he said. "Don't you think they're worth more than a dead Detrovna?"

"I want him at best dead! At worst robbed of the cache."

"He spared you. Take that as a warning. Learn something."

"He spared *you*, too," she spat. "And you don't seem any wiser for it."

"You're as crazy as you say I am," Nevsky muttered.

She was silent a long moment. The *shhhhh* of the jet's fresh air vents seemed to grow louder. Finally she said in a trembling whisper, "I missed my best chance to pierce his lizard heart," she said. "You must see to it that I get another."

He rolled his head and looked at her face. Liquid gaze and superb cheeks lay only a handbreadth from his lips. Travel, danger, and pursuit of vengeance altogether had failed to tire her. Her skin was smooth and young. Her eyes were clear. Nevsky was tired. He didn't often wish for youth, but he sensed an unappealing trend developing. Faust had been well motivated. Tenderness for her welled up, then subsided against the sea wall of the present situation. "I'm not sure I can promise you another chance. I *am* sure that, if it comes, you shouldn't take it."

Her gaze began its accustomed smolder. He tried to smother it. "I have unhappy premonitions."

"You know where I think you should stick them," she said unsmiling. She was silent a long while. Then she said, "You have given up on the cache?"

Nevsky shook his head. "Even if I wanted to, the others won't. We seem to all be working together, after a fashion."

"But Detrovna holds the high cards."

"So you keep saying." Nevsky stared down at the tops of clouds. "Maybe he does. Maybe not." He worked his way out of his seat. "My turn to pay our friend a visit."

He moved down the aisle until he found Lyubov's row. He was sitting precisely as Nevsky had left him two hours previously. Both hands gripped the ends of his middle seat armrests. His lips moved silently in prayer. His solid face was ashen. On his lap lay a common wooden ikon.

"Another hour, maybe two," Nevsky said, trying to swallow his smile. "Then—America!"

"The Devil take America and this airplane!" Lyubov growled. "I am now barely alive. Our Savior help Queen Catherine wherever they have hidden her!"

The dog was safely stowed, as Nevsky had already explained several times. At this moment Lyubov undoubtedly regretted his decision to be Nevsky's guest and jack-of-all-trades for a few months.

Earlier, though, the Russian had been open-mouthed at the chance to visit America and to work for a Nevsky as his great-grandfather had done with Sergei. He was dumbfounded at what influence Korchevko, of whom he had never heard, exercised over the bureaucracy. Papers, passport—everything!—for him and his dog arranged on short notice at Nevsky's request.

Nevsky didn't explain to him that the price for that expediting was his visiting Korchevko in his monastery, telling him everything he knew, up to and including Detrovna's possession of the cubes. He had to swear to help the Force for Leadership find the cache. That was not swearing in the casual American sense, but in the Russian one, on his knees before the holiest ikon in the monastery. He did this despite his religious beliefs being little more than odd stirrings arising at unlikely moments and largely indefinable, thanks to their patina of mysticism. Nonetheless, the oath felt sufficiently binding.

Compared to General Ostrovsky, Detrovna, and the venomous Father Fyodor, Korchevko seemed the soundest soul. However, that far from guaranteed his ascension to ultimate leadership. Who knew but that it was a drawback?

Leaving the monastery, Nevsky was well aware that by now he had promised to help all parties to find the cache. Possible? Again, who knew?

When the cab dropped him, Alessya, Lyubov, and Queen Catherine off at 138, Nevsky felt the weight of travel fatigue and the oiliness that went with it. He was thinking of a hot shower and bed.

Until he found Charity waiting impatiently, though when he had phoned from JFK, she seemed cool enough to his return. "Upstairs," she whispered. "My room."

He asked Alessya to look after Lyubov then climbed the stairs.

Charity had cleared a table to serve a desk. In its center lay the Bible from the Murrysville chicken coop. "My constant companion since you left," she said nodding toward the metal-clad volume.

"You didn't ask me how my trip went," he said.

She sniffed. "You told me enough on the phone, Yuri. The Cheka didn't find the treasure. You were nearly killed—*again*. Detrovna has the cubes." She cocked her head and looked up at him and tried to put a matter-of-fact tone behind her words. "Anyway, I was busy solving the bigger part of the puzzle while you were out gallivanting."

"What?"

"Back from the past to help you with the present," she cooed.

"You're not too old to spank, if you're jerking me around," Nevsky said.

"Me? Do that? No way!"

"Then you better do some fast talking."

She sat in front of the Bible. The ten years away had thinned her face, leaving lines and planes hinting at the intelligence once masked by the fuller flesh of youth. She pressed her palm to the raised relief metal, as though preparing to testify. "I remembered what you said your grandfather told your father and your aunt when he gave them each a Bible—one of which we have right here. 'To read it with special care if a time of great need ever comes.' So that convinced me there was *something* in here to do with the cache. Of course I didn't know what. But I knew there was…something. Know why?"

Nevsky shook his head.

"Because you told me your grandfather had them specially printed. Or more importantly—specially *manufactured.*"

"What good could you do, Charity? You can't read Russian."

She winked. "Maybe that was the best thing that could have happened."

"Explain!"

"I looked through the Bible, page after page. I took my time. I didn't assume I knew what I was looking for, so I had to look for everything. 'God' is printed in gold throughout both Testaments. Did you notice that Christ's words were printed in silver? I know enough of the New Testament to have figured that out. Interesting—"

"You want to get to the point? Or go on teasing me?" Nevsky said.

"Turned out neither of those things meant anything."

"I figured. Will you go *on!*"

"I paged through again and again looking for—I still didn't know what. Then I made a very small discovery. Some scattered words in both Testaments were italicized. They weren't the ones you might imagine, say in the Gospels."

"What words?"

"Of course I couldn't really read them. I copied them out like a schoolgirl doing a spelling exercise."

"And you asked Shmelev or Lyudmila what they were?"

She cocked her head and looked at him strangely. "Why do you trust everybody who walks through your door?"

Nevsky hated it when Charity criticized him. What he found so annoying was that she was always right. "Stick to the Bible," he muttered.

"I took my list of words to your old buddy, the ballet master Tschersky." She slipped a sheet out of a neat pile. "Here it is."

Nevsky scanned the sixteen words, one column Russian, the corresponding one English. *the, Savior, press, our, in, Christ, turn, and, three, Baptizer, times, the, faces, John, of, Moses.*

Breezily, Charity said, "It only took me a few seconds to put the words in the right order. It says, 'Press in turn three times the faces of Moses, John the Baptizer, and Christ our Savior.' At this point maybe your grandfather figured he had put quite enough obstacles in the path." She picked up the Bible whose metallic covers bore raised figures from classic Scripture. She pointed. "Moses here. John here. Christ here." She firmly pressed each thrice in turn. The *chkk* after each touch had the sound of precision mechanism. Nine *chkks*. A spring-loaded panel sprang up. In the flat tray beneath lay a folded sheet of heavy paper. Charity said, "And there, my dear Yuri, sits a big piece of your puzzle."

Despite himself, Nevsky gasped in surprise. Excitement fluttered through his stomach like a bulb-burned moth. "Well, what's on the paper?" He reached for it, but she snatched the Bible away and pressed the panel back. *Chkk!*

"I'm leaving it where it is for now," she said. "There can't be a safer hiding place."

Nevsky gave her a puzzled frown. What was going on here? "Charity Anne Day, *what does it say?*"

"Tell you the truth, it doesn't *say* anything." She took his hand. "It's a beautiful day. Let's take a walk."

35

The last two days had turned things around for Nevsky. The initial breakthrough was Charity's uncovering the Bible's secret. As well, she succeeded in turning him into a skeptic concerning all the treasure seekers' trustworthiness. Father Fyodor wasn't the only skunk in the hunt. "Sneaky as snakes, every one, is my guess," she muttered. In connection with that general theme they were making their ways to different hiding places outside 138 Morlande. They carried two-way radios, volume set low, and handguns.

Further good news came yesterday from Butch Hanson who had been trying to reach Nevsky for nearly a week. What he said was interesting enough to send them up the Allegheny Expressway in Butch's Forerunner. They exited, crossed the river, and turned toward Lake Nagle where Nevsky had found the two men who had roughed up Butch's father. On the way Butch told him that the site was now fenced in and guarded. That hadn't stopped him from successfully spying.

Within two hours they were crouched inside the fence in a heavy thicket overlooking the spoiled lake. Early July heat carried whiffs of the unnatural decay of churned aquatic environment. Along the shore the trunks of dying trees rose from the mud-colored water, evidence of its rising level. Earth had tumbled down from the adjacent high hill. Its north wall now rose nearly vertically from the scummy surface. A stream pouring down a steep wooded slope drained the lake then found the winding Allegheny River a quarter-mile below.

In silence they scanned the site. Heat made them itch and drip. "While I was away they finished up," Butch whispered. "There were maybe twenty guys working. Now I only see eight." He turned his squarish face toward Nevsky. "And two of them are my boys. Hold on just a sec. Right now we can see both of them." He passed Nevsky the glasses. "Look at the two guys who're dumping hand tools onto that pile. They're my pigeons."

Nevsky saw them. One wore his hair in a single plait hanging below a linebacker's neck. The man was an ox. The second had white hair and used a stained blue sash for a belt.

Butch made a fist and stared at knuckles like doorknobs. "Yeah, they're tidying everything up. Knowing that they're going to boogie has made me spend a lot of hours hiding out here. I missed them once. It won't happen again. I'm waiting for them to break up and leave. *Then* I'll get my hands on them."

The secrecy, the guards, and the Russian speakers gave Nevsky an inner tingling. He felt like a horseplayer with an ironclad hunch. "And you couldn't figure out what they were bringing up?"

"Hell, no! See for yourself." Butch gestured at the field glasses. "You tell me what all that is."

The woods and underbrush had been cut away to clear about two lakeside acres. On bent stalks and stumps were piled in rough order an incredible amount of what looked at first glance to be waterlogged rubbish. Some squinting and work with the glasses' focus brought Nevsky more detail but no sense to the mess.

Instead it brought elation!

His mind's gears engaged. Never mind Charity's impulsive claim that they had corroded in recent years. His grandfather's subtle clue dropping now seemed so obvious! Sybille had been ordered by Father Konstantine to use Sergey's agent in the Pittsburgh region— the old Russian sailor. Why would he have him stationed halfway around the world, except to handle his important business? Where had he ordered his son to go but to Pittsburgh? No coincidences, not with Sergei.

The cache was in the Pittsburgh area! Better than that, thanks first to Harsky, then Detrovna, and finally Butch, Nevsky knew it was *here*. Somewhere inside what of course must be the Muscovite's fence. Who else but Detrovna could have been behind land acquisition marked indelibly with the heavy-handedness of certain New York Russians? Nevsky should have tumbled *weeks* ago, the moment he heard Butch's marked thugs speaking Russian. Not really. Then he hadn't enough information or the right mind-set. Maybe getting drunk with Lyubov and Alessya on Russian soil, feeling Detrovna's rifle barrel at his temple, then facing the man's firing squad had cleared away the cobwebs—and then some! Whatever, his head was working now. He didn't have to look close-up at the lake-logged artsy objects to know that for all his money and power, the politician hadn't found the cache.

The sheet in the Bible cover had assured Nevsky of that.

"Can we work our way around to the other side of that little mountain, Butch?"

"Leave it to me. I've been all over this place. Not too many go over to that side of the property. It's been used for storage, pipe, tubing, rope. Most of the action's been right down there." He jabbed a thick finger at the ruined lake.

In less than a half-hour they were standing by the toppled foundation of what once had been a well-built little cottage. Snapdragons gone wild pushed their stalks up between tumbled fieldstones. Nevsky oriented himself to the front of the ruins. He raised his gaze to a grassy depression about forty yards ahead. He started toward it, Butch a little behind. "You mind if I ask what this is all about?" his friend said.

"My gut feeling is that you'll be better off if I don't tell you," Nevsky said.

"Could you be coaxed?"

"To maybe set my friend up for trouble from some nasty people and an eighty-year-old curse? Why should you coax me?"

"Sounds interesting as hell."

Nevsky hesitated. He might have explained if it hadn't become so obvious that the cache was Russian business in the primal sense. Butch was a straight-ahead American. He needn't get tangled in the web spun by Nevsky's grandfather, lunatic Russian hearts, and the agonies that passed for the Motherland's twentieth-century history. "I like you too much to explain," he said.

Butch shrugged and growled, "I get my two men, no matter what goes down."

"You stick with them, partner," Nevsky said. "They're all yours if you can manage it. I won't do anything to mess you up."

"Good enough."

Nevsky turned back toward...

Yes! Clearly it had once been a pond. His heart began double duty. His eyes found the center of the depression. From it emerged a stubby stone column about two feet high. He moved closer through the heavy grass. He couldn't smother his cry of delight.

From the center of the column protruded a threaded pipe barely tarnished with rust.

He turned to Butch. "Time to go. I have everything I need."

"Oh, man of mystery!" Butch laughed. But the flinty eyes above the laugh line wrinkles reminded Nevsky not to cheat him of his vendetta.

Now, the next day, Nevsky took his position hunched down in a heavy clump of hydrangea at the corner of 138's porch. "In position," he whispered into his radio.

"Likewise," came Charity's reply. "I'm angled behind a stone fence. I can see the driveway and the rear entrance just fine."

"So we get comfortable. We wait. Over and out." Nevsky knelt by the wooden lattice that kept the larger animals from crawling under the porch. He ran over the simple moves that made up the little fishing expedition he had conceived. Charity and he had announced that they were going to be out for a few hours. He sent Lyubov and Alessya over to Russian Slope, a halfway house to learning American ways. He unlocked the doors. Leaving separately, Charity and he drove their cars to the top of the hill, then around the block, left them, and made their way back to 138 through hedges and over shadowed lawns. Simple. So simple it might even work. Bite little fishies, bite, he thought.

About twenty minutes passed. He heard Charity's excited radio whisper. "Car turning into the driveway. This could be something!"

36

Exactly when had Shmelev discovered that he no longer trusted Lyudmila? He muttered a curse. Not soon enough! He should have become suspicious their first night in Pittsburgh. She had insisted on separate rooms when they booked into their motel. At the time he had charged his uneasiness to a lover's bruised ego. He had enjoyed her body frequently in the Motherland. There the slate gray mirrors of her eyes he imagined reflected lust and affection to match his own. The skilled, sinewy twisting of her body during the act he assumed arose from her desire to please him, not from mere habits formed with many lovers.

When she first refused him on American soil, he assumed some shortcoming on his part, possibly his shocking ineptness in the face of Nevsky's skilled brawling. Even now his nose occasionally throbbed. Afterward he blamed her lack of desire on the strains arising from pursuit of the cache. She had come to his bed only twice in the five weeks they had been stewing in this strange land. Even then he sensed something mechanical in her performances, like a child glimpsing springs up a magician's sleeve.

However, the excitement of trying to uncover Nevsky's secrets stunted his flowering suspicions. He and Lyudmila never believed the American knew nothing about the cache. So after some days they hid the expensive listening devices in the principal rooms of his home. Surely such all-hearing ears would snatch the key information needed to solve the vexing puzzle, though their command of spoken English was weak. At first they listened expectantly, each on a set of earphones curling out of the receiver—and learned nothing of interest. They set up four-hour shifts covering Nevsky's waking hours. So shackled, and learning nothing useful, they found the duty tedious, whether listening or relaxing. Possibly they were missing much, tangled as they were in their imperfect English.

Deep in this well of frustration Shmelev had to fight despair and an overall sense of futility. Seeking antique czarist treasure seemed an ill-formed quest. He swung thoughts toward his anchor, commitment to Korchevko and his Force for Leadership. The leader had sieved him from the sewer of Russia's human scum, Shmelev, petty thief, thug, and hired assassin if the victim were weak and defenseless. The enlightened one taught the lesser man that God forgave and that the Motherland's future was threatened unless religious men and women of purpose and action stood fast. So Shmelev had been resurrected. And since, loyal without question.

Steadied, he returned stoically to the earphones, and found a different kind of ordeal... The behavior of Alessya Harsky, the hot-blooded warrior woman, and Nevsky on his obscenely wide bed further tested Shmelev's loyalty and now his self-control. First, such eavesdropping was not to his taste. Second, it stirred his blood. He thought of throwing himself on Lyudmila who only muttered "pigs" upon hearing sounds of the lovers' unchecked exertions.

So matters stood uneasily until he passed by Lyudmila's door while she was providing Korchevko one of her regular telephone reports. He couldn't hear her words; the door was thick and she spoke softly. Yet there was something in her tone that previously he had never heard, a conspiratorial edge, possibly, or the faintest sycophant's whine. He wondered if indeed it was to their leader that she spoke.

Possibly she was in touch with one of the admirers she had met at the excellent party to which Nevsky had taken them. Often she ran errands in their rented car. She was away long enough for assignations. Shmelev's hobbled suspicions tangled with sexual jealousy. He felt hamstrung and impotent, his judgment clouded...

The timely, violent return of Charity Day, evidently Nevsky's former housemate, returned focus and life to eavesdropping. As well as a pistol, the woman had a mind, Shmelev understood. He swallowed heavily when he overheard her suggesting to Nevsky that all cache chasers might well be sneaks—or worse. He sensed his and Lyudmila's plotting unraveling before this unusual woman's attention.

Though ill formed, his suspicions about his partner remained. He began to analyze her behavior in the light of some kind of duplicity. One morning, thanks to a balky air conditioner in his room, he was sitting with her during her shift. He heard her earphones murmuring.

"What's happening?"

"Nevsky and Alessya have returned from the Motherland," Lyudmila said. "With a man called Lyubov."

Shmelev was instantly alert. He learned forward. "Is Charity Day there?"

She nodded.

"Are she and Nevsky talking about the Bible?"

In Shmelev's mind Nevsky's father's Bible plucked from some stinking chicken coop had lain like a ticking bomb all through the American's absence.

She shook her head. "Small talk," she said.

Her shift ran for two more hours. When Shmelev took up the earphones he heard nothing more than Alessya and Lyubov making domestic noises. They were chattering about America, about which he could guarantee they knew nothing. After more than a month of bafflement *all* he knew was that no Russian could be happy in this land where everything was about money. He began to think Lyudmila might have heard more than she revealed. He regretted not having used the other earphones. There was a remedy for that lost opportunity.

Vigilance.

The motel clerk drove to work in a small car. It sat unused during his nine-hour shift. Several days earlier, for a few dollars he agreed to let Shmelev borrow it. The next time Lyudmila ran an errand, Shmelev followed her—to nothing more exciting than two clothing stores and a hair-cutting establishment. But he learned something about driving in Pittsburgh's heavy traffic and positioning his car where it was least noticeable. Twice more he followed her. He uncovered neither assignations nor treachery. Possibly his suspicions were misguided.

Two days after Nevsky's return she announced a shopping trip. Once again he pulled out behind her. Quickly he recognized the roads leading toward Nevsky's home. On previous occasions they had traveled there together. Clearly today was different. He would find out why. He fell safely behind for the better part of the trip, then pulled closer, he a block behind when she turned onto Morlande Street.

She pulled into Nevsky's driveway and hurried up the stairs to the rear entrance. He left his car by the curb and his shoes with it. He rushed silently up the stairs and slipped into the house.

His ears told him where she had gone—to the room at the end of the second floor hallway. Shmelev remembered it belonged to Charity Day, evidently as it had a decade earlier. He stepped through the doorway of the next room, Nevsky's study. As he stood listening to Lyudmila making much noise it dawned on him that she must have overheard that the house would be empty for a time.

He heard a heavy object being moved on a surface. Sharp metallic clicks chopped the air. A precision device *chkked* briefly. Lyudmila did not stifle her cry of delight. In turn Shmelev's heart raced. What had she heard through the earphones that allowed her so easily to find something that so suited her? He readied himself. When she passed by the door, he would seize her and shake secrets loose.

She didn't leave the room. She picked up the telephone. Shmelev listened, first with bafflement, then with increasing understanding and mounting rage. Her local call was to Boris Detrovna, their sworn enemy! He was nearby, may his liver rot! She told him Charity Day had solved the Bible's secret. She had decoded the instructions for opening the mechanized cover. Within it lay a sheet of paper. Lyudmila was holding the paper in her hand at that moment. It was a drawing, but she didn't know of what. Possibly of something electrical. Nonetheless Nevsky and Charity had agreed that the treasure could not be found without it.

Her voice lost its business-like tone. Excitement overwhelmed her as praise no doubt rolled to her down the line. She would deliver the Bible with its paper to him at a place called Lake Nagle. Of course immediately, she said.

Shmelev trembled with rage. He set his back against the wall to steady himself. Lyudya was a traitor! Everything the Force for Leadership had done in connection with the cache had reached Detrovna through this unspeakable bitch. Now what might well be the last of an infernal number of puzzle pieces was also to be sped on its way to that criminal.

No, not as long as Shmelev lived!

He heard a thump as she picked up the Bible. She hurried out of the room and passed his doorway. Fast as a mink he was after her. He thrust his forearm across her throat and drew her roughly to him. She choked. The Bible spun down from her arms and struck the floor a blow as heavy as an angel's.

Her terrified eyes rolled up and sideways to see in whose powerful grip she found herself. "You! Shmelev," she coughed against the pressure of his arm. "You fool! Let me go!"

Shmelev knew he wasn't that bright, but he had instinct. It whispered: do not let her talk to you. Do not let her work her wiles. As well rage roiled up. She had tricked him with her loins, used him, and betrayed him and Korchevko and their cause. He did not hesitate to grip her skull with his free hand. He applied grinding pressure until her neck snapped.

Now he had a body in his arms. Not for the first time in life. He looked around. Nevsky's home had dozens of rugs tossed down on its hardwood floors. He found one and rolled the corpse in it.

He knew how to dispose of bodies—here, in Russia, or in any other country on earth. And it would not be found. Whatever secrets the Bible held were now the property of Korchevko and the Force for Leadership.

He picked up the Bible and put the rug on his shoulder. Lyudmila's car keys were in her pocket. He would use her car, and then return later for his own. He remembered the rental car had a large trunk. He crossed the rear porch and went down the stairs to the driveway. He was about to lean the rug against the car when something hard and metallic jabbed his lower back just above his left kidney.

"Stop! Don't move. If you do, I will shoot you." Shmelev understood well enough. And he knew who spoke so calmly. Charity Day. For some reason he did not doubt that, given reason, she would kill him. Until that moment he didn't know just how much he respected her.

In seconds Nevsky stood with them, breathing deeply from his sprint. He eyed Shmelev and the rug. "Is this in Russian style or what? Under this guy's arms we have a body *and* a Bible!"

37

They adjourned to the kitchen for a conference. Charity kept her .38 at the ready while Nevsky searched Shmelev. He found only a set of brass knuckles with enough points and heft to take out King Kong. "I'll keep these a while," he said. "You going to behave?"

Shmelev lit a cigarette, heaved on it. His obsidian eyes were unreadable. "For now."

"Good." Nevsky got out the Stoli. He poured two shots. He glanced at Charity. "You didn't used to drink much. Ten years of painful marriage make boozing seem a better idea?"

"No, but I don't like killing or bodies much," she said. "Pour me one, too."

There was no toasting. Putting his glass down, Nevsky said, "Shmelev, you want to tell us why you just murdered your partner?"

The Russian narrowed his eyes. His thick cheekbones seemed Alps wreathed in a fog of smoke. He said nothing.

Maybe the pump needed a little priming. "Charity and I set up Lyudmila, you know," Nevsky said.

Shmelev scowled. Nevsky guessed that not being the brightest star, Shmelev had long since learned that when confused, it was best to let others talk.

Nevsky glanced at Charity. How quickly he had grown accustomed to the new lines in her pale face! As though she had never left? Not quite. She was still a handsome woman. In any case it had never been her appearance that greatly appealed to him, rather all that lay behind her broad brow. And that invisible business called character. He said, "Charity figured out too many people seemed to know what was going on under this roof."

Nevsky told Shmelev they guessed the house was bugged. It didn't take too long to find the tiny microphones. But it wasn't clear, with so many players in the field, just who might be listening. At this the Russian's eyes widened. "I...see," he said.

Nevsky went on to explain that they set up a trap for the bugger. Talked up the Bible's secret, but never explained just what it was. They pointed out the significant detail that no one was likely to find the cache without it. What serious contender could resist that bait? So they hid and waited. And there came Lyudmila! They stayed undercover, expecting her to exit with the Bible and face their very hard questions. Instead Shmelev got to her first. With her dead, it fell to him to explain why he had transformed a partner into a corpse.

Shmelev poured another vodka. "I curse her and the grave in which she'll lie!" He waved his glass. "I drink to the torment of her soul!"

While Nevsky was translating for Charity, Alessya, Lyubov, and Queen Catherine returned from Russian Slope. The borzoi sniffed at the oddly rolled up rug lying along the kitchen wall, whimpered, then curled up on the other side of the room. When the burly peasant saw that, his cunning spoke. He stared at Shmelev. He said only, "Treachery."

Shmelev sprang to his feet. "Of course, treachery! That bitch was a tool of *Detrovna!* Because of her we have failed."

Shmelev told his tale: Lyudmila's changed behaviors, his initial suspicions, the installation of the bugging equipment, shadowing the woman without success until today, her opening the Bible, finding the drawing, then calling Detrovna to arrange to give it to him. Nevsky translated for Charity. She scowled at Shmelev. "Tell him he comes in and starts a fight he loses, then makes nice, drinks your vodka, eats your food—then bugs your house. Tell him he's a sneaky creep."

Lyubov made a fist and shook it meaningfully toward Shmelev.

Before he could say anything Nevsky saw Alessya dig her hands into her thick mane and shake them in aggravation. "*I* am the major fool," she said. "The one without memory." She nodded at the rug. "When I met Lyudmila here I thought it was not for the first time. She said we never had met and was rude enough about it. Ruder than I deserved, I thought. I tried to remember where I had seen her before. But I couldn't'!" She tugged angrily at her dark locks. "*Now*, after everything said in this house has gone into the ear of that lizard Detrovna, I remember…"

"So when did you meet?" Nevsky asked.

"Never!" Alessya's Tatar eyes flashed. "I once for the briefest moment glimpsed a photograph in the lizard's lair." She jerked a contemptuous thumb toward the rug. "*Her* photograph! She was one of Boris Petrovich's many mistresses before me." She spat on the rug, showing all that sexual jealousy wasn't ended by death.

So Lyudya had been demoted from bed to bedlam, Nevsky thought. She probably had still hoped to work her way back to soft sheets through "good" deeds. Now she was gone, but where did that leave him and the cache enthusiasts right now? He wasn't sure. He looked at Shmelev who was grinding out his smoke as though it was the last louse in Russia.

"I'm not as stupid as you might think," he said to the Russian. "If Lyudmila had reached Detrovna and given him the Bible's paper, he'd then have a schematic drawing of the circuitry of an outdated Zenith TV that Charity tore out of its direction manual."

Shmelev grunted in satisfaction. "What drawing is on the real paper?" he asked.

Nevsky snorted. "Expect me to tell you? Does it surprise you when I say I don't trust you?"

Shmelev squirmed. He saw his position: discredited. He imagined his master Korchevko's displeasure. Nevsky could read him. New cards had been dealt, more to play "crazy" as he had promised himself he would. And so come down where he had not been before: a place of personal satisfaction. It was time to continue the risky game...

"Shmelev, I want you to contact Korchevko and tell him what happened."

Shmelev shook his head. "He took me from the gutter, uplifted me, and made me worthy by serving him. Just now I showed again my beastly ways: I might have spared the treacherous bitch. I cannot tell him I've failed in both moral strength and service!"

"You haven't failed in service: no one has the cache," Alessya barked. "As for your conscience, if your master doesn't absolve you, there are plenty of churches and in them priests who will."

Nevsky gathered everyone around the table. Translating for Charity, he explained that they now held the key to the cache's location. With it he planned to bring Korchevko and Detrovna together. Alessya and Shmelev cried out in protest.

"Give the paper to Korchevko, the pious one," Alessya said. "The other deserves nothing but death!"

"That won't work."

"Why not?"

"Because I'm certain Detrovna owns the land where the cache is hidden. It's crawling with his men—and they're nasty."

Shmelev's jutting cheeks drained of color. "He *has* the cache?"

"He has the land, but his people haven't been able to find what they're looking for." He told the group that the vain search of the lake had been going on for weeks. What had been retrieved were clearly items shipped by his grandfather in the years just before the Revolution. Now they had no time to waste. He nudged Shmelev and told him to contact Korchevko before his rival found the treasure.

Shmelev shook his lowered head. "I...cannot tell him I failed, and killed." Such a small voice to come from such a powerful man!

Impatient Charity understood well enough what was going on. "Yuri, tell him that if he doesn't get off his duff, you'll take the rug, its occupant, and him right to the police. A murder charge is worse than being humiliated."

A few words from Nevsky and a paling Shmelev was ready for action. Nevsky told him to go back to his motel, check out, and then destroy all his former partner's effects. He would be moving into 138 Morlande where the American could keep an eye on him.

Shmelev nodded his agreement then rose shakily. "A small matter, Yuri Vladimirovich. The corpse. Allow me to dispose of it. I've had much practice."

38

The Monastery of St. John the Baptist, northeast of Moscow

Korchevko hung up the phone with a smile. God be blessed for putting this Nevsky on earth! The initial reports from Lyudya and Shmelev that he was a weak reed with nothing to offer to their search for the rumored cache had been proven wrong. Since his involvement much had happened. Now it was clear that the Romanov Cache did exist and shortly would be found. Seemingly it was hidden somehow in a Lake Nagle northeast of Pittsburgh. In his delight, he arose swiftly, his white-clad body limber in motion. Then he checked himself, crossed to his ikon, kneeled, and blessed himself. He devoted a half-hour's prayer for the wayward soul of the late Lyudmila Mogadam. He added a shorter plea on behalf of poor Shmelev whose loyalty and dark urges had led him to break the Sixth Commandment.

It wasn't so easy to reach his rival Detrovna. His call to the politician's organization was bounced about until a woman's voice sounded a note of recognition. Shortly afterward he had an international number—America! He dialed and reached one Gennady Efimovich Rishnikov, Detrovna's attorney. Here at last was a gatekeeper, a man in the know. In moments he was speaking to the one he sought who was well aware of the ascetic's political ambitions. The other's cautious voice: "What do you want, Korchevko?"

To position himself quickly he said, "Lyudmila Mogadam didn't keep her appointment with you."

Detrovna instinctively began to dissemble. Korchevko cut him off. "The woman is dead, murdered for her treachery on your behalf."

"Lyudmila, dead?"

"That you didn't know. We also know she told you everything about the cache that was spoken of in Nevsky's home."

"This is such nonsense—"

"Boris Petrovich, please. No one's purpose is served by lies and deception with uncovering of the cache so near." He told him it was necessary that they meet and discuss how the wealth was to be divided between them. Detrovna refused with an angry bellow. Nevsky and Korchevko were ready for this. Unless the two of them met together with the American, he wouldn't reveal what was on the paper, and the cache would elude them all. Detrovna tried bluster: he was on the verge of discovery and needed nothing from Nevsky.

"Yuri Vladimirovich says otherwise," Korchevko said. "Come, Boris Petrovich, old wisdom tells us, 'grasp all, lose all.' Let us sit down together and arrange to share." There was a long pause, nearly a minute. Korchevko knew the politician weighed his enduring frustration and greed against progress and less profit. At the same time he was undoubtedly improvising some treacherous scheme, to be later refined, against which the ascetic and Nevsky would have to be doubly on guard.

Finally Detrovna grunted, "The meeting must be here—in America."

"Of course. Isn't that where the cache lies?"

Detrovna growled like a pricked bear.

They set the time: three days hence, at Nevsky's home.

Korchevko paced the monastery's public room. He ran his hand through his shoulder-length white hair and assessed the situation. He had been here gathering himself, centering his spirit, for better than a year. During this time his Force for Leadership had grown steadily. In the ranks of his organization marched idealists to be sure, but they were tempered with practical, far more active men and women. Plenty knew the wrestling ring of Russian politics. Recently they had come to him repeatedly, saying the time for action was now. Where was the financing they desperately needed? He would soon have a positive answer to that question. Yes, clearly the moment had come for him to cast aside his isolation and lead his Force!

He would lead at least one other to America, to this Pittsburgh. He lifted the phone and spoke with Bishop Paulos. Within an hour Father Fyodor of Kolyma stood before him. With him was a towering priest with a wild black beard. A massive crucifix hung around his neck. His inner and outer cassocks couldn't hide what seemed a medical cast covering his upper right chest, shoulder, and arm, immobilizing the last. Father Fyodor nodded at the giant. "My associate here has served our bishop well for many years. He chooses to use the name 'Archangel.'"

Korchevko eyed this odd fellow. "Well, he's big enough to be one."

"May God give you His blessing." The Archangel's voice was a deep rumble. "His Son knows of your great piety."

Korchevko knelt before Father Fyodor who blessed him. Then he rose. "I have much to say to you, father." He looked questioningly at the giant.

"A man who at once falls mute and knows how to quickly forget," Father Fyodor assured him.

"Then both of you listen carefully!"

He told them all that Nevsky had shared. Detrovna was close to the treasure stashed in the final cube marked *Anastasia Nikolayevna*. He had carried the other three cubes to the cache site. Nevsky had the key to finding that final cube. It would be necessary to meet with the politician and reach an accommodation, hopefully a fifty-fifty split.

A chain of beads appeared in the priest's long fingers. "Don't you fear treachery from such a man?"

"I expect it, but I don't fear it. You, I, and Nevsky can prevent it."

"I?" Fyodor said.

"I want you to come with me. Assuming Bishop Paulos gives his permission."

To Korchevko the priest's hatchet-faced smile seemed forbidding. "His Holiness and I have reached…an understanding about my freedom to act." Fyodor frowned. "But he may not be happy to hear that our former financial agreement has been watered down by your dealing. It was to be fifty-fifty, correct?"

"I believe our final agreement was seventy-thirty."

The priest's beads chattered. "We quibble. I tell you, Korchevko, the treasure's eighty years of appreciation will amount to a final sum that will beg all our imaginations! Eighty years, my friend! There will be plenty for all. My role with you?"

"Confidant, advisor, representative of the Church, and my link to it."

"Excellent!" Fyodor nodded at the giant priest. "My associate will be of great assistance. He must come."

Korchevko nodded impatiently. "Of course. We must all leave tomorrow to be certain of getting to Pittsburgh in time for the meeting. Your travel papers are in order?"

"Very much so!" The beads rattled under the holy man's disturbing smile.

39

Ecclesiastical offices, off Prospekt Mira, Moscow

Bishop Paulos' hands were shaking. In a few moments Father Fyodor of Kolyma would once again pollute his presence. Twenty minutes ago the priest had told him in an excited phone call that he had been given important information. He needed to bring the bishop up to date at once. Paulos blessed himself and took deep breaths to gather strength. If only his spirit were as viable as his body. But the years under the commissars, his humiliations, and most recently the seductive pressure of possible riches, and the meager redemption they offered, had imperiled his spirit. Then to damn it utterly he had caused to appear this black priest who manipulated him like one of the beads often in his fingers.

Or whom he allowed to manipulate him.

Most recently he had served as a go-between for the priest and Korchevko in what he had admitted to himself was a fishing expedition. Seemingly the sea had been harvested... Moments later Fyodor was through the door. At his side towered the wounded giant around whom the rankest rumors ran. Undoubtedly this grotesque was his partner in the recent murder on the soil of the defunct collective farm. Fyodor immediately came to the point, Greek beads chattering like castanets. The cache seekers had at last brought matters nearly to a head. The general location of the treasure had been found. He gave the bishop all the details. Then he went on to say that Detrovna and Korchevko, with Nevsky as mediator, were planning to come to some kind of accommodation over the division of the wealth, no matter how temporary. "Luckily I am the confidant of both Nevsky and the pious head of the Force for Leadership," he said.

"Both of whom you will betray." Paulos forced his eyes upward to meet the priest's gaze, but found them fluttering aside like frightened birds.

"*Druzhba druzhboy, a sluzhba sluzhboy,*" the priest said. Friendship is friendship and service is service. "You should be glad to know I have a scheme."

"Yes..." The bishop's heart groaned, knowing its owner was being led yet again and hadn't the will to save himself.

"Your Holiness, it's not unreasonable to expect that the entire cache will end up in my hands, the Church's, *your* hands. Because I swear before God I have no interest in possessing it."

"*All* of it? What about the others?" Paulos asked. "They are not boys playing toy soldiers. The stakes are high. Men and women have already died chasing this chimera."

"No chimera, Holiness! A real thing. Soon to be in *our* possession."

"What's your plan?" the bishop asked.

Fyodor's hatchet face hardened. "Only I and my Archangel are required for success. You needn't know details."

The bishop sighed. "Will there be suffering? Will more die?"

Fyodor grinned. "Only if it's the will of God."

The bishop couldn't mask his grimace. "What more?" he asked in a dull voice.

The other held out his arms like black wings, a look of mock surprise wreathing his hard face. Beads dangled silently from his outstretched hand. "We need your permission—and your blessing—to go forward."

"No..." The bishop turned aside.

"Come now. We stand on the verge of your late life's dreams. The Romanov Cache will right seventy years of wrongs done our Church."

"I cannot..."

"Bless us," the black priest said.

"We do only the work of God!" the giant said. In his left hand he gripped the heavy crucifix hung from his neck and thrust it at the older man, wonder and weapon at once.

The bishop shook his head. He knew what work they did, and for whom. Even so, he weakened, as though the giant's bulk leeched out the last of his meager will. He managed to shake his head.

"Give us your blessing!" the priest demanded.

The bishop twisted aside, as though avoiding a blow. When he turned back, tears of resignation burned his eyes. He swallowed. "Yes..." He made the sign of the cross before them with his eyes averted.

And his spirit died.

When the door had closed behind the two black figures, the old man howled like a beast being butchered. His nails raked his cheeks until blood ran. For two hours he remained in that ruined state. He gathered himself somewhat and reached for the telephone.

In his years of struggle beneath the yoke of the Party he had come to know all types of men. To be sure most were pious souls of good conscience. There were a few of opposite persuasion. He had been able to do them some great favors using the modest spiritual powers and influence remaining to him. One of these men remained in his debt. Now he would clear the books. Several calls were required. The men he needed were to be the most reliable, those greatly experienced ones who kept their heads in pursuit of their goals whatever the circumstances. He gave detailed instructions. Payments were arranged: half before, half later.

He locked his door. From the desk drawer he drew the revolver given him years ago by the commissar. He hefted its malevolent weight, spun the cylinder, and eyed the cartridge bottoms, each like the head of a copper snake waiting to strike. He eased the end of the barrel into his right nostril. Even after so many months of neglect the scent of gun oil still clung to the blued metal. The front sight gouged soft nasal tissues. He grunted and pulled the weapon free.

He spun the cylinder again. It chattered a warning. Slowly he opened his mouth and pushed in the barrel until it reached the mucoused barrier of the top of his throat. His mouth felt gorged, so wickedly invaded! Just before the gag reflex he pulled the trigger.

His last thought was of the Romanov Cache enigma.

40

Lake Nagle, northeast of Pittsburgh

Even after a healthy snort of cocaine the Attorney didn't like the appearance of Lake Nagle baking in the July heat. It was churned up and angry looking, towered over by a high, wounded hill. Heat waves wriggled up from murky waters. The roughly circular shore was heaped with sodden *objets d'art* once of some value, but now waterlogged trash. The diving and dislodgements were over now. And here he had come to help write finished to what remained.

He spent several hours in the small office trailer on his cell phone, guaranteed by its provider to be untraceable. Most of his conversations were with those with whom he had originally spoken, certain Russians in New York City's various boroughs, beginning with Brudikov. These people were experts at making records disappear. Above them were more sophisticated agents who had helped initially to create Detrovna's dummy corporations within equally bogus parent ones. All would be swept away tomorrow at midnight like sand castles at high tide. Matters were greatly expedited by his having been zealous in paying these conspirators promptly over the past weeks. Criminals, too, liked to be fairly treated, with cash on the barrelhead.

At his directions the man called Stroganov handled the final local details with his own cell: having the last of the diving equipment hauled away later that afternoon, and by tomorrow evening ending the catering, local telephone and power service, and causing retrieval of the portable toilets. The little equipment and many inexpensive hand tools abandoned by the departed divers had been left where they were or piled just above the water line on the side of the hill. All this could be left to eventual scavengers.

This work completed, the Attorney met with the remaining six men. They were housed in two trailers well hidden by design in the deepest woods on the property. Stroganov mustered them in front of the larger trailer. Here was a scabby lot! The Attorney saw Russian refuse cast upon American shores— missing teeth, boorish in use of the mother tongue, the stink of cheap vodka and sweat on all of them. Without papers and English they were near slaves of their New York masters. Stroganov had handled them well: none knew anything about what lay behind the diving. Treasure hunting hadn't been mentioned, and even one imagination among these cattle was unlikely. Stroganov had assured the Attorney more than once that they remained in blissful ignorance insofar as the Romanov Cache was concerned.

The Attorney didn't like this heat. He was too much of a northerner to enjoy temperatures near thirty-five Celsius. Here in the woods it was cooler. The sheen of sweat on his head and neck began to evaporate as he called for the men's attention. He thanked them for their work. He told them he had authorized Stroganov to pay a full week's wages for only four days worked. He stood by while the bullet-headed boss distributed cash.

"There's something more I need of you," the Attorney said. "A day or two's more service—at double your regular wage."

Noises of interest arose from the rabble.

"Mr. Stroganov is leaving the project today. For the next short period I'll be in charge. My name's of no consequence. What is important is that you'll be paid in advance."

"What'll we have to do?" asked a stocky man whose black hair had been braided into a single plait that hung down well below his shoulders.

"Possibly nothing. Or possibly..." He nodded at the automatic rifles and handguns piled on the porch of the smaller trailer. "You'll have to use those, or threaten to use them, when and if I require it."

Plait chuckled. "Rough stuff?"

"I doubt it. Some unarmed civilians may need to be controlled. Whether or not I call on you, I'll pay you an additional bonus two days hence."

He outlined their orders while Stroganov passed out the advance. Plait would be the contact man. To him the Attorney gave a cell phone. He was to turn it on and leave it on. All the men were to stay hidden in the trailers. From this moment forward under no circumstances were they to show themselves until commanded.

The Attorney and Stroganov strolled back toward the office trailer, it too to be hauled away later that day. Stroganov frowned. "Why might there be trouble soon when nothing's been found?" he asked.

The Attorney's stomach did a flip. "Those precautions are nothing more than fruits of my master's paranoia. I can explain." They entered the trailer. The Attorney walked to the small table that held his briefcase. "Detrovna's been most pleased with everything you've done."

"We found nothing—or did we?" the other insisted.

The Attorney opened his briefcase. "So pleased in fact that he ordered me to present you with your bonus after all." He pulled out a wad of U. S. hundreds secured with a thick rubber band, and a pint bottle of vodka. He put them on the flimsy desk. Stroganov's heavy-lidded eyes widened at the sight of the cash. He picked it up and smiled.

"Detrovna understands that you'll depart today and never come back. And forget what was done here for no gain."

"Sure." Stroganov busied himself with a rough count of the cash. "You must thank Boris Petrovich for me."

The Attorney nodded. "I shall. Sorry, I have no glasses." He picked up the pint and thrust it at the pre-occupied Stroganov. "We'll share these spirits until they're gone."

Stroganov pinned the cash in his armpit, tore the foil away, and unscrewed the cap. He saluted with the bottle. "*Za vashe zdorovye!*" His Adam's apple bobbed like a cork. Vodka was water to him.

The Attorney stood waiting for his turn. Stroganov lowered the bottle slowly, a puzzled expression on his heavy face. "Not...right," he croaked. Then puzzlement gave way to horror. His throat made a clicking sound. He stepped toward the Attorney. The bottle fell from his hands and bounced splashing on the floor. The sudden contortions of hate on his face twisted it into a gargoyle's leer. His heavy arms rose to do damage!

The Attorney backed away in the narrow space. His right hand reached to his rear pocket where a small automatic pistol nestled, there in the event of Stroganov's teetotalling or other possible intransigencies. His fingers were trembling and the weapon didn't come readily to hand. The solid man was almost on him!

Another stride and Stroganov would seize his throat!

The heavy frame tottered, slid to the side, and toppled. The man's limbs twitched in an itchy dance. He uttered a horrid croak that made the Attorney's skin crawl. His mouth wobbled open and his eyes stared but did not see.

The Attorney leaned back against the wall and panted for a long moment, eyes ceilingward. He lowered them to the corpse. Yes, potent poison administered to silence the final tattling tongue. Poison, that reliable and soundless expediter, had left its wide track through Russian history, he thought. He managed a weak smile. As the babushkas insisted: the old ways were best.

After a pause for cocaine refreshment came a busy forty-five minutes involving iron bars and chain from the junk pile, a rowboat, oars, and a corpse.

Driving back to Pittsburgh, the Attorney mused over how well that had all gone—according to plan. How rare in this entire cache affair! Again he began to daydream about his retirement, the Roman pied-a-terre... Those light thoughts burst like bubbles in breeze. He swallowed. Had he used up all his luck today?

41

Pittsburgh, Pennsylvania

Here was a pretty bunch of fortune hunters, Detrovna thought, eyeing the group gathered around Nevsky's dining room table—he, his Attorney, the white-clad Korchevko, Father Fyodor of Kolyma, Nevsky, and at his insistence this Charity Day. Out of earshot in the kitchen, but somehow still players, were Alessya whose hate for the politician remained undiminished since she had tired to stab him a week ago, the wounded giant called the Archangel, smoking Shmelev who was at the vodka, and the artful peasant Lyubov.

It wasn't a good omen that the gathering had begun with the peasant's great dog baring her teeth and lunging at Father Fyodor, evidently intent upon finishing bad old business between them. At the final instant Lyubov controlled the animal. Borzoi and man were parted, the former growling like a diesel, the latter instinctively rubbing his partially healed right wrist.

Detrovna approached the priest and asked after his health. The other's eyes were icy. He said, "So we meet again, Boris Petrovich. Had you been more accommodating to my proposition, we might have come to this moment or one like it without...." He dropped a shoulder toward Korchevko.

Detrovna didn't share the priest's certainty in any direction. "Who can say what might have happened, or will yet happen?"

Father Fyodor snorted and turned away.

Then there was another awkward confrontation, this one between the wounded giant and the Day woman. Detrovna remembered the late Lyudya reporting that it was Day who had shot the man earlier when he attacked Nevsky and Alessya in the middle of the night. It was necessary for Fyodor to step between the lunging giant and the woman. Then Nevsky joined in, accusing Fyodor of having given the giant his lethal orders. Only the significance of the business at hand kept them all from one another's throats. An awkward truce of sorts was declared and the settling of accounts put off to a better time.

He looked around the room. Here his former lover Lyudmila had spyed well on his behalf. Now she was gone, murdered according to Korchevko. How, where, by whom he understood he would never know. She, another victim of the cache. His morbid instincts whispered she would not be the last.

This was Nevsky's meeting. The floor was his. Detrovna wondered where he would begin, the division of valuables, the secret of the Bible's paper? It was none of these. To his annoyance it was another matter completely.

"Are any of you aware there are other players in this cache business?" Nevsky asked. "They call themselves the Sons of Continuity. They go all the way back to Sergei himself, closeted away for decades like monks guarding the Imperial flame. They intend to make their own man Russia's leader. Ostrovsky is his name. His *nom de guerre* is Raptor. They're the ones who had the Nazi documents explaining what happened to the *Tatiana Nikolayevna* cube. They tipped me to Sybille Sollonier who saw the treasure in the *Maria Nikolayevna* cube."

"Saw the false treasure!" Detrovna bawled. Around the table others muttered their agreement. He felt his heart pounding with impatience. His mind's slide show served up greedy, impatient Gaichev who had the power to raise him high. *Less than a month to act!* His gaze traveled the gathering. He saw eager expectation everywhere.

Nevsky said, "With that red herring out of the way, we're assured the cache remains at Lake Nagle for us to find." Murmurs of anticipation filled the air. Detrovna glanced at the Attorney whose exhalation had more the whisper of dismay. The man's upper lip and temples were dewed with perspiration. The politician felt somewhat uneasy as well. What infernal business was this when good news seemed bad?

Korchevko stroked his long white hair. "Why didn't the czarist Nevsky fill all the cubes with faux treasure? Why just the one?"

"There's a reason. I sense it. But I don't know what it is," Nevsky said. Then he hurried on. "You must all know by now that there was nothing in the *Olga Nikolayevna* cube, or what had been there was removed. My guess is that nobody found it on the steppe before it was dug up. I don't think it ever had anything in it."

Korchevko frowned. "Again …why not have all of them empty, or all filled with false treasure—or pebbles for that matter?"

"I told you I haven't figured that out," Nevsky said. "You should understand that my grandfather had reasons for what he did." He cut off the rush of questions. "We'll talk later about the cubes—and the Bible paper. Let's get back to the Sons of Continuity."

"What of them?" Detrovna muttered.

"I think they should join us at this meeting," Nevsky said. "I think they should share the cache if we find it." A hubbub arose then, followed by a long discussion. Nevsky's points: the Sons were determined people; they were disciplined and dangerous. They might have been following him or otherwise gathering information about the cache's location. Who was to say what they might know and do if and when the treasure came to light? Finally debate wore down. A vote now was required by the principles.

Nevsky abstained. He made a point of saying he wasn't a contender for the cache. First, he wanted to help the others find it, of course. After that he sought only the murderer of a young priest, evidently done away with at the beginning of this vast circus. His suspicious glance found Father Fyodor who paid no heed. Nevsky said that if he were catalyst for finding the cache, none of it was of his design. Maybe his late grandfather's hand guided things somehow. Maybe curious events were simply unfolding in an orderly way over which he had no control. In any case, he abstained.

Shortly it would be Detrovna's turn to vote. To his surprise he found himself hesitating. He well recalled the small band of Sons fighting like Spartans.

"By all means have them join us," Korchevko said. "The treasure is vast. All can benefit."

The man's mindless piety rankled Detrovna. Behold more of this long-bankrupt Christianity! His annoyance pushed aside the Attorney's report of the deadly flashes from Sons' automatic rifle barrels. A two-way split was bearable, with the Church getting some part of the Force's share. No further dilution was acceptable. "I say no." Then all eyes turned to Father Fyodor who had the deciding vote. "My bishop gave me clear instructions. The Church's share in this affair is small enough. There are to be no further diminutions!"

Nevsky shifted, looking uneasy. He eyed the priest sourly. Clearly the American had ample reasons not trust the man and to suspect his motivations. The politician chuckled inwardly. Who at this table could be wholly trusted?

"You won't reconsider?" Nevsky asked.

"Impossible!" the priest said.

"I'm on record for saying that's a bad decision."

"Damn you and your record!" Father Fyodor spat. His ceramic beads chattered like a reptile's warning.

Matters turned then to the division of the cache. The Attorney busied himself at his laptop. Shortly an agreement was written, the device connected to Nevsky's printer, and four copies produced. The appropriate signatures were applied to the fifty-fifty split. Detrovna put down his pen on pages not worth what they weighed. He was as assured that treachery would follow ink as that tomorrow would arrive—his treachery, if no one else's. But it was too soon to finalize any plan. Such was impossible until the exact nature of the cache was revealed. His Attorney had successfully positioned their forces yesterday. No more could now be done.

As though granting Detrovna's wish, Charity Day, who had been the beneficiary of Nevsky's summary translations, spoke up. Nevsky reported that she said she had figured out precisely what made up the cache.

42

Nevsky was as anxious as anyone in his dining room to hear what Charity had to say. Time and again she had been far ahead of him in assembling handsome puzzles from ugly pieces. As she spoke, he translated for his skeptical guests.

"It's really not all that complicated," she began. "By now we have all the details we need. Here they are. Between 1909 and the Revolution Yuri's grandfather traveled around the world buying things. He bought a lot of indifferent art objects and, I believe, more important, *other* things. He went to great pains to arrange covert shipping to this country, to his man, 'the old Russian sailor,' living by Lake Nagle. Detrovna's divers have proved that beyond a doubt all the shipped items ended up dumped in the lake. Every one had the same characteristic..." She paused for Nevsky to finish translating.

All stared at her expectantly.

"They were all *hollow*, from the smallest vase to the biggest suit of armor. That was so they could hide the far more important other things I mentioned. When the many objects arrived, the first thing that happened at the lake site was that the Russian sailor emptied them of packing material and valuables."

After translation Detrovna cursed. "I was a fool for so long thinking the art worth something!"

Charity hurried on, not worrying about what Detrovna said. "So one doll at a time, one vase at a time, then another and another... After years of this the accumulated treasure was placed in the last cube, the one you call *Anastasia Nikolayevna*," Charity said. "Then the cube was hidden somewhere by the lake."

Nevsky was impressed. "So, wise one, what ended up in the final cube?"

Charity pressed a thoughtful finger to her cheek. "I've been thinking about that for some time. It had to be something that wouldn't lose its value or age or decompose in any way. Something easily recognizable as common currency anywhere that Nicholas II might have ended up—and at any time. I think Yuri's grandfather stashed...gold coins."

Nevsky remembered the many trays within the three seemingly identical cubes. They could comfortably have held coins. Why should the fourth one not also be a cunningly designed coin suppository? He recalled the dimensions of the cubes, nearly eight feet square and deep. A bit of calculation produced five hundred and twelve cubic feet. If every tray in the fourth cube was filled… That would mean a great deal of gold. Yes! He translated.

"So let it be gold!" Father Fyodor said. "Let it be platinum. Let it be *anything!* First, let us *find* it. Please, let us move to the mysterious paper Yuri Vladimirovich found in the Bible."

Nevsky translated and Charity snapped, "That *I* found in the Bible."

Fyodor growled his disrespect for her. Nevsky went to a sideboard, slid out a drawer, and withdrew a sheet of heavy vellum. "This is the sheet Charity found in the Bible." He unfolded it and held it up. "Can you imagine what's on this?" he asked.

Detrovna cursed. "Just tell us! It's been many weeks we've been in the hunt."

"OK. It's an engineering drawing."

"What kind of engineering drawing?" Korchevko asked.

"For an assembly."

"For the assembly of what?"

"A mount."

"To mount what?" Detrovna asked.

"You might ask me what it's to be made up of."

Father Fyodor jumped up. "What do I care? What's the mount *for?*"

Nevsky ignored him. "The mount will be made of certain brackets and trays from the three cubes. Every bracket and tray in them is coded. They're not all *quite* the same, it seems." Nevsky looked around. "Are you getting this? Pieces have to be removed from each cube then assembled according to this drawing." He looked around at the curious faces. "The three cubes never held any of the cache. But we need all three of them because without them the mount can't be assembled and the cache found."

"This is outrageous!" Detrovna shouted. "How could anyone expect all these steps to be taken across the decades, the continents, with always the possibility of mischance? A cube not found? An inconvenient death? The failure of memories? Ten thousand things could have gone wrong!"

Korchevko's low voice commanded everyone's attention. "When God wills something, it comes to pass, Boris Petrovich. Are we not here, now, with the cache soon to be within reach? Why question the minor miracle He has bestowed on us?"

The politician closed his mouth to avoid sputtering. He calmed himself and muttered, "God's work indeed! Just as likely that of the Devil."

"Here's what we're going to do," Nevsky said. "Tomorrow we're all going to Lake Nagle. We'll use this drawing to assemble the mount—"

"Where is this mount to be placed, Yuri Vladimirovich?" Father Fyodor barked. "And what is to be mounted?"

Nevsky looked stonily at the priest. "After we put it together, I'll show you," he said. "Before tomorrow is over, I believe we'll be opening a cube filled with gold."

43

Pittsburgh, Russian Slope

Here indeed was a country where *anything* could be had for money, Father Fyodor thought. Two weeks ago a handful of greenbacks shoved onto the greedy palm of a useful contact had led him to a certain doctor. Considerably more cash assured that the medico would ask no awkward questions about gunshot wounds. It took several hours for him to repair the worst of the damage done to the Archangel's shoulder and to cover his bandaged handiwork with a light cast that he molded from flexible plastic.

At that time Fyodor had been in another, familiar guise. It was not wise for a priest to be seen about such business. That same identity he assumed earlier this evening before a one-of-a kind specialist, a cat-toothed man whose existence was revealed to him only after energetic dispersal of more of those magical greenbacks to the right—or was it wrong?—people in this Russian community. The last of what had once seemed a heap of money squeezed from the spineless Bishop Paulos a month ago had gone to the cat-toothed man for the highest of reasons. After the deal was closed he had thrown in the use of this unused basement room for the night. "A 'freebie,'" he croaked, pocketing the wad of hundreds. After tomorrow neither the priest nor his Archangel would be troubled ever again by financial issues. The future would widen immeasurably for them to go about God's work as they saw it.

Now some immediate, lesser work was required of Father Fyodor. He beheld his Archangel without his two cassocks, shirt, undershirt, bandages and heavy crucifix. Also without the plastic cast that the priest earlier had removed so carefully. He saw the ruin of a once powerful shoulder and sutures with new white flesh beneath them. Within he understood there were screws into the bone. "Do you have much pain by now, my beast?" he asked.

The giant growled, his huge mouth in its nest of beard twisted with irritation. "It can be borne. Time will heal it."

"Excellent!" Father Fyodor turned to the wooden table. On it lay olive drab cellophane packages stamped "U.S. Army," the fruits of his dealings with the cat-toothed one. He tore the first one open. Within lay pale white foot-long bars. Each was two inches across and one thick. His source had called this material "C-4," what was available when an illicit buyer asked for plastic high explosives.

With the cast on the table to serve as a model, the priest copied it, shaping the marvelously malleable explosive. As required he opened additional packets and kneaded in the strips, adding them to the growing shape. Soon he eased what was now a sheet of explosive into the cast, bending the material to conform. Prayers came to him as he worked, and he spoke them. The Archangel had always found these familiar verses uplifting. The two chanted praise for God and His Son as the minutes passed. When the most convincing copy was completed, it weighed only twenty pounds. Fyodor attached the sealed detonator and nestled it cunningly out of sight. He also added a small, significant device with a magician-like flick of the wrist that escaped his beast's attention. The priest blessed himself, and the giant followed suit.

He cleaned the Archangel's wound and tightly arrayed fresh bandages. He fitted the shaped explosive to shoulder and chest with wide adhesive tape. "This doesn't offer the support of the other," Father Fyodor warned. "Handle your right arm as gently as you would a baby."

"I understand."

The priest patted the shaped explosives. "Here we have the highest trump," he said. "A card not to be played until the treasure lies before all the surviving contenders—after the exercise of who knows what chosen treacheries, during which we must look to our lives. We wait for that *one* perfect moment."

The giant nodded excitedly.

"Then you and I move front and center. Your fingers will be inserted in these two rings..." The priest exposed the hidden detonator and pointed to the metal circles dangling from it on two-inch wires. Two rings were required, avoiding the mischance of one being pulled in error. "I will explain the exact nature of your 'cast' and tell everyone to remove themselves from the treasure." He eyed the other man. "If they don't, we all go to meet our Maker." He snickered. "But they will retreat before my Archangel's reputation. I will disarm them. Possibly then, we will manage a quick execution for all. Save one."

"I know who!" the giant hooted. In many instances his rattling mind echoed the unspoken thoughts of the brighter man. "She! The blonde woman."

"Spared only to give to you, my beast. You will repay her for her expert pistol work. He spoke well who said revenge is best savored cold."

A high-pitched giggle escaped the giant's lips. "Cold now, but I know *then* my Heat will seize me! I will do...*wonderful* things to her. And in the end I think I will flay her."

"And such pleasures will cost you not a kopek of what in the end will be our horde. What will you do when our Church has the gold in hand?"

The Archangel pondered only a moment. "I will be founder and director of the best and largest orphanage in the Motherland—just for girls!"

Laughter neighed in the narrow room.

44

Lake Nagle, northeast of Pittsburgh

During the early morning ride Detrovna's attorney had told Nevsky that the three cubes were stored in a carelessly constructed shed at the foot of the high hill behind the lake. Upon arriving, Nevsky led Lyubov there. The short man carried a set of wrenches under his arm. In a sack over his back were metal saws, a rivet cutter, and Nevsky's choice of other hand tools and accessories.

Trooping behind came the others, minus Father Fyodor. Nevsky knew that wherever that man went, trouble followed. Maybe trouble would happen somewhere else today. He hadn't time to worry. The immediate task was to find the cache, and be done with it. He had studied the drawing and its parts list carefully last night. To his great disappointment the sheet contained not a single word about where the treasure was or how to use the assembly to find it. The best he could do was to organize the steps to be taken today, and then hope for inspiration. He set Lyubov to work opening the cubes, each at a panel he specified.

He refused to answer any questions. Detrovna, his attorney, Korchevko, and Shmelev in time fell silent. They paced the long grass impatiently. Shmelev reinforced himself with slugs of vodka from the bottle tucked inside his shirt. The bearded giant, who seldom spoke in any case, said nothing at all. He only towered, black and menacing, staring at Charity as though she were a sweet bun in a bakery window. When he first saw her again after she had wounded him, Nevsky had managed to damper the looming trouble. That it had been put off didn't mean the end of it. This Archangel wasn't the heavenly kind, able and willing to chuckle off a .38 slug through his shoulder. Nevsky had no idea how the matter ultimately would be settled.

Nevsky's eyes found Alessya who stared malevolently at Detrovna. Last night Nevsky had talked to her about curbing her implacable hatred of the man, at least until the treasure was in hand. Any lunacy on her part today would bring the whole affair crashing down to anarchy.

In an hour Lyubov, a clever man with tools, had opened the three cubes. He was peering into the gaps with the help of a hand lantern. Queen Catherine was trying to look in, too. He shoved the huge bitch away and ordered her to sit and be still.

"Can you see the identification numbers on the trays and brackets?" Nevsky asked.

"*Da*. Small and nearly hidden, as you described, Yuri Vladimirovich."

"Here are the numbers for the ones we want from *Olga Nikolayevna*..."

It took two more hours for Lyubov to remove the required pieces from the three cubes. He set each piece carefully on a plastic tarpaulin spread for the purpose outside the shed. At Nevsky's orders he polished the aluminum and removed minor corrosions with sandpaper and polish.

Korchevko strode up with Charity. In the bright July sun his white hair, leggings, and peasant blouse were dazzling. He nodded toward the tarpaulin. "This is all *amazing*, Yuri Vladimirovich. I sense you are...in God's hands."

Yuri nodded vaguely. Who knew? Maybe he was in his grandfather's hands. Or in no one's hands at all, just his own. Feeling awkward and slightly embarrassed, he said, "It's time to put them all together, Korchevko."

Studying the drawing, he called out the first two piece numbers and Lyubov found them. "They're supposed to snap together, it looks like," Nevsky said.

Lyubov busied himself. A metallic *clik* sounded as the two pieces joined. Another *clik* for the next two. Lyubov blessed himself twice against what to him seemed sorcery. The onlookers crowded closer as pieces were added to the mount structure. Shortly it stood before them, about four feet high. Its bottom tapered down to a threaded hole. From its top protruded a finely machined hexagonal nut slightly less than two inches thick.

"Now I'll show you all where it goes," Nevsky said. He led them up the hill. Queen Catherine circled ahead, running a gauntlet of discarded concrete blocks, lengths of three-inch vinyl pipe, and loose coils of woven yellow nylon rope. She followed her master to the spot Nevsky pointed out, the dried pond in front of the crumbled house's foundation. Lyubov busied himself with a wire brush and solvents to clean the threads from the pipe emerging from the concrete block. Nevsky marveled inwardly at the fineness of the machining and threading. Where had Sergey gone to have such exact work done? Shortly Lyubov was able to screw the mount onto the pipe. Nevsky peered over the shorter man's shoulder. "Turn it down flush to the base of the pipe," he ordered.

"They have set a metal disk in the cement. So it will be *just* so," Lyubov said. "As you wish it. And look here." He pointed at the disk. "Arrows on disk and mount align to show the way!"

Detrovna had crowded close. He shoved tentatively at the mount. It was unyielding. He cursed in amazement. "This is confounded good work all around, Yuri Vladimirovich. But..." He laid a palm over the protruding hex nut atop the mount. "What goes here?"

"The telescope," Nevsky said.

45

Ostrovsky lowered his Zeiss 8x30 binoculars through which he had beheld the sweating Nevsky and his greedy cohort drooling over their aluminum contraption. He smiled. Matters were going well, according to the plan he devised after the costly affair at the records center—Sasha gone! Let others unknot the cache's mystery and suffer its vexations. The Sons of Continuity would watch and wait. And when the time was right, strike!

It seemed that time was almost upon them.

He and his small force of eight Sons had been afoot in the wee hours, arriving well ahead of Nevsky's party. They had brought military equipment with them. Loyal American Sons had made its possession in this foreign land possible. It included small hand-held rocket launchers, grenades, explosives, mines, and flares, among other possible necessities. One did not want to lose an engagement, if one developed, for want of materiel. He ordered his troops to position themselves to their advantage. Radios kept all in contact. There had been a dicey moment early in their stay…

A military man at heart, Ostrovsky had ordered that the area be made secure. Surprises were bad business for those who wished to mount their own. It was Elena Petrovna who was tested. She had volunteered to join this effort because her sister had been wounded, tortured, and killed by Detrovna's people. Shortly before dawn she made her way through the site's heavier woods with the help of the scant moonlight. Ostrovsky had ordered that no lights be used and that his soldiers walk slowly and stop often. That had proved to be profound wisdom, at least for that particular moment—when the motionless woman heard a twig *snak* a few meters from her. Barely shielded by a boulder, she froze. She remained so while the tottering man unzipped and voided, some nearly splashing on her boot toe.

The discipline demanded of the Sons served her well twice, first keeping her silent, second squelching her great desire to kill the man with the Uzi she carried easily at her side. His like had ended her sister's life in horrid suffering. Composing herself with great dignity worthy of her aristocratic blood, she followed him a few dozen meters to find two well-hidden trailers looming up in the gloom. A look through the windows into interiors lit with battery-powered table lamps showed six men and signs of temporary occupancy. She wasn't surprised to see the firearms scattered about in the fashion of those who only imagined they knew weapons and how to handle them.

Earlier Ostrovsky had praised her for her work. Inwardly he had soared. She had found Detrovna's "strike force!" They were lumpish men who could be easily eliminated when the time came.

"Raptor, a question," Elena had said.

"Ask it."

"Will it be necessary for you to liquidate those swine?"

"Very likely, daughter," he said.

"I want a central role."

"You'll have it."

Her spine stiffened. Her right hand shot out. "Mother Russia will be great again!"

"If her Sons dare make her so!" Ostrovsky replied, and sent her away a happy woman.

He was blessed to have such stout, finely blooded hearts to serve the cause of his ascendancy. He was also blessed—for want of a better word—to be served by the man of quite different persuasion who had been patiently waiting in a small copse for his thanks. Ostrovsky waved the priest into the open, strode up, and embraced him. "Without your information over these weeks, Father Fyodor…" He shrugged. "The cache would have found its way into the maw of the opportunist Detrovna."

"Or that of Korchevko." The priest snorted. "Who in vain strives for that Christian impossibility, to balance piety against base greed, lust, and striving."

Ostrovsky led the priest to a fallen log. They sat. "We've been allies for many years, holy one. You've served the Sons of Continuity well."

"You've rewarded me generously." The priest's hatchet face broke into a rare smile. "Last week my mother saw the dacha you made available." He squeezed Ostrovsky's arm warmly. "She was stunned."

"Say the word and it's hers after we have the treasure."

"You're too kind." The priest was silent a moment, his ceramic beads clicking. "I did you a service for which you didn't ask," he said. "As I told you, the principles voted on sharing the cache all now are certain is made up of gold coins. Nevsky insisted that you be invited in to share."

"He did? Interesting…"

"He's wise enough to fear you and your forces. He bears you no enmity." The priest scowled. "He treats everyone evenhandedly. Except for me. And of course he has cause. I find him both puzzling and annoying. Since this affair began I sense something deep in him has ripened and ridden forth."

"I don't understand."

The priest waved his hand vaguely. "Something to do with blood and race long asleep. Those things that truly prevail no matter today's political rhetoric."

"Are you saying he's a contender for—?"

"Nothing of the sort. He says he cares only about finding a priest murdered weeks ago. By now matters have far exceeded what he first imagined. I cannot guess why he's doing what he is. I don't think he knows either. Those old realities I mentioned might now in some way have enchanted him. In any case, as I said, he wanted you to join the meeting. I clearly understood you had no wish to share any of the booty. Nor to act out a charade of cooperation that no one would value."

"So?"

"I told them my bishop had ordered me to prevent any further sharing." His laugh was a sharp croak. "As I said, the Church is to get a share of Korchevko's half. My 'no' vote ended the possibility of you suffering the inconvenience of having to present yourself uselessly."

Ostrovsky drifted off into thought. "Then when I take the cache, the Church gets nothing from all this?"

The priest shrugged. "So it seems."

Ostrovsky studied the cruel face. It was as impenetrable as marble. True, this cleric had been well rewarded for his services. Nonetheless... "To be candid for a moment, father. I can't help but understand that in my service and in others' you've show great skill in betrayal."

Father Fyodor looked directly into his eyes. "Such has been God's will for me."

"So, once more, there is no gain for you—and more importantly for your Church—in this matter past what I've already promised?"

"None."

No matter apparent truth, Ostrovsky's intuition spoke eloquently. "I hesitate to say this, Fyodor. Nonetheless, I feel compelled to warn you that one more attempted betrayal on your part will be instantly fatal."

"To be sure. To be sure." The priest was unconcerned. His beads rattled smoothly.

"Don't be so unwise as to try to seize the cache."

"Armed with what?" the priest laughed. "My only weapon is faith."

46

Lyubov was busy inside the Tatiana Nikolayevna cube. All others crowded around Nevsky asking questions about the telescope that he couldn't answer. Time had advanced to near noon. Another hot, humid Western Pennsylvania July day drew out the sweat. Usually cool Charity was tossing the hair covering her neck. Beefy Detrovna was dripping. "Hurry him up!" he barked.

"Here!" Lyubov's head and shoulders emerged. In his right hand he held a thick strut. He carried it to the tarp and attacked it with socket wrenches, searching for the best fit. He unscrewed four nuts. A cap popped off the strut's end. "Now we have it…" He tipped the strut. Out slid a tube protected by a cloth of odd weave. Lyubov chuckled. "Horse hair. Here is something that doesn't crumble in a week or two!" Carefully he unwrapped the telescope. Its metal fittings flashed under the sun, as though they had been machined yesterday.

"Mount it!" Detrovna ordered.

"Patience, Boris Petrovich." Korchevko laid a pale hand on the politician's shoulder. "Matters proceed well enough under Nevsky's hand."

Detrovna shook himself free. "We've been at this far too long. I am Boris Detrovna, not Job. I *must* see the gold!"

Nevsky turned the telescope in his hands. It was about eighteen inches long. Caps of fine wood were fastened to each end. They spun off their threads without taxing his fingers. Each lens was whole. He studied them. Both were unscratched. He turned to the others. "These lenses are fixed, not adjustable," he said.

Korchevko touched the instrument, his long fingers curling around it. "And what is the significance of that?" he asked.

"When we mount it, using this—" Nevsky pointed at short threaded rod set in the telescope's base. "—it will focus on an area. In that space we'll see what we're supposed to."

Detrovna looked around the landscape of dense bushes and scattered trees in puzzlement, like a man lost in a desert. "I don't need a telescope to see that there is no aluminum cube two-and-a-half meters on a side in sight."

When Nevsky translated for her, "Charity said, "Tell this guy that it figures a big cube stuffed with gold coins wasn't left out in the weather in plain sight for eighty years."

Instead of aggravating the politician, Nevsky carried the telescope to the mount and carefully screwed it into the hexagonal nut until it was flush. He saw the telescope was angled up toward the side of the substantial hill. He looked into the eyepiece. Detrovna was at his side in an instant. "Yuri Vladimirovich, what do you see?"

"Crosshairs centered on a blurry tree."

Detrovna cursed and stamped his foot.

Korchevko glided up to his man Shmelev. "Go to the pile of tools I saw at the edge of the lake. Fetch a saw to cut the tree down." The white-clad man's patience seemed infinite. "Bring whatever's there that might cut brush as well. The Lord's sun and rain have had their way here for a long time."

Shmelev and Lyubov took turns with the saw. The maple tree toppled in leafy surrender.

"Now what do you see?" Detrovna asked.

"Blurry bushes."

"Attack them!" the politician shouted, as though the growth was his worst enemy.

The two men wielded axes and saws. They tore at the growth with bare hands. In another half-hour nothing stood between the telescope and the side of the hill.

Nevsky put his eye to the scope. The crosshairs looked to be centered on— Detrovna shouldered him out of the way. He clamped his eye to the lens. "The hillside. Get up there! I'll guide you."

Lyubov and Shmelev scampered up through the growth, following Detrovna's directions. Well up the side of the hill Shmelev turned and shouted back. "Here there are stairs made of railroad ties fallen to pieces!"

"Yes!" Detrovna hogged the eyepiece like a selfish child. "To the right! Now, there, what do you see?"

Lyubov shouted back. "Nothing. Just the rocky hillside thick with these infernal bushes."

"Right there where you are. The crosshairs speak! The mossy stone marks the spot. Get shovels, spades. Dig in the hillside below it. *Dig!*"

Shmelev and Lyubov scampered down the hill, Queen Catherine in their wake, and returned with a mattock, axe, a pick, and two shovels. By then everyone had struggled up through the brush and was crowded around the hillside spot.

Detrovna shoved a forefinger at a twig in the brown earth halfway between the stone and the crumbled railroad tie beneath it. "Start here!" The men swung their mattocks. Dirt fell away. The earthy ellipse deepened. "Close at last..." Detrovna murmured.

Thrump! Shmelev's mattock struck something hollow. He clawed away dirt with thick fingers. He whirled toward his master Korchevko. "Wood. Maybe a door."

With an elated grunt Detrovna snatched up a shovel and joined the attack. He chopped and scraped. The giant Archangel strode forth as well. His good left arm and hand cut like a spade. He grunted and sweated with the others. Soon all the wood was exposed. A door, yes!

But more.

On it was painted the Romanov double eagle! And below, the date 1916.

So there it was, Nevsky thought. Sergey's completed masterpiece, the fourth cube completely filled and buried, just in time for the Revolution that the Sons of Continuity had feared. Mission accomplished. The cache was hidden in a safe, stable country where the czar-in-exile could access it. Nevsky imagined his grandfather's horror when he learned of Nicholas II's execution. Yet that was not the end of the dynasty. True to his mission Sergei knew of Cyril Vladimirovich's hope of a government in exile. The cache rightfully was now his. Thanks to the Cheka, Sergei and Cyril never met... Nonetheless Sergey's final moments insured that the cache moved not from Romanov hands to those of the Revolution, but to...well, Nevsky would soon see.

The red and black paints had been faded by the decades, but there was no mistaking authenticity. Detrovna said, "Behind this door stands the last cube. This one filled with gold!"

"If God wills it," Korchevko said softly.

"Untouched for eighty-two years," Detrovna's attorney breathed. He opened his briefcase and removed a measuring tape. He pulled out the tongue of flexible metal. He held it to the door vertically then horizontally. "Two and a half meters square," he announced. "Just wide enough for the fourth cube to pass." He stepped back and studied the door front. "One small matter, Boris Petrovich. I don't see the name we expected: *Anastasia Nikolayevna.*"

Detrovna said, "We'll see it on the cube when we find it inside, no doubt—" He checked himself. "And what does that matter in any case? Things painted on? Things not painted? Things that seem to be, but then are not? Gennady Efimovich, are you now trying to fill the shoes of the mystic czarist Nevsky with your nervous nitpicking?"

"I only comment," the attorney mumbled.

Lyubov explored the left side of the door with a mattock. There was the *klang* of metal on metal. "The hinges are here," he said.

Exploration found the door to be held closed by wooden pegs driven through it into an unseen vertical timber. It would have to be pried open. Luckily, there were tools…

The group fell back from the door, looking for shade among the thick bushes. Nevsky and Charity stood together. Before they could share a word, they heard Korchevko's voice. "Who are you calling?" A shout from the soft-spoken one was like a clap of thunder. Nevsky pushed through leafy clusters to see the white-clad ascetic confronting Detrovna's attorney who was holding a cell phone. Before the man could reply, Korchevko snatched the device away and hurled it down onto a boulder. It flew to pieces. "Who were you calling?" he insisted.

"Business matters in the Motherland," the attorney said.

"You're a liar!" Korchevko spat. "You'll do no more 'business' this afternoon, Gennady Efimovich! You'll stay in my sight until we see gold, and after."

Lyubov found an open can of motor oil and a rusty crowbar. He doused the hinges. Shmelev armed himself with an axe. Though the battle of metal against oak was unequal, the pegs were so stout and cleverly inserted that it took nearly half an hour to splinter them. Finally Shmelev's axe levered the door open a few inches. He spun and seized Korchevko's white sleeve. He shouted, "It's you who'll lead us all in the end. It's you who should open the door to the Romanov Cache!"

Korchevko hesitated for only an instant. He seized the door and heaved. Once. Twice. Then a third, mightier effort. The hinges shrieked like Baba Yaga's hut and the door swung open.

Nevsky never saw the two men coming. They burst from the bushes with automatic rifles leveled. "Nobody move!" one shouted in rough Russian.

"Well done!" Detrovna said. He moved quickly behind the two men. His attorney scampered to follow suit. Nevsky recognized them from the day he had peered through Butch's field glasses, the hoodlum with the plait and the other white-haired. "Search them for weapons at once," the politician bawled. Quickly Charity's .38 ended up in Plait's belt. White Hair checked out the Archangel who held up his massive left arm while his useless right stayed at his side. "I am a wounded holy man. Do not abuse me," he pleaded. Plait frisked him, left side, rear end, crotch, and legs.

Detrovna pointed to Alessya. "In her bosom she has a nasty knife. Get it!" White Hair rushed to her, tried to slide his hand inside her blouse. Her head ducked down like an adder's. She sank her teeth into his forearm. He howled and swung the butt of his automatic rifle into her ribs. Nevsky rushed at him and got a sudden look at the weapon's business end. "Far enough, hero!" Plait warned.

"Why don't you just ask her for the thing?" Nevsky said.

Alessya pulled out the narrow knife. She shoved it toward the hoodlum. When he took it and shoved it into his belt, she spat at him. "Pig! Detrovna's dim-witted slave!" she shouted.

Lyubov edged forward and threw his arms around her to hold her still. "Hot-headed sister, you roll dice with death. Calm yourself." She shrugged to throw him off, but her effort was half-hearted.

When everyone had been searched, Detrovna stepped forward, now armed with an automatic rifle brought by his men. "Not everyone is going to live to see the cache. He pointed. "Nevsky, his woman Charity, Alessya—you are to shoot them. The two Americans are no longer of use to us. My former mistress won't rest until she sees me dead. And so I simplify matters. Wait until we're through the door. I've seen enough liquidations for the present."

Nevsky stared, but wasn't surprised. This was the third time Detrovna threatened to kill him. He knew there would be no mercy this time. At his side Charity breathed, "Oh, my…"

Alessya cursed, kicked, and fought Lyubov's powerful arms. "Let her go, peasant!" Detrovna ordered. Lyubov reluctantly released her and backed away. The woman stood hissing like a cornered cat. With a sudden upswing of his weapon's butt to the side of her head, Plait knocked her spinning. She sprawled unmoving, outthrown arm in a V of bush branches.

Lyubov began a rash move.

"No!" Nevsky shouted.

The burly man skidded to a stop the instant before White Hair tugged his trigger. The slug stirred Lyubov's hair in close passage. White Hair lowered his weapon for the moment. Lyubov turned sorrowful eyes toward Nevsky. "Not to take a chance when Lyubov of the Dogs might save you?"

"That wasn't a good chance, Lyubov."

"A good worker doesn't let a good boss die."

"There's nothing you can do." Nevsky nodded toward Detrovna. "Do what he says. You might survive."

Lyubov grunted, as though he didn't want to survive if Nevsky didn't.

Detrovna made a gathering motion. "Lyubov and the rest of you come with me. We'll all see the cache before I decide your fates." They moved toward him. Queen Catherine circled nervously. He pointed at Shmelev. "You, swing the door wide." The others preceded him.

Shmelev followed orders. He peered beyond the door. "We will need lanterns, lights."

Detrovna cursed. Shmelev said to Korchevko, "Master, there was a small hand light abandoned where I found the tools. Lyubov used a bigger one inside the cubes."

Korchevko nodded thoughtfully, indifferent to Detrovna's control of the situation. Nevsky sensed the cache tugging at the man, tangling his judgment. "Get them," the ascetic murmured.

Detrovna snarled, "If you don't come back, Shmelev, your walking saint is dead. Your getting 'lost' and finding your way to the police...you wouldn't need any more English than you have to cause them to make trouble for us."

"Understood," the boar-like man said. The vodka bottle popped out of his shirt like a ventriloquist's puppet. He gulped down a generous slug and then disappeared into the bushes. In five minutes he was back. Again the group moved toward the yawning door, Lyubov looking back at Nevsky with sorrow in his eyes.

The Archangel paused and turned back to ogle Charity. Something like disappointment shifted his face's heavy planes. "A pity!" he croaked.

So the cache also stymied monsters' lewd desires, Nevsky thought.

Detrovna hurried his herd along. Over his shoulder, he commanded. "Finish your work quickly! Then guard this door. There are to be no interruptions while we're examining the gold." He called ahead to his attorney, "Gennady Efimovich, do you see the cube marked *Anastasia Nikolayevna?*" Then he was behind the door and gone.

Plait clipped Nevsky expertly behind the knees and he went down. The hoodlum's boot settled on the back of his neck. A few yards away Charity squealed. White Hair had a handful of her hair and was tripping her, dragging her down. Nevsky wanted to save her. No way. No saving her or himself. Loudly he asked her, "Sorry you came back to 138?"

"No. Damn it! *No!*" Recovering a bit, she added, "Not that it *matters.*"

Plait said to his partner. "These two first. Then we'll do the crazy bitch. She's not going anywhere."

Nevsky felt the hideous nudge of Plait's rifle barrel on the back of his neck. The last seconds of his life had come. He wanted to fault the Romanov Cache. Might as well fault Russia herself.

47

The Attorney was dismayed.

Behind the door was no cube!

Instead a mineshaft stretched ahead, the reason Shmelev had asked for lights. The Attorney didn't have one in his hand. Instead it held his small pistol. Detrovna had made him rear guard. His assignment: shoot anyone who tried to get away or otherwise provoke treachery. Ahead his master had made Korchevko carry the largest hand lantern. Lyubov had the flashlight. Their shadows bobbed ahead. Their meager conversation echoed.

The Attorney's misgivings had been calmed somewhat by the reappearance of the old, ruthless Detrovna. The heat of nearby gold had evaporated the quality of mercy that he had shown Nevsky on the ruined collective farm's grass, and who knew whatever other softness. No matter that he didn't wish first-hand observation of the three imminent liquidations. Yes! The Attorney sensed they were mounting the final pinnacle, with the entire matter entirely within their control. His master would indeed press on through to great wealth and even greater power. He might well become czar. And he, Gennady Efimovich Rishnikov, would coast to early retirement, to many cappuccinos and biscotti in Roman breakfast bars...

Still, he had very much wanted to see the final cube just beyond the door. Every moment it continued to elude Detrovna added to his uneasiness. From the open end of the shaft came the distant sound of three gunshots. Nevsky and the women were gone. The Attorney drew a deep breath. Now there would be no help from the American and his shrewd mistress should there be some...problem ahead. Please, let Detrovna not have liquidated them too early as he had the milquetoast Harsky!

The shaft angled down, turning deeper into the hill. His senses suggested it was then bending back toward the lake. Though the light was shadowed and dim, he noticed the timbers of the shaft were nothing like the rude beams of the mines he knew. These had been shaped and joined with the same pegs that sealed the door. The ceiling and walls had been smoothed and treated in some cunning fashion. A brush of his fingertips failed to dislodge a crumb of dirt or even a puff of dust. Possibly this wasn't a mine at all, rather a carefully constructed tunnel.

At first the air had been dry. Now it was becoming moister. He knew the shaft's downward plunge had carried it below the lake's water level. Confirming this suspicion was the appearance of wooden gutters filled with gravel and pebbles set into the floor at its edges to provide drainage. The floor's center was now slightly mounded, so any water would ease down into the gutters. There appeared side tunnels or shafts of the same size as the one he walked, similarly guttered and mounded. One opened to the right, another left, possibly fifty meters between each. Where did they lead? What purpose did they serve? He dared not investigate them. He had neither time nor light.

These other tunnels made him uneasy—as did the water now seeping from the walls. There wasn't much flow, but he remembered Boris Petrovich talking about the energetic divers having increased the lake's depth. Conceivably they were in danger here, well below the water line already, and angling steadily downward. Yet underwater mines and tunnels were disturbing places under the best conditions. Soon this one must end at the final elusive cube. Still they tramped on. More water seeped in. Cold drops fell on his head. He didn't like that. Nor did he relish the sound of Lyubov's bitch's increased whining. Finally the group came to a halt.

The tunnel ended—before a wooden barrier marked with the infernal Romanov double eagle!

Detrovna howled a curse. Korchevko blessed himself. Lyubov, Shmelev, and the Archangel muttered in disappointment. Shmelev felt the need to steady his nerves with another gulp of vodka.

"Why didn't we bring the *tools?*" Detrovna asked. "Who would have thought we would be stymied once again? Now this too must be broken down!"

The Attorney couldn't contain his uneasiness. "Boris Petrovich, show some caution here. This barrier could be holding out the lake itself!"

"Nonsense! The final cube filled with gold is behind this wood." Just to be sure he thumped the double eagle with the barrel of his automatic rifle. A comforting hollow sound boomed in the confining tunnel. The Attorney sighed with relief. His hands were trembling. His palm on the scored butt of his pistol was slick with sweat. For the love of God let them find the cube!

The previously used tools were required again. As before, Shmelev was chosen. Again Korchevko gave his approval. Off went the burly man, reinforced by another swallow of spirits, to scoop up the implements just beyond the tunnel door. Lyubov, Korchevko, and the Archangel milled uneasily before the barrier. The giant cast repeated glances up the tunnel. The Attorney guessed he was anticipating the arrival of his compatriot, the missing Father Fyodor. In what direction had that suspect cleric disappeared, today of all days, and for what purpose?

Despite his determined optimism, the Attorney understood anxiety and tension still reigned, even at this penultimate moment. Today death had already claimed three treasure hunters. Rifle at the ready, his master glowered at his captives. His power over them was a stifling fog that smothered conversation into infrequent mutterings. The bitch's steady whining grew annoying, no matter Lyubov's efforts to silence her. Nerves were stretched as tight as submarine hatches.

The Attorney studied the barrier. Not only pegs held this one closed. Its edges were sealed with tar or some other black, crusty, and thick creosote derivative. With Detrovna well armed and the three men close by, the Attorney was free to walk back up to the first side tunnel, Lyubov's flashlight in one hand, briefcase in the other. As he had gathered, this tunnel was identical to the other ones that mirrored the main. He walked swiftly, nearly at a run. After about fifty meters the tunnel ended.

It was blocked by a barrier identical to that at the end of the main tunnel. The double eagles seemed to leer down at him.

He hurried back, anxious to share what he had found with Detrovna. But as he reached the group an inner voice urged him to say nothing to his master because it could certainly vex him to violence. More likely: the Attorney wished so mightily for the final cube to lie behind *this* barrier and no other that he dared not speak. An indefinable sickness, not unlike a sense of doom, grew within him. These long minutes of infernal moleing in the earth seemed to lead less to treasure and more to…trap.

Further complications could not be endured!

His eyes were glued to his watch. He tried to ignore the water drops oozing from the ceiling, splashing down, and draining sluggishly into the gutters. Where were Shmelev and the tools? He glanced at the barrier as though at a feared enemy. Weapon in hand, Detrovna paced before it like a prison guard on duty. What was taking Shmelev so long? Possibly Korchevko was sharing the Attorney's uneasiness. He sank

slowly to his knees and began to pray determinedly. The
dampness oozed its way up the white cloth of his loose leggings.

"What's on your menu that God will order from?" Detrovna
asked with a laugh. "Gold for your cause? Angels to help you
carry off your share?"

"I pray for wise leadership for the Motherland and for
blessing on all our wicked souls." Korchevko turned to look up
at the Archangel. "Join me, father. Matters have grown rank
here and we need God's mercy."

The giant pressed a hand to his massive crucifix. "Don't
fear, my brother. Our Savior is with us. All will be well!"

As if on cue, there came Shmelev, burdened down. Lyubov
rushed to meet him, as anxious for matters to conclude here as
any of them.

"On your feet, Korchevko!" Detrovna nudged the ascetic's
shoulder. "We need fewer prayers and more light."

The Attorney added Lyubov's flashlight to the scanty
illumination. Axe and pick in hands, the burly men attacked the
sealed barrier. The Attorney was grateful for their stout backs.
Even better, experience with the construction of the first barrier
speeded their progress. Here, though, there was an additional
problem. Over decades the black sealant had hardened to
cement-like strength. Shmelev swung a pick at it. Black bits
darted off. He grunted, his breath coming faster. He swung
again, and again. Lyubov's axe bit into the oak like an iron
tooth. Their shadows heaved on the red double eagle. In their
sweaty exertions they seemed demons at darker work. Finally
Shmelev delivered an extra powerful blow that opened a small
hole. A curious rush of air whistled through it for just a
moment. The two men continued their assault, metal thudding
on wood.

"Faster! Harder, men!" Detrovna urged. "I know the
Anastasia Nikolayevna cube stands within arm's length waiting
to be broken and plundered."

Lyubov's axe broke through. With practiced strokes he
opened a wider hole. Despite Detrovna's shoving the smaller
man aside to peer through, the Attorney caught a glimpse of
what lay beyond. At his side the bitch's whine peaked to what
seemed a shriek in the narrow space.

He staggered aside. His heart told him he would never feel
Roman sunshine.

Ten meters further on was another, identical barrier.

48

"No one-two-three for you, Nevsky." Plait centered the rifle barrel on the back of the prostrate man's neck. "You're dead *now*—" Nevksy clenched his teeth for his trip to oblivion.

He heard a heavy *thukk* above. Plait uttered a short, muted scream. His weight fell on Nevsky who squirmed wildly in an adrenalin-charged fit of fear and loathing. Running boots flashed past. He looked over the hunting knife protruding from Plait's back to see White Hair swinging his rifle away from Charity's head toward an onrushing Butch Hanson.

He wasn't quite quick enough. Butch's left hand seized the barrel and jerked the weapon away as though from a boy. He flung it aside. His big hands, fast as a mongoose, now gripped the White Hair's neck. "You don't know me, but I want to tell you why you're dying. Remember the old man who wouldn't sell his property? Remember how you and your buddy there broke his arm? You thought that was bad luck for him." He increased the pressure. Choking noises came from White Hair's sagging mouth. "I'm his son come to say that was really bad luck for *you*." More pressure from the large hands brought popping and snapping from White Hair's throat. Nevsky looked away. "You lived a lot longer than you deserved," Butch whispered. "No more safety in numbers for you, trash." Long moments passed. White Hair gave a short chicken-like squawk. Nevsky looked back as Butch threw down what was now a corpse.

Nevsky got up shakily, trying to balance on Jell-O legs. He turned toward Charity. She was on her knees, saying, "Oh...oh...oh..." with hands pressed to her face. "We were both going to *die*. I have to thank you, whoever you are. Thank you for...being able to kill." She turned away from the corpses.

"Lady, they were ugly men all the way through," Butch said. "I know. I've been studying them for weeks." He snatched up a fallen automatic rifle and fired three rounds into the air. "Bang-bang-bang! You're dead," he said to the two. "In case anyone's paying attention."

Nevsky introduced Charity to Butch then staggered over to the bush into which Alessya had tumbled. He freed her arm from the branches and knelt. She had an apricot-sized lump above her ear. On it was an abrasion oozing blood. He laid a hand on her long neck. There was a pulse. Concussion? Brain damage? He didn't know. Right now he could do nothing for her. Too much was going on.

Butch dragged the dead men into the bushes and came back to the couple. His pale eyes showed no remorse as he accepted Nevsky's profound thanks. Charity added still more of her own. Uneasiness stirred in Nevsky's gut. Butch had been his friend for years, but he had never really known him well. Nonetheless, he understood ruthlessness and skill in killing when demonstrated for him. Now he saw that Butch Hanson was not a man to jerk around. So when he asked, "What the hell has been going on around here, Yuri?" Nevsky felt very much under the gun for not entirely clear reasons. "I have a feeling you know," Butch added.

Nevsky felt the need to put him off a while. "Let's first hear about how Cavalry Hanson came to the rescue just as the injuns were closing in," he said.

The three stepped into the shade. Butch spoke tersely, without emotion. Earlier he had helped his mother pack up for her move to Florida. During that time his quarry left the site. He didn't find out the two men had gone on some kind of errand until he had set himself up once again to spy on them, and saw them return. After that they didn't leave again. Annoyed by his missed chance, he intensified his vigil. The effort seemed about to bear fruit the day before yesterday when the work crew was reduced to seven—then six when one of them was rowed out to the middle of the lake and slid over board wearing cast iron shoes. His two targets were among the remaining six men. He imagined he could ambush at least one of them before long. Unhappily they were confined to quarters for the rest of that day and the next, it seemed, because none appeared after the man with the briefcase left in his car.

Now Nevsky understood the sudden appearance of the two deadly hoodlums. Detrovna's attorney had called them on his cell phone. He swallowed heavily. That meant there were four more still around to work the politician's will.

Butch hung around well into yesterday evening. Only when it was clear that none of the men was going to leave his trailer did he doze for a few hours in his hidden car. Before dawn he was up, looking to stake out the trailers in hopes one of his targets would emerge to be taken. And what did he see? A woman in camouflage carrying an Uzi was peeking through one of the trailer windows!

She had the look of a soldier. That changed Butch's plans. With great caution he scouted the property he knew so well. In time he found eight soldiers, all out scoping the terrain. He was furious that their presence might further delay his revenge. To his surprise they all gathered at a distant corner of the property, evidently waiting for orders. He returned to the trailer area and hid himself. The arrival of Nevsky's party proved a wild card. Maybe simply killing his quarry on the spot wasn't the thing to do. When Plait and White Hair came out at midday, he chose to follow them. He guessed he might be able to do Yuri some good. And indeed he had. "Lucky day for you, Nevsky," he said.

Charity let out a slow breath. "Yes. Lucky, lucky!" She shook her shoulders, as though to throw off the touch of the hand of death. Then she frowned. "Eight soldiers!" She looked at Nevsky. "They must belong to that group you wanted to be a part of things. The Sons of Continuity."

"Well, they're that now," he said, sensing a certain inevitability.

Butch looked at Nevsky. "Your turn. What's happening here?"

Nevsky hesitated.

"Let me guess, Yuri. What they were looking for in the lake turns out to be behind that door over there."

"That's pretty much it," Nevsky said evenly.

"So what's all the fuss over? Must be something pretty valuable. All the trouble somebody took to get hold of this property, hire the people, do the diving, and haul up all that fancy trash. Couple days ago I saw a guy get cement shoes. Today you each almost get a round in the back of the neck." He nodded toward the door. "And some pied piper with an AR leads a flock into the mountain."

"Butch, it's about some old Russian stuff that people today are taking pretty seriously." Nevsky took a deep breath. "We talked about it before. It's about something I don't want you to get mixed up in."

The big man snorted. "I'm already mixed up in it. If I wasn't, you'd be dead!"

"Don't get me wrong. I'm not ungrateful," Nevsky said. "It's that this business is all...tainted and twisted."

"So..." Butch frowned.

"I want you to leave here now. For your own good."

Butch opened his mouth.

Before he could speak, Nevsky said, "I want you to trust my intuition, Butch. Please. There's deep danger here."

Butch shook his head in bewilderment. "Hey, man, there are soldiers and civilians walking around here packing heavy artillery. What are you going to do about them?"

"I hope I don't have to do anything."

Butch scowled. "I don't get it. I saved your lives. Your lives are still in danger, and you're trying to give me the push."

Charity said, "It's not 'the push.' You're a wonderful guy, Butch. Forever a hero in my book. I'll always be in your debt. We both will be. Yuri's saying that it's a lot more dangerous here for you than for us."

Butch began to ponder, so Nevsky was grateful for Charity's womanly persuasion. "I go, what happens to you?" Butch asked.

"I don't know," Nevsky said. And he didn't. "Leave now. Then come to my house in a couple days. We can talk then. I'll tell you the whole story."

"Suppose neither of you is there."

"Then you can decide if you want to invite the police to come out here and have a look."

Butch glanced toward the bushes hiding the pair he had killed. "Don't think *that* will happen." He walked over and pulled his heavy knife out of Plait's back. He jabbed it deep into the soil to clean it. "You sure about what you want?"

"Yes."

"*Really* sure?"

"Absolutely," Nevsky answered.

Butch smiled uneasily. "Yuri, the talk around town has always been that you're a little… weird."

"So you have another anecdote to support that view."

"I guess I do." From his belt Butch pulled a Smith and Wesson .45. "Why don't you take this as a good luck charm?"

Nevsky shook his head. "Enough guns and lead are around here already to fight a banana republic war. Don't really need more."

Butch shrugged and smiled. He offered Nevsky his hand. He shook it. Charity gave him a warm hug. "Thank you so much, in every direction," she said.

"Good luck," Butch said starting off. "You're going to need it."

Nevsky called after him, "Butch, no hanging around. No more patrols. Please just slip off the property."

"Will do." Butch waved and disappeared into the bushes. His voice floated back. "I don't think I'm going to see either one of you again."

"See you in a couple days!" Nevsky called bravely after him.

When he was gone, Charity whispered, "Was sending him away like that a *good* idea?"

"Seemed right to me. He doesn't belong here. Anybody with a gun who sees him shoots him."

"And what you told him about this being a *tainted* place?"

Nevsky looked into her questioning blue eyes. "I'll stand by that."

Charity's started. "Look! Somebody's coming out the door!"

It was Shmelev. The two rushed to the burly man. He was astonished to find them alive. He touched Charity's shoulder just to make sure she wasn't a spirit. They offered no explanation of their survival. They rushed to ask him if Detrovna's group had found the cube.

He slipped out his vodka, unscrewed the cap and had a good pull. Then he hastily lit a cigarette. "I do not like being under the earth," he explained. He told them about the tunnels, the deepening dampness, and the long descent to the barrier bearing yet another Romanov double eagle. It had to be breached. He had come for the tools. His eyes darted about nervously. He had already spent too much time talking to the two. His master Korchevko's life was forfeit if he delayed. He threw down his smoke and slammed it with a heel. He rushed back up the hill, snatched up the axe and pick, and hurtled out of sight behind the door.

"Now what, Mr. Mumbo-Jumbo?" Charity said. Her voice was shaky, her narrow escape much on her mind. "What's going to happen to us when they come up out of that hole and everybody starts shooting at each other over the treasure? Maybe they'll shoot us, too!"

Nevsky scarcely heard her. He was thinking. There was no cube beyond the door! *No cube...* Ideas fluttered in his mind, but they refused to come to rest for identification. He was missing an important connection with the obvious. He paced, Charity watching. He sensed he knew everything he needed, but couldn't push his brain over the hump beyond which lay the final answer. He needed to think like his grandfather. That wasn't easy... His memory patrolled the slights-of-hand and misdirection of the last eighty-plus years. Abruptly, as though through sorcery, an idea popped up.

One that might fit the final pieces together.

He needed confirmation. He looked at Charity. "We have to go back to the telescope," he said. "I never got a clear look through it."

"I was thinking maybe we should run for it," she said. "When they all come out of that hole with the gold, I know there's going to be big trouble"

"They haven't found it yet, have they?"

"Well, no..."

"I have to help them. Everything goes back to my family, from Imperial Russia to now. First my grandfather who started it all, now me to finish it. I hope you understand."

"Well, not exactly," she said. "But..."

"I know we're very close to the end of all this," he said. "I'm asking you to hang in just a while longer. Let them do what they want after we find the cache. We'll just clear out. To handle the last of my 'responsibilities' I need to look through the telescope again."

"If you think that'll help us get out of here alive... " Charity said skeptically.

They angled down the hillside through the piles of pipe and rope lengths toward the drained pond. A man stepped out of the bushes and blocked their way. He wore a business suit and a full beard.

It was Timofy Grushkin who had sat with Nevsky at repentant Father Ruslan's bedside—and was never seen again.

49

Nevsky now wished he had taken Butch's .45, but only for a moment. In Grushkin's wake came a man in camouflage holding an Uzi. It was pointed at Nevsky's chest. Too many weapons on this earth, he thought, and far too many aimed at him these days. Familiarity in this case failed to breed contempt.

"How convenient that you sent off your protector," Grushkin said. "For strategic reasons the Sons cannot fire their weapons just now. As to taking that man hand-to-hand..." He smiled. "We would have to lose several Sons for no worthwhile reason."

Nevsky gathered himself as well as he could. In an unsteady voice he managed to say, "Where have you been keeping yourself, Timofy Teodorovich?"

"Going here and there about the world, as is said," Grushkin laughed.

Nevsky saw nothing funny at this moment. He glowered at the bearded man. "Odd how things work: I think you're the reason for everything."

"For 'everything?'" Grushkin asked.

"I might have never really gotten involved in finding the cache if you hadn't murdered Father Alexei. And none of you would be here today if I had done that."

"You think I tortured and killed that pleasant young holy man?" Grushkin asked.

"I know you did!"

"Not exactly." The bearded man chuckled. His luminous blue eyes sparkled.

"What does that mean?"

"I'm told you used to be some sort of a detective. Do some detective work."

Nevsky stared at him, puzzled. For sure there was something he wasn't getting.

After a few moments Grushkin said, "Is your mind not working well right now? Well, you've had a hard few weeks. Would you like me to introduce you to Father Alexei's murderer?"

Nevsky was baffled. He shrugged. "Go ahead then."

Grushkin turned his back. His giggle chilled Nevsky's blood. He fumbled at his collar, gripped something and heaved upward. In an instant the rubber mask with its attached beard was dangling from fingers held above his head. He turned back.

Father Fyodor of Kolyma!

"You!"

Father Fyodor giggled on as he put fingertips to his eyes and popped out blue-tinted contract lenses that fluttered down to the dirt. He tossed the mask into the bushes. "My alter ego matched with a most convincing change of voice. Very useful when I went about un-priestly doings. Not needed any longer. The search for the cache draws to a close." He smothered his mirth, drawing a deep breath. He gestured at the soldier. "You see I'm in the Sons of Continuity's camp. The Raptor and I have cooperated for years." He chuckled. "In fact I'm also working under an agreement with the pious Korchevko. And for the Church, too! I'm working for *everyone*." He threw back his head and howled with delight.

Of course he and Ostrovsky were in league! Nevsky thought. That was how weeks ago, when the general and he traded information, Ostrovsky already knew about the Kirgiz cube, but didn't dare admit it. The disguised priest had told him about it soon after the episode at Father Ruslan's bedside. Nevsky had been a dunce not to have figured that out.

Rage flashed up from Nevsky's heart. He lunged at the priest, curses on his lips. Charity cried, "Yuri!" She flung herself in his path, tripping him up. The soldier's finger slipped from the trigger guard to a more lethal position. "Are you *stupid* or something?" she asked. Nevsky was on his knees. She hung on his shoulders so he couldn't rise.

A commanding voice that Nevsky knew said, "Listen to a woman's wisdom and calm yourself, Yuri Vladimirovich." General Ostrovsky stepped forward out of the bushes. Behind him were four soldiers. "To die now when the cache is about to be uncovered would be a senseless tragedy. I appreciate your role in helping the Sons to this moment. Enough blood has already been spilled, some of it unwisely, I must admit." He touched his goatee thoughtfully. "Then, behind every great fortune stands crime. Do I have your promise to control yourself?"

Across the lake came long bursts of fire from at least three automatic weapons. There was no return fire, only screams. Fyodor and Ostrovsky smiled. "That would be the surprise liquidation of Detrovna's four remaining men. The attack was led by my most determined trooper, Elena Petrovna." He punched a number into his cell phone and put it to his ear. "Report on the operation!...Excellent...All of them,

Elena?...You're certain?...Of course...Throw the bodies in the lake at once...Send somebody to pick up the box of flares...Then all of you join us...We're near the opened door on the side of the hill...Again, good work!" He turned back to Nevsky. "Excuse me, Yuri Vladimirovich. A necessary interruption. Are you willing to be reasonable and tell us what you've learned?"

The ranks were thinning in this affair, Nevsky thought. A deep-rooted instinct whispered that further thinning still remained. "All right," he said. He climbed to his feet and glowered at Father Fyodor. "Get him out of here. I don't want to look at him!"

Ostrovsky shook his head. "We saw Korchevko's man Shmelev talk to you. We both need to know what he said. Did they find the cube?"

Nevsky told them everything he knew, but kept his uncertainties to himself. He chose not to look at the black priest.

Ostrovsky further straightened his already ramrod spine. "Excellent! They're on the cusp of success. And now we make our move!" He turned to the priest. "It's as we planned then, Fyodor. Do as you suggested." The priest nodded, left the group behind, and moved alone toward the door in the hill. The rattle of his ceramic beads diminished, then was lost to the ear. Ostrovsky turned back to Nevsky and Charity. "You and your associate Day won't have the pleasure of seeing the cache as we open it, Yuri Vladimirovich."

Nevsky frowned. "Why not?"

"Because you failed to be honest and straightforward with the Sons around the issue of Sybille Sollonier's information. Moses, despite all he did, failed to tread the Promised Land. Likewise, no matter your efforts and past perils, you won't be among those to first behold the treasure. You see, my friend, I don't forget treachery, no matter how modest. If your grandfather hadn't been the sole genius among the original Sons, I would deprive you of a great deal more than the first look at what I'm sure is a monumental amount of gold. Possibly later you will be allowed to see what we find."

Nevsky translated for Charity. She snorted indignantly. "You'd think by now he'd know nothing in this whole cache chase goes well without you. I'd think that would include finally looking at the elusive thing."

Ostrovsky of course understood not a word. Nevsky was about to translate, but something checked him. He said nothing. The general motioned to the nearest soldier, a handsome young man with corn-colored hair. "Keep them right here until we come back with the treasure."

The four soldiers, one a woman, moved up the hill to join the others. She saluted Ostrovsky. He returned it. He saw to the distribution of flares to his soldiers, and then led them toward the door into the tunnel.

Nevsky looked at Charity. "Might as well sit down," he said. They found a patch of grass under a high bush. He eased down and turned in an effort to sit comfortably on the rough earth. His angle of vision differed from that of the man assigned to guard them. He saw two men moving silently up the hill toward them through the deep screen of bushes. They moved as fast and silently as bats.

They weren't ordinary men.

50

Father Fyodor knew nothing about the tunnel down which he strode. He had no light. He ran his hand along the smooth wall to keep his direction. No matter that awkwardness. The only important thing was that the Romanov Cache lay at the end of this incline behind a wooden barrier—the last of the many barriers of all types that the cunning czarist Nevsky had erected before those who sought what he had hidden.

Moving through the darkness made him uneasy. Men needed to use their eyes. Even so, he hurried on. No time for qualms. There was work to be done. His fingertips found no resistance! A tiny flash of panic arose. He made himself move forward three, four paces. Ahh, contact with the wall again. Good. Clearly another tunnel had branched off the main. He discovered others in his blind descent. In time he glimpsed dimness ahead. His anxiety subsided. He came closer to the splash of battery-powered lights. Understanding Detrovna had a weapon and might well be trigger happy in the heat of the final moments of the search, he called out.

He saw. The barrier was down! The treasure had been found! Wait a moment. There was another, identical barrier beyond the first. The treasure was still hidden. The men gathered before it gave him scarcely a look. Shmelev and Lyubov were attacking the second barrier with axe and pick. Detrovna and Korchevko looked on while the peasant's whining bitch turned in small circles.

"Welcome!' the Archangel croaked. There was sweat above his beard on the wide planes of his heavy face. Detrovna too was sweating. His attorney's collar had long since wilted. Even Korchevko's white clothing looked matted. Fyodor saw this treasure hunting had become ever more anxious business.

"Well, Boris Petrovich?" he said.

The politician looked quickly at the priest's unfamiliar clothing, frowned, and then turned his eyes back to the two laboring men. "Any moment now…"

"Good to know." Father Fyodor slid the automatic down the sleeve of his business suit into his hand. He shot Detrovna through the neck. The gunshot punished eardrums in the confined area. He whirled and shot Detrovna's attorney just above the right eye. The shot was so clean that the man didn't even drop his briefcase. With it still in his hand he crumpled soundlessly. The shots' concussions rolled up the tunnels and echoed back as fading moans.

The Archangel whooped with delight.

Fyodor swung the pistol toward Korchevko, lowered it. The man was an ally in a manner of speaking. He needn't die now—soon, but not now. The two shorter men were needed to continue the attack on the final barrier. For now the killing was over.

Korchevko stared at him. "Who *are* you that you can do such things?"

"A very special person who has just increased *your* share of the cache."

"Everything…has gone wrong. Far worse than wrong!" Korchevko blessed himself. Lyubov and Shmelev did the same. These two men were wide-eyed and trembling. Shmelev sucked up all but the last of his vodka and slid the bottle back inside his shirt.

The Archangel chuckled to see their fear. "They all wish they were back in the Motherland with their mommies," he grunted.

Fyodor saw their dazed eyes, their fear of him and this damp tunnel. He slid his beads out and began to work them steadily. "You want to get out of here and away from me?" he asked. "Then knock down the Romanov eagles! And we'll all soon be happy men." He snatched up dead Detrovna's rifle. On a hunch he frisked the fallen attorney, found a small pistol, and dropped it into his own suit pocket. He pointed at Shmelev and Lyubov. "Keep working. I'll be right back." He turned up the tunnel toward Ostrovsky and his forces. They had waited, of course. Had the Raptor or one of his soldiers appeared, an ugly gun battle would have been a certainty, with lives needlessly lost. So it was left to Fyodor to expedite. And so he had. With the situation under control, he called loudly up the tunnel, "Come ahead, Raptor! Come and uncover the Romanov Cache!

51

Nevsky nudged Charity's shoulder and inclined his head slightly toward the two approaching men. She started, but concealed the motion by then adjusting her hair. The guard was about five yards away, his eyes fastened on them. So he didn't see one of the silent figures raise a curious rifle-like weapon. A silencer hissed and the young man fell. No blood, little damage. A rubber bullet had nicked his skull.

Nevsky waited for the weapon next to be turned on him. Instead the two men scanned the immediate vicinity with care and then approached. They were dressed identically in gray ski-like outfits, tight pants, shirts, and sheer gloves. Each carried a medium-sized backpack. Further, they *were* identical: same height, weight, and face. Each had heavy brows, pale blue eyes, and chin jutting like an outcropping. They both looked at him. "You are Yuri Nevsky?" one asked in Russian.

Nevsky nodded. "Why didn't you stun me, too?" he asked.

"You are not armed," the other twin said.

"How do you know me? I don't know you."

"We were told about you. And many other things about this place and the search for the cache."

"Who told you?"

The twins shook their heads together. "We are late coming. Almost too late," one said. "Travel in a strange land isn't easy."

Charity said, "Yuri, what do they want?"

"Good question." He asked them.

"We're looking for Father Fyodor of Kolyma and another devil called the Archangel."

Nevsky translated for Charity. "Why do you want to find them?" he asked.

The twins together drew fingers across their throats.

So someone was after ending the black priests' capers, but not those of any of the present cache players, Nevsky thought. He who had loosed the demons now sought to cage them forever with paid assassins—a longstanding Russian tradition. He remembered the night this quest had begun. Father Alexei had brought him a letter from...Bishop Paulos, who had later tried intimidation to get cache information from him. The bishop had been a distant player in the game, but one nonetheless. He smiled. "And how is Bishop Paulos these days?"

"He isn't with us any longer," the assassins both said together in eerie chorus. "He died by his own hand."

"How can he pay you, then?"

"His agents still act for him," a twin said. "A bargain has been made, and will be kept."

Important time was being wasted, Nevsky realized—theirs and his. He needed to send the assassins on their way. He told them everything he knew about the tunnels and all the people in them. Among all those obstacles they would find their prey. They slid off, fast and confidant, to set up an ambush near the tunnel entrance. Nevsky imagined they carried in their packs a variety of weapons, silent and otherwise, and well knew which ones to use, and when. The black priests were as good as dead. He said to Charity, "Stay here. I'll need you."

He hurried downhill toward the mounted telescope. Of course it pointed at the hill. He had seen that before Detrovna had shoved him aside. Nonetheless, he knew he needed to look through it again. He skidded to a stop before it. He drew a deep breath to steady himself. He glanced back up the hill. The assassins had already made themselves invisible. They were in hiding now and as disinterested as the Sphinx in any of his doings. He turned back to the precision instrument. Its brass winked in the sunlight. He bent his head down to the dime-sized eyepiece. There was the hill, there were the crosshairs centered...not just where the door had been exposed, but above its top by two feet.

The crosshairs marked the middle of the mossy rock Detrovna had identified and used to decide just where to dig.

He called to Charity. "Can you get up there above the door? There's a rock there. Scrape the moss away if you can."

The slope was steep and she had to dig her feet in. She clutched at sumac saplings. She angled over to lean for support with one spread palm on the heavy oak door. "Hang on, Yuri. Need a scraper." She was close enough to the stone for Nevsky to see her enter the telescope's narrow field. She found a bit of flattish rock. With awkward one-handed strokes she attacked the deep moss. *Klik-klik-klik.* "Something carved into the rock, Yuri. I recognize Russian letters..."

Nevsky saw them exposed a few at a time. Gray rock, peeled back heavy green. She didn't have to finish the job.

On the rock was carved *Anastasia Nikolayevna!*

In an instant he understood. The "fourth cube" was the tunnels!

There were many tunnels according to Shmelev and presumably many other barriers. Breaking them down willy-nilly wasn't the way to go because there were no cubes behind any of them! They had to be told—now!

As he moved his eyes away from the telescope he saw a moving figure. It was Alessya! She had regained consciousness and had just snatched her dagger from dead Plait's belt. She rushed toward Charity who was badly balanced on the slope. The powerful woman dragged her down and set one knee on her chest. Nevsky started to run back up the hill, but was far too slow and far away to get there quickly. He heard Alessya shout, "Where is Boris Detrovna?"

Charity hesitated. She did understand "Boris Detrovna," if nothing more. In an instant Alessya's knife was at her neck. "Once more, where—"

Charity thrust an arm toward the tunnel. "In there!" she shouted in fright. "He's in there!" Alessya sprang up like a panther. Blood dribbled down the side of her wounded head.

Nevsky shouted. "Don't go in there! There are a dozen people down there and—"

But she was already in the tunnel, knife in her grip.

Nevsky plunged in after her, doubting he could catch her soon enough. He had to run as fast as he could anyway. To tell them what they were doing down there was *all wrong*!

52

Ostrovsky ordered his seven soldiers to drive their glowing flares into the sides of the tunnel every twenty meters. Clutching his own flare, he led them in a hasty descent. The sound of Fyodor's pistol shots echoed in an all clear. Detrovna and his toady were out of the way. Now there remained only the two lumpish men and the last contender, Korchevko. The Raptor began to plan ahead just a bit. The white-clad one might be more useful alive than dead. Conceivably he could be persuaded to accept something like a prime minister's post. The czars and later-comers with similar powers had employed seemingly impressive men in such a fashion. It bore further thinking. He was still in something like a satisfied reverie when the tunnel ended. He heard Fyodor's invitation to descend further and soon behold the cache.

Water now trickled down from the ceiling, little rivulets that found everyone's head and shoulders. The flares showed enough water had entered the tunnel to half fill the gutters.

He didn't like what he saw ahead. It wasn't the corpses of the politician and his lackey that troubled him.

One shattered barrier had fallen. Lyubov and Shmelev were attacking a second with axe and pick, encouraged by the automatic rifle in the priest's hand. Why were there *two* barriers? Ostrovsky wondered. Was not one enough to hide the final cube? See the guttering ended just before the first barrier! Hear the dog whining miserably!

No sooner had he come to a halt than Shmelev's axe pierced the oak.

A curious rush of air came through the hole.

Hairs rose on the back of Ostrovsky's neck. He eyes found the tarred edges of the fallen barrier, moved up and saw the same sealant on the newly pierced one. He interrupted Fyodor's greeting with an urgent shout. "Was there such a sound when the first one was opened?"

The priest frowned uncertainly. Lyubov said, "The same? Yes, I heard it."

Ostrovsky cursed. He had learned of such barriers. Pirates and sailors often made them. Fyodor had told him that an old Russian sailor had manned this outpost for Nevsky. He had done more than just that! He and an unknown crew long ago had partially drained the lake or erected temporary dams. Then they closed the end of each of the tunnels with a series of heavy, airtight wooden doors or planks like those before him, the outermost undoubtedly waterproof set well below the ken of Detrovna's divers. Air was pumped into them, and then they were sealed with the tar-like cement. Only when that work was completed was the water restored to its original depth.

No one who understood this would ever break the wooden seals without first again lowering the water level. To do so would be to fall into a dreadful trap!

"Stop!" he shouted. "Strike the wood once more and I'll kill you!"

53

Father Fyodor scarcely could have imagined how well matters were falling out. He had heard of the suicide of Bishop Paulos who once had expected some share of the gold. He and his Archangel had tittered long and hard over having destroyed him. Moments ago, acting not on his own volition, but at the Raptor's orders, he had liquidated Detrovna, the most troublesome contender. Now only the Raptor and the overmatched Korchevko stood between his Church and the treasure. He glanced at the ascetic. As he did so, a thin stream of water shot out of the wall by his bush of white hair. The priest wasn't troubled. Soon the Raptor's troops and the rollers they would certainly improvise would be easing the loaded cube uphill out of this dampness into sunlight.

When the cube was outside, he would explain the exact nature of his Archangel's cast: twenty pounds of high explosive. He would promise that no one would be hurt. All would watch the giant slide his fingers through the lethal rings. He imagined the terror gripping a dozen throats. Everyone save he would stand quietly with the Archangel some distance away. He would be opening the cube. He would stand shielded behind the fortress of heavy gold. And then... He reached into his pocket and fingered the electronic device mated to the smaller detonator tucked beside the ringed one. He would arm it, press the button, and...

Goodbye, Archangel and everyone else.

Except him.

Here was the Raptor with his minions! Then came his command to stop attacking the barrier. What was this? The cache *had* to be uncovered. As he stood in puzzlement, three more spouts of water emerged from the walls. These had considerably more force. Some uneasiness invaded his hopes. Indeed, they were far under the lake. Could this all-out assault on solid oak have been an error? His beads chattered frantically in his fingers, as though speaking for themselves.

Grinding arose behind the barrier. The tunnel shook. The barrier shot toward him! He stumbled in attempted retreat. The eagles towered over him then descended like avenging angels. A curtain of water obscured everything. A split beam slammed into his side, crushing his ribs like straws. Water filled his lungs.

He understood that God had found someone else to do his work.

54

Nevsky charged down the tunnel lighted with fizzing flares, Alessya far ahead of him. Her youth and long legs sped her down toward her quarry. He began to shout warnings, though he was still too far away for them to reach the toilers. He wasn't in good shape. His breath was short and his legs shaky on the tunnel floor. How far to the tunnel's end? A hundred yards? Fifty? Now he saw the side tunnels appear in the uneven light, threatening glooms to left and right in turn. He smelled the dampness. Still far ahead he saw the cluster of flares and beyond them...

The tunnel shook.

There came a mighty roar, and screams. Water was rushing up toward him!

He had arrived far too late with his warning. He skidded to a halt, turned and ran back the way he had come. Adrenalin freshened his legs. Behind him the tunnel was collapsing. From the side tunnels ominous groans emerged. Possibly they, too, were going to collapse. He had to reach the level of the lake's surface. But could he? And even if he did, the surging water might well rush above it and batter him until he smothered in it.

He sprinted with all his strength. Forget the complaints from his knees and hips. The sound of the water grew closer. He heard the hiss of dampened flares. He had covered ground. Maybe, just maybe, he could escape dry...

Then he was tripped! Furry legs entangled his. Queen Catherine, too, was bolting for her life. He tumbled down, out of control. His head and hands slammed into a wooden gutter. Before his eyes lay pebbles and gravel. Pebbles and... His right hand lay on them. He scooped up a handful and leaped up. He jammed them into his pocket. The dog was gone. It had outrun the water.

Not he.

A wave like a seashore breaker knocked him down and washed over him. He rolled beneath the onrushing water. He tried to get to his feet, but went down again. The tunnel was filled with an onrushing tide. It rolled him along. He struck the side of the tunnel and breath was forced from his lungs. He breathed in water and choked. Panic clutched him. He lunged upward, struggling to his feet. For a moment his head was above the water. He sucked in a desperate breath.

Then he was under again!

He tried to swim clumsily up the tunnel, smothering the urge to cough that would fill his mouth then lungs with water. His head struck the ceiling. He saw stars. No air! He was going to drown!

He held his breath stubbornly. With weak arm strokes and kicks he tried to swim ahead. No good. The turbulence twisted him around. His fingertips scraped the wall. He was swimming sideways. He kicked away from the wall, legs like lead. His shoes weighed him down. He wasn't going to be able to reach the air...

He was thrown to the floor. His face dragged along the rough mud. The water surge had receded! He scrambled up to his knees, and then rose on legs like balsa. There might be another surge! He wobbled toward the patch of daylight beyond the door. The tunnel floor trembled. He staggered ahead. Soon the door was only a few yards away.

A violent earth tremor shook him off his feet. He fell to his knees and kept going on all fours. He lunged up then lurched forward. He burst through the doorway into the July glare. He shouted to Charity who stood on the far side of the hill, "Run, run!"

She hesitated only a moment then turned and scampered. Following her at full speed was Queen Catherine. Nevsky ran after her, angling around the hill, away from the door. The earth shuddered again. A rumbling sounded above and behind him. Still at full run, he turned. A massive portion of the hill fell away and crashed down, tearing out bushes and uprooting small trees. Boulders tumbled like dice. He heard anguished howls. The assassin twins were being buried alive.

The cascade of rock and dirt, scouring the landscape, rumbled on down into the lake. Waves heaved up and battered the far shore. Loose pebbles and gravel trickled down from above. Then, near silence.

Nevsky slowed, and then stopped. He turned and surveyed the ruptured hillside. It seemed the worst was over.

55

The Archangel was no lover of water even on the sunniest summer day. He did not drink it or bathe. So this underground dampness, dripping and trimmed now with infernal sprays from all directions, was as disturbing as an honest man. Before the fascist Ostrovsky had fully descended with his troop, the giant had begun to ease back up the tunnel. Even the lowest beast understood the need to reach high ground before impending flood.

Backing as he was, he was startled to see the Amazon Alessya fly by him intent on mayhem with the shiv she swung. He saw her dart among Ostrovsky's soldiers before any could act, even if they wished to. She screamed to see Detrovna fallen with a ruined neck, lying behind Fyodor, well this side of the barrier. She flung herself to her knees and raised her knife. "Die again!" she screamed. "Die a hundred times!" The Archangel chuckled as she worked her blade in and out of his body like a berserk seamstress. As though the corpse could be made deader. Here was a passion to kill that matched his only when he felt his Heat.

He wasn't truly surprised when the water burst through the wood. He bolted up the tunnel. He was strong and his legs long. The nasty borzoi bitch sped by him, her whine like a siren, showing him what speed afoot really was. Indeed, for the water caught him! He was knocked down and tumbled about. His head struck the floor. Lights lit behind his closed eyes. He sucked in water and coughed it out. He was tossed head over heels. Flares flushed from their lodgings, but still alive through chemical magic, darted about in the flood like creatures from the ocean's deepest floors. His wounded shoulder was smashed against the wall. The pain drove in like a lance. He stifled his instinctive howl. To open his mouth was to drown.

Even so, this Archangel wasn't so easily drowned. He heaved to his feet, clawing the wall with his good hand. Heavy going, yes, but... Abruptly the water dropped to his waist. He rushed forward, heaving against the flood. He took four more strides and the water receded to his calves. Now he could run! In darkness his long legs ate up the meters. He ran headlong into a solid face. The impact crushed his nose and snapped something in his repaired shoulder. The pain was like a devouring flame. He staggered to his feet and groped, to the tunnel's top, then to each side in turn. His way was completely blocked. He screamed.

He had collided with another of the czarist barriers!

Despite the darkness he understood. His tumbling about had led him to turn the wrong way. He had blundered into one of the side tunnels! He turned back. Too late!

The flood was rising. It was up to his shoulders. It forced him back to the barrier. He tore the heavy crucifix from his neck, gripped it by its base and slammed wildly at what he knew from the other barriers were the accursed eagles. Moaning echoed from beyond. The arm of the crucifix lodged in the barrier, imprisoned by a knot or seam. He howled in frustration and heaved, to no purpose: He was immobile in His Passion. The Archangel cursed the czar and his poisoned treasure.

Now the growing flood had reached his neck. He turned his back to the barrier. Rivulets tickled his beard. He stood on tiptoes. The water was in no hurry. Tunnels collapsed in the distance, shaking the earth. In time a wave splashed over the top of his head, and then fell away. The water crept up slowly, steadily in the total blackness. It stirred his thick beard. He tipped his head back to raise his nostrils above the tepid flow. He sucked in a mighty breath—just in time. His nose was under, his eyes, his brows, and soon his entire head. What matter that he still lived? Could a man hold his breath for thirty years?

He knew his time had come. His Heat seized him with a greater strength than ever before. It surged up like Hell's fires themselves.

The Book said there would be no more water. The world would end next in fire.

His world would. He dropped his hand to the base of the cast, found the two rings, and tugged down hard.

56

The rumbling explosion deep in the earth made Nevsky start wildly. Instinctively he sprang further away from the hillside. The ground rocked beneath him, throwing him down onto the grass. He staggered to his feet. A second fit heaved the earth, as though in an earthquake. He sprang away, searching for both balance and haste. The hillside that had seemed solid began to slide away beneath him. Boulders bounced down, like marbles from an emptying bag. From the depths below the lake a rumbling grew in strength.

He screamed. He was in the air, falling...

He toppled into a tangle of leaves and branches, striking his head on a heavy limb. A tree had been nearly dislodged by the shifting earth. It hung over the deepening precipice supported by a few ropey roots. Already a hundred feet of empty air yawned below. He hung upside down. The blow to his head, rather than dulling his vision, seemed to have sharpened it. He saw with clarity past even that granted by this sunny July afternoon. Before him the hillside opened like a conjuror's coat.

The earth's innards erupted. Amid this chaos he saw them! First, Korchevko in radiant white, tossed into mid-air, arms upthrust, white hair glowing like a halo. Here was a real archangel or John Chrysostom himself! Next, Detrovna wallowed waist deep in a rush of stool-colored slurry. Behind him with her Needle flew Alessya, mother of passions, her flailing arm stabbing the politician still. His attorney tumbled after, attending his master even at Armageddon, briefcase firmly in hand. Ostrovsky stood spine straight, arm raised in his salute. *"Mother Russia will be great again..."* His soldiers warred, though they were kin. Sturdy Lyubov of the Dogs strode rich black earth. Shmelev waved his vodka bottle and brass knuckles, cartwheeling like a tumbler. Did Nevsky glimpse the assassin twins lurking off to the side, hiding behind a huge airborne boulder? Of Father Fyodor of Kolyma and his Archangel there was no sign. The earth had closed upon them.

Then all were gone in a deafening rumble of shifting elements. Down plunged the greater part of the hill into a lake that could not contain it. Its far shore gave way. Earth, stones, mud, and heavy boulders gouged the hillside below. The deep flood's descent to the Allegheny River a quarter mile below tore out trees, bushes, and deadwood. It swept away vehicles belonging to the contenders and their men and tumbled them end over end like toys. The river swallowed them up as well. The massive torrent rushed on, scourging all before it. Its long vibration touched Nevsky's tree till it vibrated like a thick reed.

He swung upright, his head ringing. He looked up toward the bank where the tree clung. Roots were giving way! Below was a full seventy-five-yard drop into a torrent decorated with tumbling stones. Death would come in that fall or in the turbulent water itself.

"Yuri!" It was Charity peering over the edge of what had become a cliff. In her hand was a length of the cast-off yellow nylon rope. She had coiled it into clumsy loops.

The tree was loosening. He felt it shift. Vertigo clutched at his innards. Such a fall!

Charity advanced to cliff edge. "Catch!" She tossed the rope.

And missed.

The rope end fell among the braches at least six feet from where he was tangled. It would only slip away when the tree let go. He heaved himself free of the branches and made an awkward lunge toward the yellow lifeline.

Too far away!

His movements loosened the roots further. He fought back vertigo. He would have to try again. Surely that effort would dislodge the tree. But there was no choice. The tree heaved— and twisted! The rope curled around a stout limb. He still had some distance to cover. He made an awkward scramble. The tree shifted again. His stomach flew toward his mouth. Hold it! The movement had drawn the rope taut. He had caught a break. Charity had earlier tied her end around a stump or tree behind her. Above she was shouting, but her words meant nothing. He lunged twice. Now he had the twisted nylon in his hands.

He looked up the rope angled about thirty degrees. He was no Army ranger, but up the rope he had to go, hand over hand. He had no time to waste. If the tree let go, the rope could never hold it. How strong were his out-of-shape arms and hands? He took a deep breath and swung out over the chasm. Hand over slow hand he went, eyes averted from the tumult below. He had made it to the halfway point. He dangled, swaying sickeningly with his effort. It was horrid to have nothing beneath his feet. Water from soaked clothes trickled down his ankles.

"Hurry, *hurry!*" Charity shouted.

He couldn't spare the breath to explain that what he was doing *was* hurrying. His wrists ached dreadfully, his shoulders more so. If only he had thought to kick off his shoes...

Charity was kneeling and leaning impossibly forward. He realized she had a rope around her waist, the other end probably fastened to the same tree as his strand of yellow hope.

"Come on!" she urged.

He swung himself forward. Blood ran down onto both wrists. He advanced one hand, swung, and then reached out with the other. One of his dangling feet touched fresh earth. He drew himself forward and tried to get a leg up over the grassy edge. Couldn't. Charity was leaning out, fingers curled to claws. "One-two-three kick!" she said. "I'll grab your leg."

He twisted and kicked hard, but the high point of his ankle's sweep was just below her grip. He cursed. The tree shifted further. The rope was stretched straight as a laser. They tried again. He felt the touch of her fingers, but his leg dangled free still. He looked up pleadingly.

She was gone!

Surely no one was alive now to drag her away and leave him to drop to his death. Or was there? He thought of diabolical Fyodor. Had he somehow survived and...? He hung on with fading strength. He looked down. The lake was emptying. Its exposed bottom was peppered with boulders. To fall was to die.

"Time for our last, best effort!" Charity was back! She leaned over the abyss with a loop of rope dangling from her right hand. He closed his eyes, clenched his teeth, and swung his leg through the air.

She snared it!

She dragged his left leg up. He took another handhold forward. His heel was digging into the dirt. He felt her fingernails sink into the flesh of his thigh. "Roll...right...on...up!" She guided his left hand from his rope to the one that circled her waist. He rolled and she heaved back with all her strength. He clawed the grass. Safe!—and just about to vomit.

Behind his shoulder the rope snapped like a whip end. The tree spun down in a leafy whirl toward the stone-strewn mud, the yellow line spiraling behind like kite tail. He rolled far from the precipice before daring to rise to his feet, soaked and shaken. He felt sick. His world whirled. He put his hands on his knees. Charity untied the rope from her waist.

"Did I say thanks?" he panted.

"No, but then you've always have been an inconsiderate wretch."

They both turned to where lake and hill had become wasteland. The smell of moisture, mud, disturbed earth, and the puzzling acrid stink of spent explosive hung in the air. Water still trickled and loose stones clattered down from the shallow C-shaped shell—all which remained of thousands of cubic feet of earth and stone.

"My God!" Charity breathed. "Everything's gone. Every*body's* gone!"

The death and destruction were certain, but there was an important uncertainty to resolve. Nevsky couldn't forget what he had seen while upside down and dazzled.

He put his hands on Charity's shoulders and looked straight at her. "Did you see them when the hill was exploding?" he asked.

She frowned. "See who?"

"All of them. Korchevko, Detrovna, the whole lot…" He waved vaguely toward the birds soaring in the abyss. "Parading and flying along with the dirt and water."

"What?"

"I saw them all for a moment."

"I was looking, too," Charity said. "I didn't see anyone, Yuri. Because there wasn't anyone there."

57

Pittsburgh, Pennsylvania

Even though Nevsky was sitting in 138 Morlande's smaller living room, the sound of busy roofers two floors and an attic distant still reached his ears. He thought that a fine noise. New slates meant another fifty leak proof years, more than enough for his needs. Exit the roofers Friday, enter the painters Monday. The bids to scrape, patch, and paint had been high; this ark did go on and on. No matter. At the moment money, as they said, was no object.

Of course it was the emerald that made it all possible. It had been a bit complicated. First he had to contact "Volodya" Tschersky on Russian Slope. From him he went to "a special man from Odessa," a newly arrived émigré who used the nickname "Stones." To say he was a gemologist was to say Hank Aaron was a baseball player. His specialties went far afield indeed, to the most skilled overseas lapidaries ("These wizards could cut a piece of coal into a jewel."), to the pulse of gem trade, and to the world's richests' precious stone "want" lists.

Nevsky made an appointment to see Stones. They met at the Garden Ring bakery-café. Stones was short and balding, in his mid-forties. Tufts of black hair stuck out above ears whose lobes were decorated with large diamond studs. They ordered tea and black bread with butter. He insisted on speaking English to improve what he claimed was his sketchy command of the tongue. "English is this world's lingua franca, Yuri Vladimirovich. The tonal scale in the music of commerce." He was quickly to business. "You said you have a stone…"

From his pocket Nevsky took a small cotton-filled box. He put it on the table and took off the top.

"Ahh…." A handkerchief flew into Stones' hand. Onto it he tipped the lumpy bit bigger than Nevsky's thumbnail and nearly an inch thick. His other hand dropped into a shirt pocket and came out with a hand loupe. He peered intently at the crusty stone, rolling it back and forth. "So fine a raw emerald…" he murmured, partially to himself. He looked up sharply. "This is from Colombia, no?"

Nevsky shrugged. "Possibly." He remembered that his grandfather had "shopped" all over the world.

"You do not know?" Stones' chuckle had the reverberation of a pond side bullfrog. "Of course not. A stone from Colombia...where drugs and money mix with...uncut precious stones?"

"I was told you weren't an inquisitive man," Nevsky said. "Only one that knew all that mattered about what you're holding in your hand right now."

"To be sure. To be sure... I learned to be so in our 'new' Russia where thieves who stole from the state with both hands are still anxious to convert their spoils into easily portable valuables." He looked back at the emerald. "This can become such a beauty!" He picked up a table fork and outlined the stone's shape. "I think a lozenge cut would be the most advantageous. See the line here..." He hefted the stone. "The finished gem should weigh eleven or twelve carats, on a guess."

"Is that considered good size?" Nevsky said.

The froggy chuckle. "I understand I have much to teach you, Yuri Vladimirovich."

In time they made their deal. Stones would arrange for the emerald to be cut and find a buyer for it. He wanted fifteen percent of the selling price. He dropped to twelve when Nevsky told him he had other stones of similar quality.

When they parted, Nevsky went to St. Basil's church. He found Father Teodor. To Nevsky's delight the priest told him that old Father Ruslan was still alive, mending in fact. He emptied his wallet into the priest's hands. "For the old one," he said. "I'll send you checks." He declined to visit the man until he was stronger. There would be time.

In these days of instant communication and jet travel Stones was able to work quickly. Such high quality merchandise never gathered dust, the balding man explained two weeks later as he counted out many hundred-dollar bills onto related documents resting on Nevsky's dining room table. Let him know when he was ready to sell again, he said, and off he went.

A slate escaped the roofers and fell just beyond the window. Queen Catherine, lying at Nevsky's feet, growled and stirred. "Easy..." Nevsky scratched the borzoi between the ears. She put her head down again and made a sound something like a sigh. No question she missed Lyubov of the Dogs—as did he. Her first few days at 138 Morlande after the Lake Nagle events were marked with complete loss of appetite. She went to the downstairs doors in turn and scratched to go out in search of her lost master. Nevsky was thinking about taking her to a vet until the day she slipped past while he was taking out the trash. She found a squirrel too far from its tree and snapped its spine with one bite. After that she went to her dog dish with enthusiasm.

Nevsky picked up the day's *Post-Gazette* to see if there was any news to add to his skimpy pile of clippings concerning what reporters had called the "Lake Nagle mine explosion." From the beginning the matter had suffered the usual fate of an event distant from populated areas: not much coverage. In the best tradition of contemporary journalism, some of the facts were correct, but the larger truth utterly escaped discovery. The explosion was attributed to mine gases oozing up from the earth's innards. The lake's destruction was clearly explained— less so the discovery downriver of the bodies of two unidentifiable "hunters" wearing camouflage, and an unlucky "hiker," similarly without identification. Three cars and one truck were pulled from the river. All were rented vehicles whose drivers oddly enough could not be traced. All contained a few small arms. As did two SUVs found nearby. The exact ownership of the land around what had been the lake could not be pinpointed. The opportunity for an ambitious investigative reporting project remained unseized so far. Today's paper carried not a word of that event, by now pushing toward three weeks past. The world was ready to call it history. OK with him.

Charity returned from a clothes-shopping expedition. She held up fall fashions for him to appreciate, slacks, tops, and five light sweaters. He did his best to be appreciative. Despite the long years passed since his bad marriage, he hadn't lost his husband-like skills. She put down the last of the garments. "Still living lush off the emerald," she grinned.

"And a fair amount of 'lush' still left," he said

With passing time the horrors of that day of death and convulsion had abated to some degree. When they were able to turn away for a time from the darker side of the calamity, they managed a teasing banter over which of them had been most misdirected by his grandfather. He said it was she, who thought there was a fourth cube filled with gold coins. She countered by saying if Queen Catherine hadn't tripped him and literally stuck his nose into a small bit of what was the Romanov Cache, he would have never understood what it really was.

Not gold coins from the go, of course. Give anyone a glimpse of those and the coveting gene flipped its switch to "on." Also, gold was too heavy. Raw gemstones were far lighter than gold, so easier to hide in mediocre *objets d'art*. They were also far more valuable in terms of volume. They were the perfect choice for maximum value in minimum space.

Importantly, they weren't too noticeable—at least not to even one of the contenders or their supporters in the tunnels. There thousands of jewels-in-the-rough lay mixed with gravel and poured carefully into the wooden gutters for display, as though in an upscale showroom. All that was missing were the special jeweler's lights that made even the humblest shiny seem major. Hadn't Shmelev told them that the walls and ceilings had been curiously treated? None of them understood that had been done so that not even dust drifted down to dim the Romanov's future. One didn't have to be Stones to sift the wheat from that chaff. A child could do it. Toss the pebbles; keep the "gravel." Had history unraveled differently, a minion of the czar or his legitimate successor could have regularly visited the site, removed what was needed, and begun the lapidary and sale process. Piece of cake.

As to his actually recognizing the exact nature of the cache, Nevsky thought he would have done so, had Detrovna not forced the issue in the wrong direction. From the time the contents of the three cubes had been revealed—one empty, one filled with pebbles, the last with jewels, albeit faux—all the needed clues were there. As in so many of his grandfather's doings, ambiguity prevailed. The clues could be interpreted countless ways. But the simplest seemed to be that jewels and pebbles would be together in an empty space. Had matters proceeded carefully beside Lake Nagle, first the stone would have been cleaned off and its inscription read. The door of *Anastasia Nikolayevna* would open into just such a space—the tunnels. Then one had only to look for pebbles and jewels. But of course it hadn't gone like that at all. After Charity cleared the stone he understood at once that the tunnels shouldn't be damaged in any way. His grandfather's last twist had been to create a watery doomsday machine to destroy unknowing interlopers. In Nevsky's headlong rush to catch Alessya and warn the others to stop breaking down the barriers he had found no time to notice pebbles near his feet.

He and Charity put their gentle needling aside in favor of vigorous disagreement over the straightforward physical realities that she saw in everything and his perceptions touching, however unclearly, on the unseen. To her the unraveling of the cache puzzle over decades—no matter how fragile connections between its actors, objects, and events—involved nothing more than fortunate coincidences and "things just working out that way." He perceived deeper waters flowing, the invisible glide of race, the agony of Russian history, sorcery, or the enigmatic hand of Sergey's God.

Charity listened patiently as he attempted to explain, but words didn't come easily in describing what in fact he really didn't understand. When he got too deep for her, she had a fallback position, a killing phrase. She would say, "I didn't see *any* of those Russians flying out of the hill that you did, Yuri." They would then change the subject.

Their differing opinions received further testing with the unannounced arrival of Butch Hanson the promised two days after the Lake Nagle events. He joined them in the kitchen. He declined his host's offer of vodka. Here was the man who had saved both their lives. No matter, Nevsky could not explain the uneasiness he felt. "I'm here for the explanation you promised," Butch said. "About everything that was going on that day at what used to be Lake Nagle." He had heard the explosion and later read the papers.

"The big hill collapsed, Butch. One of that mad bunch was carrying dynamite or something like it. Everybody you saw was crushed or drowned. They're all dead. Buried or washed away. They never found what they were looking for."

Butch dug for details, clearly dissatisfied with what he was being told. A little frown flourished on his wide brow. He interrupted Nevsky. "I guess you'll be going back there from time to time, Yuri."

The hairs on the back of Nevsky's neck did a little jig. "I'm never going back there, believe me!"

Butch shook his head almost sadly. "Sorry to say, I don't believe you."

"Why?" Charity asked.

"Because I went back after the emergency people left. And I found something…" From his pocket he took an irregular shiny slab as long as his forefinger and about an inch thick. He put it on the table. Yellow and green color bands ran through it. "I wouldn't have ever noticed this if it hadn't been wet."

Nevsky sat silent. This wasn't going to a good place.

"I took it to a jeweler." Butch looked pointedly at Nevsky. "You probably aren't surprised to hear it's a rough opal. Cut into polished stones it'll be worth pretty big money." When Nevsky said nothing, he added, "The jeweler said there aren't any opals in the ground here. They come from countries like Australia."

"What's on your mind, Butch?" Nevsky said.

"Thinking you and everyone else were looking for jewels."

"And you understand what happened to everybody except the two people sitting here looking at you?"

"What's that supposed to mean?" Butch's big shoulders shifted restlessly inside his three-button shirt. "I know you wouldn't threaten me…"

"Last thing on my mind for a guy who saved Charity and me from bullets in the back of the skull. I'm trying to say again what I did when we were all there. That place is…unlucky. Whatever stones are scattered around I think are unlucky, too. I'm telling you the truth when I say I'm never going back there."

"Even if you might pick up a fortune if you looked real hard?"

"That would be the *last* reason," Nevsky said.

"Well, I'm thinking of going back," Butch said.

"That's up to you."

Butch looked at Charity. "And what do you think, little lady?"

Charity hesitated. "I…Yuri and I don't agree about the place or exactly what happened. I—don't want to say, Butch."

Butch got up. He folded his arms. "Yuri, I think you're trying to scare me. I'm thinking whatever's laying around is fair pickings."

"Up to you," Nevsky said.

Butch departed, leaving all three of them somehow dissatisfied. They would never have a chance to iron out the issue. A newscast reported that Butch was shot with a Saturday night special in a Shadyside wine bar three nights later. His assailant was an innocuous hairdresser who went berserk. He was under a therapist's care. Possibly he had made a serious mistake when taking his meds…

Nevsky turned off the TV and covered his face with his hands. Butch… A good man lost too young. Their savior! It took Nevsky better than twenty minutes to steady his wits against a wash of grief.

Curse or coincidence? In either case only he and Charity remained to tell the tale of the cache—which he was certain they would never do. As to the decimated treasure itself, he meant it when he said he'd never go back to that tainted spot.

Charity said "coincidence" so often over the next days that Nevsky shouted at her to be quiet—something he had never done before. They had remained at odds since. Shopping must have soothed her soul. After she packed away her loot she wandered with feigned aimlessness into the little living room. She sat down at the desk. As she often did, from the desk drawer she removed the Pirates 1971 World Series ashtray in which lay the five pebbles and three remaining virgin stones, two large diamonds, and a ruby. Too bad that other stones had fallen out of Nevsky's pocket while he was upside down seeing—or not seeing—the hill disgorge its victims. She rattled them around with a forefinger.

"I just can't get over it. This is all that's left!" she said. "All the effort, time, and rubles your grandfather spent to create the cache and hide it. Then he was shot for his trouble. So was your father. His sister was murdered in some horrid way. And so many others died tangled up in those dreadful cubes. And then what happened three weeks ago... First, such hope eighty years ago, and then...sacrifice, calamity, and monstrous loss!"

"Think of it as Russian history writ small."

"Oh, Yuri, don't be so...flip. I guess I'm trying to say I'm sorry for—all of that."

He smiled. "Don't you think that's all too much for one little lady to apologize for?"

"Of course. But I'm apologizing just the same."

"Accepted."

Peace was restored on the domestic front, Nevsky thought. Another, more subtle peace had been granted him over the weeks since Father Alexei's steps creaked on the porch during the hour of the wolf. That peace had to do with his once-tattered soul, the *dusha* to which the holy man had directed hermit Nevsky's attention, and then urged him to do good works. And as so often happened, those "good works" had twisted into a complex tangle of death and discovery as enigmatic as the cache itself.

No one could remain the same after being thrust, however imperfectly, into the role of his own grandfather. Consider, too, the destruction of his isolation when the sudden company of a gaggle of Russians was thrust upon him. In his imagination now before him stood shapely Lyudmila, neither a candle for God nor a stick for the Devil; Shmelev with his cigarettes and vodka; and of course Alessya who had bestowed upon him the gift of cinnamoned ecstasies—now so sorrowfully lost. He still felt the strength of Lyubov of the Dog's embrace on the earth of what long ago had been his family's lands. Tears like those he shed then dampened his face now.

Twice he had felt icy gunmetal touching the skin of his head and neck with ugly death a trigger twitch away, and hadn't begged to live. He had smelled the Devil in dark disguise, and heard an Imperial Guardsman murmur knowingly of the Bible. Finally, he had hung upside down to behold what he understood to be a privileged vision of an enduring people with bewildering ways. Yes, his *dusha* had received a polishing up that rivaled that of the czar's emerald. Gone was the whining Yuri sucking the bones of long-gone losses. A better man was going forward. With a perfected soul? No, that would never happen. Because he was a Russian.

He wiped at his tears with the back of his hand. They oozed on determinedly. He knew too well all that for which he wept.

Charity rose and hurried to him, tissue in hand. "No sniffling, Nevsky!" she ordered, wiping away the wet. "You have things to do. It's your day to take Queen Catherine for her walk."

THE END

Farmington, Connecticut
Wednesday, September 20, 2006

Dimitri Gat has been a published writer of detective stories and thrillers for more than thirty years. His 1982 novel, *Nevsky's Return*, was voted one of the best ten mysteries of the year by the *New York Times*. His co-authored *Some Are Called Clowns; A Season with the Last of the Great Barnstorming Baseball Teams* is considered one of the best fifty baseball books of all time.